FAR FROM THE OIL LAMP'S GLOW

D1784341

ART P. Ó DÁLAIGH

The sequel to
The Glow of the Oil Lamp

Order this book online at www.trafford.com/07-0843
or email orders@trafford.com

Most Trafford titles are also available at major online book retailers.

Note for Librarians: A cataloguing record for this book is available from Library
and Archives Canada at www.collectionscanada.ca/amicus/index-e.html

Printed in Victoria, BC, Canada.

ISBN: 978-1-4251-2552-3

*We at Trafford believe that it is the responsibility of us all, as both individuals
and corporations, to make choices that are environmentally and socially sound.
You, in turn, are supporting this responsible conduct each time you purchase a
Trafford book, or make use of our publishing services. To find out how you are
helping, please visit www.trafford.com/responsiblepublishing.html*

*Our mission is to efficiently provide the world's finest, most comprehensive
book publishing service, enabling every author to experience success.
To find out how to publish your book, your way, and have it available
worldwide, visit us online at www.trafford.com/10510*

 www.trafford.com

North America & international
toll-free: 1 888 232 4444 (USA & Canada)
phone: 250 383 6864 ♦ fax: 250 383 6804 ♦ email: info@trafford.com

The United Kingdom & Europe
phone: +44 (0)1865 722 113 ♦ local rate: 0845 230 9601
facsimile: +44 (0)1865 722 868 ♦ email: info.uk@trafford.com

10 9 8 7 6 5 4 3

In memory of my parents,
Mick and Sarah Daly
&
'The Three Wee Pagans'

"It is not often that a sequel is as good as its predecessor but this one certainly is".
Dr. Loreto Todd MA PhD. July 2007

ACKNOWLEDGEMENTS

Three years ago I published *"**The Glow of the Oil Lamp**"* with feelings of some trepidation and even dread. It was a very personal piece of work and I was nervous because it was impossible to know how it would be received and to some extent I expected the worst. I was, therefore, rather bewildered and delighted after the launch when people kept stopping me, phoning me and writing from all over the world to say how much they had enjoyed it. They kept telling me that it was a 'fabulous read', 'most enjoyable', and 'a wonderful book altogether'. I have completely lost count of the times when someone said, 'I am not a reader but I could not leave it down'. Perhaps the most satisfying thing of all was that most people, young and old, assured me that, more than anything else, they had enjoyed the humour.

I was particularly gratified and hugely surprised by the unsolicited response of academics since I had consciously written it for 'ordinary people'. Dr. Loreto Todd, who is one of the leading linguists in the world wrote:

Everybody who reads *The Glow of the Oil Lamp* will open a box of delights, that provides food for thought as well as a walk down memory lane. It is a book for young and old, for male and female, it is a kaleidoscopic overview of a life that was rich in love and cheerful companionship.

Whatever our views on that period of lost innocence, few of us could fail to be impressed by Ó Dálaigh's book. It captures a child's view of the world with sensitivity and humour.

Dr. John McGurk, who is Emeritus Professor of History at Hope University, Liverpool wrote:

You have captured that rare thing in writing, the sensitivity and innocence of childhood as well as bringing many of your readers back to their own early years with humour and candour.

Between early September, when the book was launched, and Christmas of that same year, at least four or five people each day contacted me to express their appreciation for having provided them with a great deal of enjoyment and even now I meet people who assure me that the book has given them lots of pleasure. Many people finished off by saying, "I can't wait for the next one; when will it be ready?"

I was quite determined at first that there would be no 'next one' but people were so gracious and at the same time so demanding that finally I set to work and the result is, *"Far from the Oil Lamp's Glow"*. It is a continuation of the story begun in its little brother but I hope that this book can stand on its own. In other words I don't think one has to have read 'The Glow of the Oil Lamp', in order to fully understand this book though those who have, will probably feel more at home with it. My first words of appreciation are, therefore, to the many people who have demanded that I write the sequel. I hope they all enjoy it as much as they have enjoyed its predecessor because to a large extent it is their book; without their pleading it would not have existed.

Aidan McKavanagh was the editor of 'The Glow of the Oil Lamp' and he was good enough to read a first draft of this book and encouraged me to continue, assuring me that it was well worthwhile. To Aidan goes a sincere word of thanks.

It would be totally remiss not to say a word of appreciation about that late gentle, courteous, kindly and very gifted lady, Sheila Madden of Tullysaran. Sheila never failed to enquire how sales were progressing each time I met her, nor to suggest that I had done the world a great service in writing the book. Over a period of eighteen months she bought thirteen copies and each time she made me feel that I was doing her a great favour. Her sudden death was a great shock and marked a tremendous loss to the community.

I have been very fortunate in the recent past in meeting Malachy Ó Neill from near Armagh, a young man of exceptional talent. A couple of years ago Malachy joined the committee of The Ó Neill Country

Historical Society and the warmth of his character was soon obvious to everyone. I quickly discovered, however, that if a scene were described to him he could capture it perfectly in cartoon form with a few strokes of his pen. His illustrations appear with some sections of this book and I am deeply grateful to him for his work and friendship.

Rea McGrail McGonnell and Barney Hughes were good enough to get pictures for me which went back to our school days in Blackwatertown. For their help and for their constant, friendly support I wish to say a very heartfelt word of thanks.

I have used a cartoon by Fr. Eamon McCreave OSM as the main illustration on the cover of this book and I wish to express my sincere thanks to him for allowing me to do so.

To my wife Maureen and to Sinéad and Grainne our daughters, I wish to express my gratitude for all the help along the way and especially the proof reading, although the 'slagging' has been hard enough to bear at times. I dread to think what our son Michael and his wife Karen will have to say when they read some parts of the text.

Tommy Jordan was involved in the stories in 'The Glow of the Oil Lamp' almost as much as I was myself. It was a great relief, therefore, when he assured me that he really enjoyed the book and he even went so far as to promote it both at home and in America and apparently gained some positive notoriety because of his participation in it. He is not so deeply involved in this book but I hope the passages where he is involved will bring back some long forgotten and hopefully pleasant memories. Where Tommy is involved, laughter is never far distant.

Once again that young man of endless talents and wicked sense of humour, Martin Ó Brien, agreed to act as editor for me. (*He had previously edited 'Fifty Years in Ireland' some six years ago*). Not only was it invaluable to have one of the keenest legal minds in the land peruse the manuscript in depth, but Martin questioned every line, indeed every word and punctuation mark, in detail. In spite of an incredibly heavy workload both at The Queen's University of Belfast and in the Law Courts, he spent endless hours making sure that the text was as perfect as it was humanly possible to make it.

One of Martin's great strengths is that he can be bluntly, even savagely, honest. I always knew that if he felt that the work was not up to standard, that it was no worth bothering with, he would tell me in no uncertain terms and that is one of the reasons why I was so glad to have him on board. I can only say a hundred thousand thanks to him and hope that he gets as much satisfaction from this book as I know he did from 'Fifty Years in Ireland'.

Art Ó Dálaigh.
Sessiamagaroll 2007

CHAPTER 1
A WARM WELCOME

The huge doors closed behind me and I found myself in a long bleak corridor and standing beside the college caretaker whom I had met a few weeks previously. He directed me up stone stairs to the left and told me I would find my dormitory on the top floor of the building. I lugged my case up the flights of stairs and found myself in an immense room with beds in neat lines and bedclothes stacked on top of them. In the centre of the room was a double bank of wash-hand basins and for some reason I counted them. There were forty. A note on the door told me where my bed was and instructed me to make it and to be sure that the job was well done or I would be in trouble with the Dean. I had begun life in Saint Patrick's College, Armagh.

The long hot summer of 1949 had seemed to me to be never ending because I was looking forward to starting a new life as a boarder in the college and I could not wait to get started. I still loved and enjoyed the rural peace of my native townland of Sessiamagaroll but I was filled with a mixture of dread and excitement in trying to imagine the totally different way of life, which lay before me. I suppose I realised that I would miss being away from my parents and especially being cut off from my lifelong friend and companion Tommy Jordan, but these feelings were pushed into the subconscious. The anticipation of making new friends and the problems of fitting into a new environment tended to banish all other thoughts from my mind.

At that time, even in our rural backwater, a feeling of impending disaster hung over the community. The Second World War had ended four years previously when the Americans destroyed two Japanese cities using the new and terrible atomic bomb. Nearly every family now had a radio and were being constantly informed that a dreadful evil threat was growing daily in the east and it seemed that it would only be a matter of time before another and even more terrible war would break out. Stalin and his powerful red army posed a greater problem than Hitler and the Nazis had done. Few people, if any, would survive the weapons with which the new war would be fought. All the sacrifice and loss of life of the previous decade appeared to have been in vain. Most people got on with life and enjoyed it but probable doom lay like a dark cloud on the eastern horizon.

When I entered the dormitory, or dorm, as we learned to call it, one boy was already in the place. He came over and told me his name was Jim McNally and he came from near Portrush. We sat on beds and chatted and Jim told me that he had two elder brothers at the college and they had given him a fairly full picture of what life was going to be like.

The first thing that he told me was that we had to be up at half past six in the mornings and I could see that he was not joking. While my father had always assured me that any decent man should be up before six in the mornings or he would lose the best part of the day, I had paid little heed to him. I know that Da really believed this for he was usually up around half past five. In spite of this I was of the opinion that for me eight was a far more sensible time to get out of bed and even an hour or so later did not do any harm on the odd occasion.

In the next hour or so the other boys in our year group arrived and started to settle in. Many of them, like Jim, had older brothers in the school and those of us who were greenhorns followed their example in getting their beds made and putting their things in order. It was probably the first time in my life that I had made my own bed but after watching those around me I thought I had made a reasonable attempt at the job. I was quite pleased with myself.

The task of getting everything in order was finished and everyone sat around talking and getting to know each other. It was then that a huge priest burst into the dorm. He wore a long black soutane, with a matching black cape about eighteen inches long, fitted to the neck and falling over his shoulders. The cape was open at the front and he flicked the ends over his shoulders so that the lining on the inside of the garment was outward. The lining was like shining silk and I thought it made his entire habit look most attractive.

"Silence," he roared and swung the long, thin cane he carried so that it swished into the lower part of his soutane. Silence was immediate and as he stood gazing around, only the bated breathing of the boys could be heard in the room.

"I want to introduce you boys to my best friend", said the priest and he swished the long cane once more. "I want to assure you all that you will come to know my friend very well if you do not do exactly what I say, or if I catch you misbehaving. I can tell you now that if you do step out of line I will catch you because I know what boys are going to do even before they have thought of it themselves. I am the Dean of Discipline and don't be in any doubt that you will be disciplined".

Having completed this friendly introduction the priest stood for a few moments in silence. He then started to walk slowly along the aisles between the beds examining each one in detail. He stopped at a boy's bed near my own. He raised the cane in the air and brought it down on the middle of the cover. "This bed is a disgrace", he shouted. "Get this bed tidied or it won't be the bed my friend will be dealing with".

The priest moved to the bed beside mine and commented that it was well nigh perfect. I began to pray earnestly that mine would also pass inspection as that boy's had done. The priest stopped beside me and looked at my handiwork. He then looked at me and scratched his dark hair with his left hand whilst holding the cane in his right. He slowly moved his left hand to his chin and began rubbing it as though in puzzled thought.

"What might your name be?" he asked, gazing at me as though I were some creature from outer space.

"I am Arthur Daly Father", I answered, trying as best I could to keep my voice steady. The priest looked down at me even harder.

"And where might you come from?" he enquired. I knew now that he was not pleased with my work.

"I come from Sessiamagaroll Father", I answered, wondering why I was getting this special attention.

"Now where might that place be?" The priest asked the question in a sarcastic tone as though our townland had no right to exist. "Would that be somewhere in the darkest part of Africa?"

"It's out near Benburb, Father". I answered, now really puzzled as to where all this was leading. From the far side of the dorm whispers and titters could be heard as he stopped to study my answer. He jumped in the air and swung the cane round his head.

"Silence", he roared. "When I say silence, I mean silence. The next boy who opens his mouth will get six on the bottom". There was a deathly silence in the dorm and he turned his attention back to me.

"Does nobody in that part of the country make

beds?" he asked and paused briefly. "Or maybe they all lie out in the hay stacks or behind the whin bushes".

"All the people make their beds Father", I whispered, feeling very foolish indeed.

The priest reached out and grabbed the bedclothes from my bed and threw them at my feet. "Get that bed made as it should be before I finish this inspection", he said fiercely, gazing down into my eyes. "And you", he said to the boy whose bed had passed inspection, "give this nincompoop directions as to how civilized people make a bed. You have my permission to speak while you are giving directions".

The priest moved on and we began the task of trying to get the bed made to a satisfactory standard. The boy explained that the corners of the sheets had to be folded so that they held the sheet in place. It was a technique that nurses used he explained, and his sister, who was nursing in Belfast, had taught him how it should be done. By the time we had finished, five or six other beds had been stripped and the priest had now completed his examination. He paced slowly along the aisles until all the beds were to his satisfaction.

"The next time I find a bed not up to standard", he announced in a hard voice, "you won't be getting help from the person beside you. My friend will be dealing with you". Again the cane swished though the air. "Now I want every boy to stand at the bottom of his bed and face the door. You are going to have a nice walk round the junior ring before you go to bed. Now who knows where the junior ring is?"

A few boys whose elder brothers had given them a tour of the college grounds put up their hands in silence. The priest picked the one nearest the door and said, "lead the way down to the junior ring like a good fellow and the rest will follow as I direct you".

As we made our way down the couple of flights of stairs to the main hall a boy beside me said, "I come from Cookstown and my name is Jim Long. What do you think of Gammy? He was right and tough on you about the bed".

"Why do you call him Gammy?" I asked, having worked out that Jim was referring to the priest. "That's what everybody calls him", answered Jim. "I don't know how he got the name but he's a real savage. All the boys round Cookstown who are at the college have told me about him. For dead sure he's a savage".

We reached the main hall and I got a bit of a shock. It was now full of huge boys walking around and chatting to each other. They looked to me like fully-grown men and one or two of them made a swipe at some of our group as we passed them. Some of us also got a good kick on the bottom although no one touched me.

We made our way out to the back of the building and found ourselves beside the handball alleys. I had seen them when I did the entrance exam but from the other side. Jim explained that the ones I had seen first were for senior boys. The two alleys we could see now were for juniors. We turned to the left and the boys scattered into groups and started to walk round the oval of concrete that was the junior ring. It was about three hundred yards in length, or circumference to be more exact and I was to spend many happy hours walking round it with my friends. Jim McNally joined us and we sauntered round the ring for half an hour or so until Gammy called us in to go to bed.

"Could you tell me", I asked while we were sauntering round the ring, "what the handball alleys are for?"

"They are for playing a game called handball", answered Jim Long. "You will see boys playing on them tomorrow or the next day. Handball is very important in the college for if you are any good at it you can get an extra fry".

I thought back to a conversation that I had had with my uncle Pat when he assured me that we would only get a fry on Saint Patrick's Day. Even though Frank Conlon, my neighbour, had confirmed this, I now came to the conclusion that they had been taking a hand out of me.

"You know", I said to the two Jims, "my uncle tried to fool me that we would only get a fry once a year and a man who had been here as a student some years ago told me that my uncle was right. They must have taken me for some fool".

The two boys started to laugh and then informed

me that I had not been fooled and that a real fry was served only once a year.

"You see", said Jim McNally, "every other morning we will get a piece of bread fried in lard. That is what we call a fry and since it is tasty everyone looks forward to it. The boys challenge each other in a game of handball for a fry and the boy who wins takes the other boy's fry the next morning. There are some boys who are really good handballers and they clean up. It is looked on as a cowardly thing to do if you refuse a challenge for a game of handball".

I decided on the spot that this was a game at which I would have to try to become proficient. We arrived back up at the dormitory to find Fr. Gallagher chatting to a senior boy.

"Silence", he shouted once more. "You have all had a good chance to do your talking and from now until tomorrow morning I do not want to hear a word out of you. It's half past nine and it's time to get ready to go to bed. Make sure you wash your faces, your hands and your teeth and then get into bed silently but say your night prayers first. And I have a nice surprise for you. Tomorrow morning you are going to have a sleep in. You will not have to get up until seven o'clock but remember that is only for the one day.

"I now want to introduce you to your prefect. His name is Tom Woolsey and he will be in charge of you for the rest of the year. Tom is a fifth year and he is doing his Senior Certificate exam at the end of this year so he needs his sleep. If your prefect has to report any of you to me I can assure you that you will be sorry boys. Now into bed and I don't want to hear a sound".

It would later become clear that we had been extremely lucky in having Tom Woolsey as prefect. Tom was one of nature's gentlemen and during the rest of the year he was always kindly and helpful. As the year went on we heard news from the other year groups that one or two prefects were unfair and vindictive. In the entire year Tom never reported anyone to the Dean though if things became ridiculous he would tell people off. He went on to Maynooth and became a priest to serve in the Archdiocese of Armagh. Some years ago he suffered an untimely death and was greatly mourned and missed by all who had known him.

Fr. Gallagher sauntered between the beds and made some of the boys wash themselves a second time because he said they had made a bad job of it in the first instance. I managed to escape his notice and got myself tucked up in bed under the harsh glare of the electric light. The light was switched out and I lay on my back thinking of all the new experiences I had had in one evening.

I was really doubtful about whether or not I had been lucky to pass the exam. Even on a warm September evening everything about the place had seemed cold and harsh and bleak. I sensed that life was not going to be any bed of roses. I pictured my father and mother sitting chatting by the fire at home, bathed in the soft glow of the little oil lamp and gradually I drifted off to sleep.

Perhaps many people who read this account will think that the word savage was well chosen when applied to the Dean. I certainly thought so when I was at the college. My later life as a teacher, especially in a secondary school, has made me change that opinion. It seems to me that he was making a dramatic presentation in order to avoid future trouble and in many ways his bark was worse than his bite. He was a man of his time and in that era it was believed that corporal punishment, dished out in abundant measure was good for both body and soul.

Every teacher I have ever known detests having to do 'duty', which means that for a time one is in charge of the entire school. If one is going to find trouble it is sure to happen on duty rather than in the classroom. Teachers are allocated duty on one day per week, usually with three or four others to help them, or the team may be on for a week with a period of six or seven weeks free. Even with the help of one's colleagues it is regarded an onerous and unpleasant task.

Fr. Gallagher, however, was on duty day and night for an entire year and the only break he got was a half-day on a Saturday afternoon. He was responsible for the safety and welfare of four hundred boys, some of whom were really young men. We were aware of him wandering the dormitories at all hours of the night. I do not know how much sleep he got but it must have been short and broken. On top of all this he taught mathematics throughout the school and I am sure he had a fairly full timetable.

I do not know who had devised the system, which prevailed in all colleges like Armagh, but it strikes me that it was the perfect way to break even the strongest and most determined of men. Looking back on it today I marvel that the President, Fr. Sheridan, could be so hard and unthinking with his fellow man and I know that he showed neither gratitude nor appreciation for the work the priests did. They had made a choice to serve their God in a life of hardship and so hardship was contrived and embraced rather than avoided. It was a savage system on the clerical teachers and it is little wonder that Gammy was seen as a 'savage.' It was probably the only way that he, or any other man, could have hoped to survive and he was lucky to be very big and strong both mentally and physically.

CHAPTER 2
'LOVELY' GRUB

The Dean wakened us with a loud 'Deo gratias' at seven o'clock on Monday morning. He explained that this was the Latin for 'thanks be to God' and was said in gratitude for having safely survived the night. He ordered us to get up, to get washed and dressed, and to go down quietly to the chapel. Fifteen minutes was given to complete these tasks and to appear in the chapel, which he told us was at the far end of the bottom corridor. There would be older boys going there and he suggested we follow them.

We arrived down in the chapel to find the pews lined with boys from the older classes. We were told to stand in the middle aisle at the front. We were welcomed by a priest who was standing at the gate in the middle of the altar rails and who greeted us with a big warm, friendly smile.

"I am Fr. Kelly", he said softly, "and I want to welcome you all to your new home. Like the other six priests here I am a Vincention or a Vin as most people call us. The first thing we have to do is get you all into your proper places here in the chapel.

Anyone whose surname begins with the letter 'A' please make his way up here beside me".

In a few minutes he had worked his way through the alphabet and we had taken the places, which we would occupy for the rest of the year. I found myself at the end of the second pew, nearest the aisle. Task completed, one boy was still standing in the aisle. Fr. Kelly looked at him and then walked over to stand beside him.

"Tell me son", he said softly, "does your name not begin with any of the letters of the English alphabet?"

The boy looked at him with a puzzled expression on his face while the rest of us tittered. Indeed all of the rest of the chapel tittered.

"My name is McAllister Father", he answered, "and I was not sure whether you wanted me to come up with the Ms or the As".

The whole chapel burst into howls of laughter, which the priest silenced by holding up his hand.

"That is a very good point son", he said quietly to the boy. "I must say I had never thought of that myself. We always, however, take the first letter of your entire name. Now do you know which to choose?"

"My name begins with M", replied the boy in almost a whisper.

"Good man", said Fr. Kelly. "That's right, and so we will have to find your right place. Now you will often find that in this school you will be expected to remain in alphabetical order. I hope that you will know from now on exactly where to go". The boy assured him that he would.

"Now boys", continued Fr. Kelly, "I hope you will all remember your correct place and that you will always come into the chapel quietly and with great respect. In the days to come you may find yourselves missing your parents and family. It is an emotion that can be very strong and it is called home-sickness. If any boy feels he needs help or he wants to talk to someone, you will find my room at the far end of the main corridor on the left. Now for a little while I want you to sit quietly and talk to God in your own way".

I was never aware of anyone taking Fr. Kelly up on his offer of help but maybe some people did.

The next half hour was given over to meditation and private prayer and from time to time Fr. Kelly suggested which subject we might meditate upon and which prayers we might say. He continued to speak in a soft, kindly voice and told us that his job was to organise everything to do with practical religion. He was overweight and even on that first morning I realised that he was not in very good health. In the years to come he would sometimes appear and say a Mass on a side altar. We quickly realised that he could say his Mass very quickly and later some of the boys timed him to eleven minutes! He did not teach and apart from the occasional morning appearances we seldom saw him.

At a quarter to eight a priest came out of the sacristy to the left of the altar led by two senior boys in soutane and surplice. Before beginning the Mass he turned and stood facing us.

"My name is Fr. Tom Dougan", he announced, "and like you boys at the front I am a new boy here. I was ordained a few months ago and this is my first appointment. I will be teaching quite a bit of Latin and a smattering of other subjects. You might like to know that I come from Armagh and a few years ago I sat where you are sitting now. It is my privilege to be chosen to say the first Mass of the year in the college".

He turned and faced the tabernacle and began the Mass. It lasted about half an hour and we were then kept for ten minutes of thanksgiving before being told to leave the chapel in silence and proceed to the refectory for breakfast.

The refectory, or 'ref' as we called it, was a big room set with rows of tables. From the floor of the main corridor a set of four steps led up to the great, dark, heavy wooden door. It was only six or seven yards from the entrance to the chapel.

The Dean was there before us with his cane and had a huge bunch of keys hanging from his belt. He showed all the first years where their tables were and what position each pupil should occupy for all meals. Gammy then led us in saying grace before meals and we sat down to our first breakfast.

We were just about to begin breakfast when we

were interrupted by a bellow from Gammy who had wandered down to the back of the room.

"Get up to the front immediately", he bellowed, "you have been here long enough to know that behaviour like that will not be tolerated".

A big, strong boy rose from his seat and walked quickly to the front of the room, followed by the furious Dean. They reached the front and stood facing each other beside a table on which there was a big bowl filled with eggs.

The Dean took up his cane and told the boy to hold out his hand. The boy looked up at him and said, "it was a mistake Father and I did not mean it. I don't think I should be punished for that".

Gammy straightened himself up to his full height and went slightly red in the face. He addressed the boy in a rasping voice.

"I will not take that sort of language from anyone", he snarled. "You may have forgotten how to behave over the summer but that is not my business. I am now going to give you a choice. You can go straight to the President and I can assure you that you will be expelled and sent home in disgrace. On the other hand you can take your punishment like a man. I was going to give you two but now you are going to get an extra four for impertinence. The choice is yours but if you wish to know I would prefer you to go to the President".

A second went by. Slowly the boy held out his right hand.

Gammy raised the cane high over his head and took a step backwards. The cane swooshed downwards through the air and caught the boy along the tips of the fingers making him wince and push his hand under his left armpit.

"The other hand", ordered the priest quietly, but in the deathly silence his voice could be heard in every corner of the room. Again the cane swooshed and again hit the very tips of the fingers. Six times the process was repeated. The boy moved to turn away in obvious agony.

"Where do you think you are going?" asked Gammy.

"I was going to try to take my breakfast", answered the boy squirming with the pain in his fingers.

"Oh so it's more impertinence, is it?" asked Gammy, "Do you think you are going to get away with that? You know that you have to apologise for giving me all this bother and for your bad conduct".

"I didn't mean to be impertinent", muttered the boy. "I am sorry Father".

"You will go straight out to the chapel and spend the next half hour in meditation there. That is unless you would rather visit the President?"

The boy turned and went out through the door and disappeared down the steps on his way to the chapel. The other four hundred or so of us began breakfast. The new boys like myself, were in a state of shock and disbelief.

In the centre of each table was large rectangular

dish filled with porridge and there was also a fairly large jug of milk and a big pot of tea. A plate held twelve slices of bread, one for each boy at the table. Beside it was a dish with twelve pieces of margarine circular in shape and about a quarter of an inch thick. I had been used to my mother's lovely country butter and I did not like margarine but there was nothing I could do about that. I had to learn to accept it. This was to be our breakfast for the next five years and if one takes away the porridge, it was also our lunch and our evening tea. Dinner, which we got after school, at half past three in the afternoon, was somewhat more substantial but seldom very tasty. On Sunday mornings we got two sausages, which were so overcooked that they were scarcely recognisable. Still we thought them a treat.

I had noticed the big dish of boiled eggs on a table at the front of the ref. Boys rose from their places and went up and picked out an egg. I liked eggs and I decided that a good egg would be a fine addition to the breakfast. I rose and made my way up to the table only to find that each egg had a name written on it in pencil. Fr. Gallagher came over to me.

"Oh, so it is my bed-making friend from yesterday, he said, looking down at me with a slight smile on his face. "And what might you be doing up here, might I ask?"

"I thought I would like an egg, Father", I answered feeling very foolish.

"Did you put an egg out last night?" he asked.

"I didn't have any eggs, Father".

"Oh, so how do you expect to find an egg if you did not put one out last night to be boiled?"

"I thought that there were eggs for everyone", I answered, feeling that I was getting into deep water. The priest looked at me and shook his head as though really perplexed. Then he called for silence in the ref.

"This boy comes from far out in the country", he said loudly, "but he thinks that eggs come from heaven or maybe he thinks they appear out of thin air".

The entire ref burst into laughter and now I felt really foolish. He allowed the laughter to continue for some seconds and then he demanded silence again.

"Seriously", he continued, "it gives me a good opportunity to explain things to the first years. If you want an egg with your breakfast you have to ask your parents to supply you with them and they will be kept in the lockers outside the door of the ref. I will open the lockers just before bedtime and you can get your egg and leave it here to be boiled. But make sure that you write your name clearly on it with a pencil".

He turned his attention back to me. "So out in that place where you live", he said with a big smile, "it would appear that the people don't make beds and they don't know much about hens".

"We have hundreds of hens at home, Father", I answered quietly.

He looked at me in a friendly way and gave me a light punch on the shoulder. "You can't know everything on your first day", he said, "but you have given me the chance to explain things. Now go and finish your breakfast".

He sauntered down one of the lanes between the tables and I made my way back to my table. I was just about to sit down when one of the senior boys who had been up to claim an egg, reached over and grabbed five or six slices of bread from our plate and walked on. Everyone at the table looked at each other in wonder. A boy at the next table who was a second year, turned round and whispered, "say nothing and eat whatever is left. If you clash on big Pat, the senior boys will kill you". All the boys at his table put their fingers to their lips to warn us not to say a word. We were left with six slices of bread, which we shared out as best we could.

The Sunday sausages led to an incident a couple of years later, which became the talk of the school. Malachy Connolly was one of our year-group and he came from a neighbouring town where his parents had a shop. He was friendly and popular but he made it clear that he had two pet hates.

"I can't see any sense in all this religion business", he announced. "I think that it is all a cod and I am taking nothing to do with it. I intend to use the time in the chapel to have an extra sleep".

"And I can't understand why people would waste their time and energy running round a field chasing a piece of leather filled with air. That's another thing that I want nothing to do with".

The authorities must have known about his antipathy to religion and sport and it has puzzled me all my life as to why he was not expelled from a Catholic seminary. He never made any secret of his attitude and he announced his unbounded admiration for the Communist party and for the regime, which at that time ruled the Soviet Union. We were warned constantly by the priests that that regime was totally evil and would lead the world to destruction. Satan himself had designed it and no one should be in any doubt that he was still in charge.

Malachy had been used to very good food at home and he did not take kindly to the spartan diet of the college. In particular he took a special antipathy to the sausages and sent two of them off to the Russian Embassy in London to have them analysed. How he managed this feat I do not know since all letters and parcels were censored. My mother got used to receiving some of my letters with part of the text blacked out, because I had made some comment with which the President did not agree. She said it was like being back in the wartime when letters from Glasgow were treated in a similar fashion.

Seven or eight pupils in each year-group were day-boys who lived near the college and came in each morning. We very quickly realised that these pupils were seen as a lower form of life and they were tolerated rather than accepted by the clerical staff. Boarders were encouraged to see themselves as of a much higher quality and many of the pupils took their cue from the staff and looked down upon all day-boys. They often asked them, however, to post letters in the town if they knew that such letters would never have passed censorship. The authorities realised that this was an obvious loophole in the system and day-boys were often searched either coming to school or leaving. Malachy may well have used this unlawful channel to communicate with the Soviets.

"I have sent off two sausages to the Russian Embassy", he announced. "I bet you when they are analysed they will be found to be not fit to be eaten by human beings. I can't wait until I get the results back".

We could not wait either. Day after day passed and there was no word back from the Communists. Three or four weeks went by and still the desired letter did not arrive in the post.

"I bet you auld Gussy has got hold of my letter", said a disappointed Malachy, Gussy being the nickname of the President; or rather it was a familiar form of his first name, Augustus. "We would be nearly better in a Nazi camp for they poke their noses into everything here. I sent away the sausages but I could have sent any of the stuff we are given. Even a decent dog would not take most of the rubbish we have to eat".

As far as I can remember it was either five or six

weeks later when Malachy announced that his reply had at last arrived. I am still mystified as to how it too, managed to get past the censors.

"They say that the nutrient quotient of the sausages was found to be reasonable", he said in a disappointed voice, "but the taste factor had been ruined in the cooking. There is no point in sending them any other samples for they would all end up the same".

CHAPTER 3.
'ENLIGHTENMENT'

After breakfast we were given half an hour or so to stroll round the junior ring or to play handball if we could find a place on the alleys. A bell was rung then for class and the older boys made their way into the school building. Yet another young priest called on all the new boys to line up in front of him. He surveyed the group with a big friendly smile on his face. He was fairly tall and quite handsome with a mop of curly sandy hair. I heard later that if he took a service in the adjoining cathedral it was always filled to the doors with young women!

"I'm Fr. Devine, Boys", he said, "and I am going to take you up to the study hall so that we can get you sorted into classes and then get the work started for the year. Fr. Dougan said Mass for you earlier and, like him, I have just arrived here. Those of you who choose Greek as a subject will get to know me quite well. Come now and follow me".

We were divided into two classes called ones and twos.

The twos were supposed to be the better class

and it was there I found myself placed. Our next task was to decide which subjects we would study. English, religion and mathematics were compulsory for everyone but then we had choices. One had to decide between history and geography, Greek and science, Irish and French. In most cases it worked out so that the classes were fairly equal and everyone got the choice he had picked. I chose history, science and Irish.

There was a choice between woodwork and art and I was very keen to get woodwork. We were given a sheet of paper and a set of coloured pencils and given the task of drawing a scene around our own home. Half an hour later the sheets were collected and examined and I was informed that I was in the art class. It was the one decision which was made by the staff and I was deeply disappointed. I felt like kicking myself for not making a total mess of the picture.

It took until lunchtime to get everything arranged and after lunch there was a break of half an hour. Our first class in the afternoon was mathematics and we got a bit of a shock. Our teacher was Gammy. He proved to be a very good teacher and although he was tough and expected very hard work, he was fair. In class, as throughout the school, he had no favourites. He could be harsh but he treated everyone the same. Punishment for class work, or rather the lack of it, was administered by the Vice-President who was Fr. Kenny, and even Fr. Gallagher had to send boys to him if he thought they needed to be punished though my memory is that he seldom did.

The next class was Irish and this time we met a lay teacher. He came in and addressed us in the native language, "Dia dhíbh agus fáilte romhaibh." He explained that it meant 'hello' and 'welcome.' He told us that his name was Sean Ó Baoill. He then went round the class and gave everyone the Gaelic version of their name and address. He had been going fairly quickly until he came to me.

"Is your family ever called Dawley?" he asked.

"It is Sir", I replied, "but I think that some of the neighbours use it as a slight insult or as some kind of nickname".

Sean looked at me thoughtfully. "You might be right", he answered, "but really they are using the old version of your name, which is Ó Dálaigh. It is pronounced exactly like Dawley and you should be very proud of it. Your people were the bards and poets of ancient Ireland".

"But I was interested in that address of yours; that townland of Sessiamagaroll. That is out near the village of Benburb isn't it?"

"Yes Sir", I answered, "It starts about half a mile from Benburb".

"Do you know a man called Proinsias O'Conluain?"

This had me stumped. I had never heard of anyone with a name like that.

"No Sir, there is no one in our townland with a name like that".

Sean looked at me and smiled. "Maybe you would know him as Frank Conlon", he said. "He is an old friend of mine and he works with Radio Éireann. His programmes are in the Irish language, or Gaelic, as I would like you to say".

"His family are our next door neighbours", I answered excitedly, "and their house nearly touches ours. I was talking to him in the summer time".

"Maith thú", said Sean and moved to the boy sitting beside me who happened to be Arty McAnerney and who lived very near to Sean in the city.

"Well Arty", he said, "and since I know you have done some Irish in the Brothers, could you tell me what I said there to your friend?"

"You said 'good boy' or 'well done'", answered Arty. I was to come to know him as the brightest boy in the class. Nothing seemed to give him any trouble and I was later to feel envious of him because he coped brilliantly in all subjects while I had to struggle. But for some reason I took to Sean Ó Baoill and from that day on, his classes were simply too short for me. I would often study Irish sometimes to the detriment of other subjects.

Then we had Fr. Dougan for history and again I was delighted. It was a subject I had always loved and our teacher proved to be understanding, helpful, and very kind. And he stayed with us for the last class too because he also took us for Latin.

Our first day of classes was over and we went to dinner.

After dinner we had to tog out for football and Fr. Divine came into the dorm and told us that he and Fr. Dougan were in charge of the first years. He waited until we were togged out and then he led us down a steep hill, at the bottom of which we had to cross a railway line by means of a narrow bridge. He told us that this was the Keady line and it was not long before a train came along, puffing out lots of steam but going very slowly.

The huge level area in front of us was divided into several different pitches. The senior field, away to our right, was nearest to the Moy road and was for the fifth years or for any exceptional footballers from the fourth year or even the third year. The polygon was between the senior field and the little bridge and was the fourth year domain. Third years had to cross the railway line where it ran along near the Moy road and make their way to the polo grounds, which was their pitch. To our left was the pentagon and it was for first and second years.

One other pitch remained in the corner opposite the bridge. It was small and had not got goal posts to compare with the others. It was called the patch. It was reserved for those first and second years who were not capable of coping on the pentagon.

I had been very excited at the prospect of playing football in togs and real football boots. I felt a pang of sheer dismay, however, when I was told to go to the patch. I had been recognised as being one of the best footballers at primary school; perhaps even the very best. It was somewhat of an insult to find myself cast amongst the 'also-rans' of the game. But in the first session I learned that while I was amongst the better players on the patch, I was far from being the best. It was only one of the instances where I would learn that life in the big pool was to hold many uncomfortable surprises for a fish from a very small pool.

Football lasted just over an hour and then we had to get changed and ready for first study. The entire school took their places in the study hall at desks, which were allocated in alphabetical order. The first years were at the front and since my name came early I found myself in the second row from the very front. A priest was on duty. He explained that there was to be total silence while we worked on tasks, which had been allocated during class time.

"My name is Fr. Murnaghan", the priest informed us, "and those of you who know me will assure the others that I don't stand for any nonsense. This is a Catholic seminary and if any boy does not like the way we do things he has an easy option. He can take himself out of the college gates and find someplace he does like, if that is possible. And if there are any such boys I will soon find them and out they will go".

He started to walk down the middle of the hall between the desks.

"That's Tojo", whispered the boy next to me, "they tell me he has a right few slates short of a roof".

"Did some boy dare to talk after all I have said?"

the priest demanded, rushing to the front of the hall. "The boy who spoke will come out here to me immediately".

There was dead silence and no one moved.

"Oh, so we have a coward amongst us!" said the priest. "There is some boy here who has not got the guts to come up and admit what he has done. That is one of the most disgraceful things that any boy can do. Now I will give him one more chance to come out or I will have every first year boy punished".

The boy rose from the seat beside me and slowly walked up to the priest. He was quite tall and gangling.

"And what might your name be?" asked Fr. Murnaghan.

"It's Chris Coulson, Father", the boy answered in a very low voice.

"And where might you come from?"

"I come from Fermanagh, near Newtownbutler", Chris replied.

"Maybe there is something wrong with your ears?"

"I don't think so Father, I can hear fine".

"Oh, so you simply don't pay any attention to what you do hear?"

"I'm sorry Father. I know I did the wrong thing".

Fr. Murnaghan stood studying Chris for quite a while and then turned to look at the rest of us.

"Would the boy to whom this boy was speaking please stand up now?" he said.

I rose slowly from my seat, wondering what was going to happen next. Fr. Murnaghan stood gazing at me as he had at Chris.

"What is your name?" he asked slowly.

"It's Arthur Daly, Father".

"And where do you come from?"

"We live out near Benburb, Father".

"And why did you not come out here along with Chris?"

"Well, Father, I did not say anything".

"No. Maybe not! But you were part of the conversation were you not? Were you afraid to own up to that?"

I knew that there was something wrong with the priest's logic but I also knew that I was in a situation where I could not win. Since I could not think of anything reasonable to say I stood looking at him blankly.

"Do the two of you think I should send you to the Dean for punishment?" Fr. Murnaghan asked the question as though he expected 'yes' as an answer. We were both silent, and though I can't speak for Chris, I felt very uneasy indeed.

"Oh, all right", said the priest at last, "we will say no more about it this time but if it ever happens again you will be in serious trouble. Now get on with your work".

Fr. Murnaghan was not very tall but was rather stout. It was his round face, which caught my attention, however. It was made up of patches of different coloured skin and there were lines round the edges of each patch. When he got angry or excited some of the patches seemed to glow deep purple while others went a deathly white.

I was to learn later that he had been in an horrific road traffic accident when he was young. He was so badly injured that he was not expected to survive. His face was a patchwork of skin grafts. He had sought refuge in deep prayer and made a vow that if he did get better he would become a priest. I would later see him suddenly go down on his knees while walking in the corridors and I came to the conclusion that Chris had been right. The roof was not fully complete!

I never discovered why he got the name Tojo. It may have been because he had a slightly Japanese appearance but I am not sure.

There was a raised desk in the left-hand corner at the very front of the big hall. The deputy-head prefect took his place there facing us and it was his job to help keep an eye on the front half of the hall whilst doing his work. He was the eye in the back of the priest's head. The head prefect had a similarly raised desk in the middle of the room to perform a similar function though he faced forward like all the rest of us. A third raised desk was at the back of the hall for the person on duty but I was to learn that only a few of the priests or lay staff ever used it. They preferred to wander silently between the desks making sure that there was absolute silence, and sometimes checking work that they had given in class. First study lasted until a quarter to seven and then it was time for supper.

"That has been a long day", I said to the boy beside me at the table. "I'm tired and I'm glad to see it over".

He looked at me and laughed. "Oh, so you think it's over", he said. "Well, I'm afraid you're in for a bit of a shock. We still have second study to come".

"Are you taking a hand out of me?" I asked. "What are we going to do with more time to study? I have all the work we were given done long ago".

"Oh aigh", he replied, "but we only had a couple of classes today. Tomorrow we will have eight and you will get work to do in every one of them. You are not on your holidays now you know".

He was right. We had a short break and then another study period lasting from half past seven until nine o'clock. Again there was a short break and a bell rang to summon us to get ready for bed. My first full day was over and I lay shading my eyes from the harsh electric light above my bed. Fr. Gallagher came in, called for silence, and switched out the lights.

That day was a pattern for all the days in the next five years, except that September's warmth was pleasant compared with the bitter cold of the depth of winters to come.

CHAPTER 4
IGNORANCE OF THE LAW IS NO EXCUSE

Saturday was a half-day with four lessons in the morning and football or other games in the afternoon. If the weather was very bad we had a library session in the study hall. For the third and fourth period of the morning we had physical education in the school gymnasium. Our instructor was Paddy Hamill who was a teacher in one of the primary schools in the town. I was to learn later that he was a noted historian and above all a Gaelic speaker who spent his life promoting the language. To me in that first year he was simply a very athletic and handsome man who inspired me greatly.

About two months into the year he kept a number of us behind at the end of class because we had impressed him with our work on the vaulting horse and he wanted to teach us how to do fly springs. I was totally delighted to be one of the chosen few. It meant, however, that when we went up to the dorm to change the others were already at dinner, which was served early on a Saturday. We were not in the slightest worried because we had simply obeyed the instructions of a teacher. We saw ourselves as budding gymnasts and were wildly excited. We changed and went down to dinner.

The heavy door of the ref was firmly closed and since I arrived first I turned the handle and pushed on it. It refused to budge. I knocked on it and pushed even harder. The door opened a few inches and Fr. Gallagher's face appeared in the narrow slit.

"Why are you pushing and thumping on the door?" he asked, as though he thought I should be somewhere else entirely.

"We were trying to get in to dinner, Father", I answered as calmly as I could.

"Get away out of this", he growled. "There's no dinner for anyone who comes to the refectory at this time of the day. Grace has been said long ago and everyone should be here for that. Now get out of my sight".

"But, Father, Mr. Hamill kept us back to do extra P.E".

"Not my business, what Mr. Hamill does. You're late for dinner so you can do without".

He tried to close the door but I had my foot in the space.

"How dare you try to keep this door open in spite of me! You are some cheeky boy to even think of that. Stay there just for one minute and I'll try and teach you a wee bit of manners".

I stood there dumbfounded. A few seconds later he threw the door open and appeared carrying the cane. He ordered me to the bottom of the steps.

"Hold out your hand".

I held out the hand and the cane swished down.

"Now the other one".

Again the cane whistled downward and he glared at me.

"Don't ever dare to try to prevent me doing what I want to do", he said in a rasping voice. "I said there was no dinner for any of you boys today and that is exactly what I meant. Now, do any of the rest of you want to feel the cane? If not then go and spend your time on the alleys or the junior ring but get out of my way". He turned went bounding up the steps and entered the ref, slamming the door behind him.

"Well that was most unfair", said Arty McAnerney who happened to be one of the group. "It was not our fault that we were late and I'm starving. How are we going to last out till suppertime? Are your fingers very sore, Arthur?"

"They are not exactly comfortable Arty", I answered with a rueful grimace. "They are stinging like the very devil but sure that will pass. But I am famished too. That P.E would give anyone a bit of an edge to his appetite".

We wandered out to the back of the school and discussed the plight in which we found ourselves. There was nothing we could do, however, and we decided that we would have to make the best of it until supper.

Once a month each boarder was allowed to have

his parents visit him for an hour or so on Saturday afternoon. This was known as 'getting a call'. If the parent made a request the pupil was allowed to spend the visiting time down town in the parent's company. Even if permission had been given to go down town the visit began in one of the small rooms, which were beside the President's office. It meant that when we were called we had to go through the great doors from the main corridor and into the foyer, or 'holy of holies,' as it was known, because the President's office was there. It so happened that on that particular Saturday I was due for a call and my mother duly arrived not long after our confrontation with Gammy.

My mother had to walk to Benburb and get the Armagh bus, which left the village at half past ten. She then had to spend a couple of hours in town because visiting did not begin until two o'clock. Since the return bus left Armagh again at half past three she had to have her shopping done before coming up to the college. On this particular Saturday she was loaded with parcels.

"Have you got anything to eat, Mammy?" was my opening address as soon as we were alone.

She looked at me in surprise. "What's wrong?" she asked. "Did you not get enough to eat at your lunch?"

"I didn't get any lunch, Mammy. A few of us were late down to the ref and the Dean would not let us in".

"What were you doing that you were late? Were you up to something against the rules?"

"No Mammy. We had P.E. for the last class and Mr. Hamill kept a few of us behind because he thought we were very good and he wanted to give us extra training. We could not have got down any sooner".

"Dean or no Dean, he's not going to get away with that", she said, rising and heading for the door. I ran over and stood at the door to prevent her opening it.

"There is nothing anyone can do about it, Mammy", I said anxiously. "If you make a fuss about it I will be expelled or I will be in real trouble".

"Well, if they expel you what odds? If they are not going to feed you, you'd be far better off somewhere else. I'm going see Fr. Sheridan".

"Please, Mammy", I begged, "please sit down there and listen. There is no point going to Fr. Sheridan because he will not help. He will back up the Dean. And anyway if you make a fuss I will never live it down. But have you got anything to eat?"

My mother slowly cooled down and opened some of the bags she had with her, scolding all the time about how this was no way to treat anyone's decent rearing. The first thing I saw was a loaf and I grabbed it. My mother looked at me and I could see the concern and anger building up in her once again.

"Don't worry, Mammy, this will be great. But have you got anything else because I want to slip something out to my pals. They are starving out there".

She bent down and searched in one of the bags

and took out a lovely fresh apple tart. She had got up early and baked it specially that morning. Such a luxury was not allowed and would have to be hidden. It is nearly sixty years since that Saturday but I can still smell the delicious fragrance of that lovely tart and feel my mouth watering at the sight of it. I could not believe my good luck and I felt as though I were in heaven. Gammy could keep his dinner.

We made a parcel of apple tart sandwiches and I managed to slip out and give them to one of the starving boys to be shared. I knew that if I had been caught in the act I would have been expelled immediately so I had to be very careful. I was certainly a very popular fellow amongst the group that weekend and some of them remarked that I was particularly lucky to have a mother who made such beautiful tarts.

My mother complained bitterly for the rest of the visit. "I still think I should go and kick up a stink", she kept saying. "I can't see why I should wear myself into an early grave trying to pay for your keep and then they won't even give you a bite to eat. I was delighted when you got in here but I never thought they would treat anybody's decent rearing like this".

"It's all right Mammy," I kept saying. "There's no harm done and you have saved our lives. All the boys have got a big sandwich and they are happy. Please don't try to do anything about it".

I was rather relieved when that visit came to an end and the great heavy door blocked my mother's little figure from my view. I knew that she was very angry and annoyed and I feared that she might go to the President in spite of me. At the same time I always feel a deep pang of emotion as I think of how she was always there when I most needed her.

That night as I lay in bed before going to sleep I pictured my parents sitting close together on either side of the fire chatting in the ever moving shadows cast by the dancing flames. It all seemed very far away in the chill of that late autumn night.

Another event of a somewhat similar nature springs to mind. It happened some months later and must have been in the late spring or early summer because it was a lovely warm sunny day.

Arty and I used to spend some of our spare time playing shove halfpenny on a bench, which was near the handball alleys. On this day we came out for our usual game and as we went towards the bench we noticed a motorbike parked just off the alleys. It was black and chrome and was glittering brilliantly in the sunshine.

"Do you know much about bikes?" asked Arty, whose people had a garage in town.

"I know a right bit about push bikes but I know nothing at all about machines like that", I answered. "It looks like it is brand new".

"Come on down and I'll tell you a wee bit about it", said Arty. "We won't go near it nor touch it, but I'll explain all the parts to you".

We went down and walked round the bike slowly

with Arty pointing out all the different parts and explaining their function. At no time were we within six or seven feet from the machine. Suddenly the Dean's voice bellowed out from a window on the second floor of the building behind us.

"What are you two boys doing interfering with that motorbike? Come up here to my room at once".

We walked up the steps together and made our way up to Fr. Gallagher's room. On the way Arty remarked, "Gammy sounds very angry. But sure we weren't interfering with the bike at all. We didn't go near it".

"I know that, Arty", I said, "but you know as well as I do that there's no talking to him when he takes a notion into his head. We might be in trouble".

"Ach, we couldn't be", laughed Arty, "sure we were only looking at it".

We arrived at Gammy's room to find him standing at the door with the cane in his hand.

"Can people not leave a bike in the school grounds without it being interfered with by boys like you?" He demanded.

"Father, we were not interfering with it", said Arty. "We were only looking at it and I was explaining all the parts to Arthur. But Father, we never touched it".

"Did anyone tell either of you to go down and examine it?"

"No, Father", we answered in unison.

"So that means that you did not have permission to go anywhere near it?"

We could do little but agree that this was so. He gave each of us six slaps and told us to leave things alone that did not belong to us. I do not know who owned the bike; I do not know why it was there: but I certainly remember it, and I'm sure Arty does too.

CHAPTER 5
HOMECOMING OF A CARDINAL

At about the time that we entered the college it was announced Archbishop John D'Alton was to be made Cardinal and a few weeks later he went off to Rome to get the red hat. There was great rejoicing and the Catholic parts of Armagh city were festooned with flags and big banners welcoming him home. On the night of his homecoming we were given permission to go down town in groups to join in the celebrations. It was the only time during my five years in the college that we were allowed such freedom and we could hardly believe it was happening. Shopkeepers must have wondered what was taking place as they were invaded by hoards of escaped prisoners keen to spend all the money they had on sweets and other treats.

I was going out of the college gates with three or four of my friends when my aunt Maggie, my father's sister, appeared beside us. She too had three or four of her friends with her and they were all in high spirits. Maggie worked as a housekeeper with Fr. Dan McDonald and at that time they were based in Galbally. I had only met her once or twice before because she was always away working when I happened to be at granny's house. She introduced me to all her friends and was obviously delighted that she had a nephew at the college.

"And who are these boys that you have with you?" she asked.

"This is Arty McAnerney", I said.

The eyes of all four women gazed at Arty.

"Lord, isn't he a lovely boy", said one. "And such a mass of beautiful fair curly hair".

"And where do you come from, Arty?" asked Maggie.

Arty explained that he lived in the city.

"Oh, so you are not a boarder here then?" one of the women said.

Arty explained that he was a boarder even though his home was only a mile or so away. The women looked at each other and shook their heads in wonder.

"And who are your other two friends?" asked Maggie.

"Phil Stewart and Paddy McGuckin", I explained.

"And where do you boys come from?" one of the women enquired.

"We both come from Ballinderry Bridge", replied Phil.

The women began a discussion with Phil and Paddy about the priests who were in their parish at that time and explained that Fr. McDonald was very friendly with both of them. They were all deeply into religion and were keen to show that they were on familiar terms with priests all over the country.

"Come on down town with us", said Maggie at last and we'll see if we can get you something for a wee treat. We know that the usual food in the college is poor enough".

We wandered down into the heart of the city and the women bought us sweets and then took us into a café to have a mineral and a bun. The city was thronged with people and it was difficult to get served but they managed to get us the treat.

"Well, boys", said Maggie, when we had devoured the buns, "I'm sure you don't want to spend all evening in the company of a crowd of old fogies like us. We'll let you go now to enjoy the rest of your time out".

As we parted company Maggie slipped a pound note into my hand. I looked at it and gasped. "That's far too much Aunt Maggie", I said trying to get her to take it back. I knew that a priest's housekeeper did not earn much money at that time. She insisted, however, and each of her friends gave me five shillings as well. It was an evening of generosity and pleasure that I would not forget. The big bonus for me was that I would not have to ask my mother for as much pocket money for some time to come. We did catch a glimpse of the new Cardinal in his flowing crimson robes but the importance of the occasion did not make a great impact on us.

A week or two later we got a really great surprise. One morning all the older boys were talking of there being a banquet for us that evening. I had never heard of a banquet and I asked some of my friends what it was. They did not seem to be much better informed than I was but they knew that it was some sort of special meal.

That evening we went down to supper to find the ref decorated from end to end in banners, flags and bunches of balloons. Some were in yellow and white, which someone informed me were the papal colours. There were lots of others in crimson to celebrate our new Cardinal. All the tables were covered in lovely cloths and there were big jugs of orange drinks and even flowers on each table. When I got to my place and looked at the cutlery setting I got a shock. There were so many spoons and forks that I wondered what on earth the half of them could be for.

"What are all these knives and forks and spoons for?" I asked the boys beside me.

"What are knives and forks usually for?" one of them asked as though he thought I was a real gulpin.

It was soon agreed, however, that nobody had a clue as to what all the extra cutlery was for or as to how it should be used.

Fr. Gallagher called for silence and said grace. When he had done that he called for continued silence.

"A lot of you boys will never have seen tables laid

like this before", he said. "I think that the best rule I can give you is that you work from the outside in. We are to have soup first so the spoon for that will be on the outside of the group. I will try to help you out as I go around the ref. Now enjoy the meal that the new Cardinal has decided to give you. I think that deserves a round of applause in his honour".

It was a really beautiful four-course dinner. I had never even dreamed of such a meal and I certainly enjoyed every bite of it.

"That was some feed", I said to Arty and Phil as we came out of the ref. "It would be great if we get a dinner like that from time to time".

It was never repeated but I have always felt grateful to the Cardinal for the treat and I'm sure all the other boys felt the same.

We were told a story about a famous incident, which had taken place in the college seven or eight years before our time. The previous Cardinal, Cardinal McRory, was having some sort of banquet or party and a group of the senior students found out that lots of beautiful food was stored nearby in the Cardinal's residence and decided that it was only fair that they should have a share of it. They decided on a midnight raid.

As the story was told to us they made their way out of the dorm and slipped across to the Cardinal's palace and managed to push open one of the windows. They found a room where all sorts of food and drink had been left in readiness for the following day. They took all that they could carry and returned to the dorm to have a feast. Some of them tried out the alcoholic drink and were affected by the liquor to such an extent that they forgot to keep quiet. The Dean of the time was alerted by the noise and found the dorm in chaos when he entered.

It was a clear case of multiple expulsions if the rules had been applied. The boys were in their final few months, however, and the leaders were all part of the most successful football team that the college had ever produced. The merry making was quietly forgotten but had become a part of college folklore by our time.

I have been assured since that the food had been taken from the school ref, but that had never been suggested to us. Raiding the Cardinal's residence made a far better story.

CHAPTER 6.
DAYLIGHT ROBBERY

We did not need a lot of pocket money but from time to time the teachers in various classes asked us to buy extra things that would help in our courses. On a Saturday too, ice cream was sold from a stall in the main hall and it was nice to be able to have a slider now and again. It meant that if my mother could not get into town she would send me a ten-shilling note in a letter.

A time came when mother was not so well and to my surprise the usual letters arrived but with no money in them in spite of repeated requests. I was broke. At last my mother appeared for a call one Saturday and I saw immediately that she was quite annoyed.

"What are you doing with all the money?" she demanded as soon as we were alone.

"But Mammy, I haven't had any money for five or six weeks", I gasped.

"What do you mean you have not had any money for weeks? Sure haven't I sent you ten shillings nearly every week this long time? You know well that I can't afford it. I have bother enough getting money for your clothes and fees. I can't give you money like this and you should know that".

I could see tears in her eyes and a redness in her cheeks. I put my arm round her shoulder and hugged her.

"Mammy, I don't know what has been happening. I know that you have not got much money and I try not to spend much. But there are wee bits and pieces that we have to get from time to time and there's not much I can do about that. But Mammy, all your letters for the past five or six weeks have come with no money at all in them".

We discussed the matter and decided that someone was taking money out of the letters and one obvious suspect that we could think of was a postman. The other possibility was that the college censors had taken the money when they were examining the incoming letters.

"I'm going to see the President this minute", declared mother, rising angrily from her seat. "I can't afford to have my few shillings stolen by someone who has far more money to spend that I have".

"Mammy", I said, standing in front of her, "you can't just go and see the President. You have to have made an appointment. He won't see people just like that".

"He'll see me", said mother angrily, "even if I have to knock down the door".

"Please take it easy, Mammy", I pleaded, "I'll go and see the Dean and I'll explain to him what has happened and he will get the thing sorted out. Please do not try to see the President".

My mother sat down again and looked at me. She was still very annoyed and obviously not too sure that I should be left to handle this situation. At last, however, she agreed to my request but demanded that I take care of things immediately. She gave me a ten-shilling note, which I knew might well be the last one she had.

The next morning I went up to Fr. Gallagher as we were leaving the ref after breakfast.

"Father", I asked, "could I have a word with you?"

He looked down at me and a big smile lit up his face. "A man from the wilds of Tyrone can always have a word with me", he said, giving me a friendly punch on the shoulder. "What is it that is annoying you?"

"There's something funny going on, Father", I said. "My mother has been sending me money for the past few weeks in her letters and the money has been disappearing".

"Go on up to my room, Arthur, and wait at the door", he said. "I'll be up in a minute to talk to you".

I went up to the Dean's room and stood outside his door as directed. It was five minutes or so before he came bounding up the stairs with his cane in one hand and the big bundle of keys in the other. He threw the door open and told me to go in.

"Take a seat on that chair there", he said, going behind his desk and sitting down on his own chair. He rubbed his hand across his forehead as though he were feeling very tired and looked at me. It struck me at the time that though his eyes were on me his mind was elsewhere.

"So you have been losing money from your letters", he said slowly and quietly. "Now how long exactly has this been going on?"

"It has been going on for the last couple of months, Father. My mother sends me a ten-shilling note every few weeks for pocket money. About two months ago I had asked for some money and none came. It was only when my mother came on a call yesterday, that I discovered that three or four notes had been taken from my letters?"

"Did you not notice that the letters had been opened?"

"I didn't pass much remarks on that Father, because sometimes they are opened by the President".

The Dean looked at me and nodded. "You have a point there", he agreed. "But has your mother told you how much money has disappeared?"

"I think it's about two or three pounds, Father. But that is an awful lot of money for my mother to lose. Some people might not miss it but my mother has very little money in the first place".

He sat for a moment and looked at me thoughtfully. I felt rather uneasy under his steady gaze.

"Would you agree to help me to find out where this money has been going?" he asked at last in a kind and gentle tone and sounding as though he were asking a great favour.

"I will do my best, Father".

"Have you ever heard of your word of honour?"

"Yes Father, it is a kind of very solemn promise".

"Would you keep your word of honour if you gave it to me?"

"I would indeed, Father".

He leant across the desk towards me and spoke as though sharing a great secret with me.

"I have a fair idea who is taking the money, he said, "but I need your help to prove it. I am now putting you on your word of honour that you will not mention one word of this conversation to anyone. And I mean anyone, even your best friends. Do you think, Arthur, that you could give me your word of honour on that?"

"I give you my word of honour surely, Father. Wild horses would not drag one word from me".

He leaned back and laughed. "That's a fine promise", he said, "and I know you will keep it. Now go on about your normal business and I will have some news for you in a day or two".

The boys knew that I had been quite a while in Gammy's room and they asked me all sorts of questions as to what had been going on. Was I in serious trouble? Was I going to get expelled? Did I get six slaps on each hand? I managed to give evasive answers, which gave the impression that I was in trouble but did not want to talk about it. Slowly their curiosity died away.

A couple of days later I was walking along the

main corridor with some of my friends after leaving first study. Fr. Gallagher's voice suddenly bellowed above the gentle hum of many conversations.

"Daly, get up to my room at once. Hurry along now Boy".

Everyone gasped. I was clearly in serious trouble but there was no reason for it that anyone could think of. I could feel hundreds of eyes on me as I turned and made my way up the stairs. I stood outside the door of the Dean's room and wondered what was to befall me now.

A few minutes went past and he came bounding up the stairs in a very business like fashion. He had a big smile on his face.

"We are going on a trip", he informed me, "and it comes under the rules of your word of honour. You are not to tell anyone what is about to happen. I have got Father Devine to look after the ref while I am away. You are going to miss supper but do not worry about that. The boys are all in the ref now so I want you to go down to the foyer and wait for me there. Go on now, Arthur, and I will be with you in a minute".

I could not work out what under heaven was taking place. I made my way along the main corridor wondering where we were going and why. I pushed on the big double doors and entered the 'holy of holies.' Just as I arrived Fr. Sheridan came out of his room and glared at me.

"What are you doing here, Boy? Don't you know that this area is totally out of bounds?"

"Fr. Gallagher told me to come down here and wait for him Father. I don't know why he sent me here".

"Oh, yes, that's right", he said and went out through the main door of the college without another word. I stood there perplexed. Two or three minutes went past and then the Dean appeared in his usual bounding fashion, his soutane fluttering around him.

"Right Arthur", he said, "we are going out to your house and I have a taxi waiting. The President has agreed to my plan and I want to see your parents. Hurry on now or we will be away all night".

I gasped. I could hardly believe my ears. I was stunned and while I was delighted at the opportunity of a visit home, I could hardly take it in. I went out through the door in a daze with the Dean on my heels.

We got into the taxi and the driver started off. "I think you said we were going out to Benburb, Father", he said in a questioning voice.

"That's right, Peter", answered the Dean, "and from there, Arthur will guide us to his house. But Peter as far as you are concerned this trip never took place. I do not want you to mention it to anyone. It is most important that you do not breathe a word of it to anyone".

"Lord, Father", laughed Peter, "you sound like someone out of those spy stories. Are you sure that we are not going to be kidnapped or shot or something?"

"Don't worry, Peter", the Dean answered, "but remember to keep your mouth shut".

We arrived at our house and Fr. Gallagher told me to warn my parents that there was an invasion. I jumped out of the car, pressed the latch and opened the door. I remember being amazed at how small the door was and how strange it was to operate the latch again. When I appeared in the little kitchen my parents looked as though they had seen a ghost.

"God bless us and save us all this night", gasped my mother, "have you got the road out of the college? What under heaven have you been up to now?"

"Fr. Gallagher is here", I stuttered. "He has come out to have a word with you both".

My father had just finished his dinner and was sitting in his chair by the fire. My mother had finished clearing away the dishes and was tidying up. There was a lovely odour of cooking in the little kitchen. The huge bulk of the priest appeared behind me.

"God bless all here", he said, "I'm sorry to interrupt you in this way, Mr. and Mrs Daly, but I felt that I had to have a word with you in private".

Da got up from his chair and held out his hand. "You're more than welcome, Father", he said, "You'll have to take a cup of tea. Lord, Father but you are a mighty lump of a man; what height would you be now?"

"I'm six foot three in my bare feet", laughed the Dean.

"And built like a battleship", continued Da. "Sarah,

make a cup of tea there. And my name is Mick Father; nobody ever calls me anything else. Take a seat there and make yourself at home".

"I'm delighted to meet you Mick", replied the Dean in a friendly way, "but I'm afraid we have not got much time. I have a taxi man waiting out on your street. But give Arthur something to eat if you don't mind. I had to bring him out without any supper and he must be starving".

"Bring the man in and don't leave him sitting out there", said Da, heading for the door.

Fr. Gallagher put his hand on Da's arm to stop him. "I would do that normally", he said, "but I don't want anyone to hear what we are going discuss. I'm afraid he'll have to be left out there. But we won't be long. By the way Mick, where do you work yourself?"

"I'm working on a building site in Dungannon", replied Da. "I had been working in Benburb but this job came up a couple of months ago. We are building an estate of houses that they call the White City".

Fr. Gallagher looked at him clearly puzzled. "And how far away is that?" he asked. "How do you get to your work from here?"

"Och, sure I go on the bicycle, Father. There is no other way of getting into Dungannon from here. It would be about eight miles".

"Heavens", the priest gasped. "And you ride the whole way, do a day's work, and then have to ride home again in the evening".

Da laughed. "Ach, Father, sure it keeps the old

bones from getting stiff". The priest looked at him and shook his head.

My mother already had the pan on the fire and began putting big slices of bacon on it. She cut slices from a Scotch dumpling, which was sitting on the middle of the table to go with the bacon. I knew that I was going to enjoy a lovely supper on this particular night.

While all this was going on I was sitting in a kind of daze and looking all round the room. I could not get over how small it seemed after getting used to the huge rooms in the college. It was warm and cosy in the soft glow of the oil lamp hanging above the fireplace and in the ever changing, dancing light from the big fire itself. Fr. Gallagher too was obviously enjoying his respite in the family atmosphere.

My mother stopped her work at the pan and turned round to face her guest. "You'll take a wee bite, yourself, Father", she said. "It's as easy to make for two as one and sure it's never nice for a body to have to eat on his own".

The big priest looked up at her and smiled. "You know", he said, "I really shouldn't. Fr. Sheridan would kill me if he knew. But with that odour from your cooking no human being could refuse. But only give me very little for I've had my supper".

Mother's face gave the impression that she had won a big prize. She was very proud of her cooking and to cook for a priest was something only to be dreamed of. She busied herself setting the table with her best dishes and in a short time called us to the table. The meal was absolutely delicious.

"This meal is totally delightful, Mrs Daly", said the Dean, with a big satisfied smile. "But what is this stuff that you have with it? It's delicious; it's the food of the gods. I've never tasted anything so gorgeous in all my life. I've really eaten far too much".

I knew that these words had made my mother's day and that she would savour them for many years to come. She loved people to praise her cooking and these words from a priest were the icing on the cake.

"That's Scotch dumpling, Father. Only the Scotch people can make it right and I learned the art from my mother when I was a wee lassie in Glasgow. Mick here would crawl a mile on his knees for a bite of it".

"Now", said Fr. Gallagher, "we will have to get down to business. As you know money has been disappearing and Arthur has told me what has been happening to his letters. I think I know who is responsible but I need your help to prove it. I want you to write a normal letter to Arthur here and address the envelope as you usually would. Mr. Doherty, the science teacher has treated a ten-shilling note for me and I plan to put it in the letter. I will post the letter in Armagh and then wait to see what happens. I hope you don't mind".

They assured him that they didn't mind at all and my mother got a bottle of ink and a pen and sat down at the table to try to write as normal a letter as possible. It took her some time but eventually she finished and handed it to the Dean. In the meantime Da had discovered that the Gallaghers came from Donegal, that they were hard working people and that the priest had two sisters married in America. He was also able to find out what made up a normal day for the Dean in the college.

"By God, do you know what I'm going to tell you Father?" he said, in obvious surprise, "you'd be far better off carrying bricks in a hod like myself. That is a holy tarra of a job altogether".

"I suppose you find it hard enough to find the money for the boarding fees?" remarked Fr. Gallagher.

"Well, indeed Father, it's not easy", said my mother earnestly, "and I hear they are going up".

The Dean nodded slowly looking from one of then to the other.

"You know", he said at last, "we have six priests who earn teaching salaries. Each of us only gets a few shillings a week of pocket money. All the rest goes towards the upkeep of the school. Only for that the fees would be double. Not many people know that and I don't want you to talk about it but it may give you some consolation to know the real situation".

Da looked at the priest and scratched his head. "Well that's a tarra to man altogether", he said. "Do you mean to tell me that you do all that work and you don't even get your pay? Lord Father but you are nearly worse off that the prisoners in the Crumlin Road in Belfast".

Fr. Gallagher looked at him and shook his head. "You are right in one way, Mick", he said with a laugh. "But the prisoners are there against their will. We chose the life we live so we might be dafter than they are. Now we'll have to be on our way".

The journey back to Armagh was uneventful but I had the devil of a job trying to account for my absence from second study. My pals and indeed everyone else in the class were mystified as to where I had been and were not satisfied with my explanations. They sensed that something had been going on.

The next time my mother came on a call the Dean made a point of seeing her. He explained that a postman had been taking the money and he had stolen the note, which had been planted. His hands were discoloured and he could not deny what he had done. He had a wife and young family and the Dean gave him the choice of returning all the money he had taken or the College Authorities would go to the police. He chose to return the money and Fr. Gallagher gave my mother back the amount that had been taken from my letters and thanked her for her help.

The episode had two lasting effects. For years to come my father would talk of "yon big priest who was out here one night, do ye mind?" He never failed to express his total admiration for the man and to emphasise to me how lucky I was to have such a fine character in charge of me. "Be God, Da", I said a couple of times, "you might not be so fond of him if you were on the other end of his three foot cane".

The other result was, however, that I got a glimpse of a very different side of the man they called a 'savage' and I am still very thankful for that.

CHAPTER 7
A BRIGHT GLOW IN THE TWILIGHT

About three or four weeks after entering the college, homesickness struck. It wasn't too bad during the day because the time was taken up with class work or study and the companionship of friends. At Mass in the mornings, however, it descended like a dark cloud and but for the shame of it I could have cried my eyes out or even bawled out loud. It was like being in a dark tunnel and not being able to see the end of it. The one consolation was that as I glanced sideways at my fellow students, I could see them wiping their eyes and I knew that we were all in the same boat.

The other time when the cloud closed in was when I lay in the silence of the dorm after getting into bed. Sleep did not come easily and as I lay looking up at the high ceiling I was overcome by a desperate desire for my own little bed at home and for the joy of sitting with my parents at the fire listening to their chat and stories as we sat in the friendly flickering light of the fire with the gentle dancing shadows on the walls. It all seemed very far away from this harsh and demanding way of life in which

I found myself. Tears streamed down my cheeks in the darkness and it was little consolation to hear the forlorn whimperings from the neighbouring beds. I wondered night after night why I had been looking forward to coming to this place during the long days of the past summer.

This awful feeling lasted about three weeks and then it cleared as quickly as it had come. I still had pangs of longing for home now and again but not in the same intensity and not particularly in the chapel nor in bed. I had settled into college life.

At about the time when the homesickness passed the annual college retreat was held. It was a three-day time of prayer and meditation and sermons. All normal work was suspended. And it was a time of total silence; at least it was supposed to be. We were ordered to keep silence at all times, even during the breaks and at meals. We were assured that it was a time of exceptional grace and opportunity when one was supposed to be alone with God. Whilst it soon became clear to me that most of the boys hated it, I rather enjoyed it. Maybe it was because I was an only child that I found it quite pleasant to be alone and I loved the challenge of keeping total silence. It was a new experience to nod to one's friends while out walking in the grounds but not to speak.

A team of priests was brought in from other parts of Ireland to lead the retreat. They were Vincentians too and apparently spent most of their time giving missions.

In the first couple of days their talks were filled with fire-and-thunder and I found myself shaking in my shoes in dread of the awful fate that lay in store for anyone who would dare step even slightly out of line. I had been to missions at home with my parents but these sermons made an impact on me that I had never experienced before. It seemed that God was always round the next corner waiting to clobber anyone who offended him in the slightest way and I was certain that he had good reason to clobber me rather than some of my neighbours.

On the final day of the retreat the tone became much more gentle and a way out of all trouble was opened up to us. A good confession would heal all the self-imposed wounds and we were assured a gentle and loving God was waiting to welcome us back into his friendship with open arms. At one point a priest stopped suddenly and stood looking all round the chapel. His eyes seemed to search into every corner as though looking for something or someone he knew to be there but could not see. Everyone waited with baited breath, wondering what was coming next. The dramatic pause seemed to go on forever.

"There is a boy sitting down there in this chapel", he said at last, letting his outstretched arm and his pointed finger move very slowly over the crowd, "and he is in deep and lasting trouble. He feels that he has made bad confession and he is very worried about it. I can see him now and I beg him to come to confession and take this chance of lasting peace. The chance may never come again".

I tried my best to make myself as small as I could in my seat. "This man knows about me", I thought. "He must be getting a special message from God. What will everyone think if he exposes me in public?"

My mind went back to the day when I had made my first confession. I had been at a Protestant school at the time and the priests of the parish ruled that I could not go to confession with everyone else who had been attending their own Catholic school. As a special privilege to my parents, Fr. Soraghan, the parish priest, agreed that they could prepare me for the big day and that he would test me to see if I was ready. If I passed the test then I could go to confession to him in his own house in The Moy.

I passed the test and for years afterwards my mother claimed great praise for the job she had done in my preparation! She was the equal of the trained teachers in the school. There was nothing wrong with my mother's teaching but facing the priest in this manner, however, proved to be somewhat overwhelming even though he was kind and gentle. I felt that I had made a bad confession and I had been carrying the guilt like a heavy burden ever since.

I can still feel the sense of relief and gratitude that I felt coming out of confession on that final day of the retreat in the college. I felt as light as a feather and that I could have flown over the school. In my heart I felt relieved and happy and it had all been so easy. It is little wonder, therefore, that I still see that retreat as one of the highlights of my life.

On the second night of the retreat I was just about to drift off to sleep when the lights were suddenly switched on. Fr. Gallagher was standing beside the switch with his cane in his hand.

"The boys of this dormitory are a disgrace", he shouted angrily. "I could hear lots of talk outside in the corridor and that in the middle of the retreat. Will all those boys who were talking stand out at the end of their beds immediately?"

Two or three boys did stand out. The Dean studied them for a few seconds.

"There were a lot more boys talking than that", he said firmly. "Every one of you stand out and as I come towards your bed, lean over the end of it. I am going to give each of you four strokes of the cane on the bottom. I will not put up with this sort of behaviour at any time and in the middle of a retreat especially".

It must have taken ten minutes for him to administer the punishment to every boy in the dorm. If it did nothing else it certainly made me aware of how thin the material of my pyjamas was. We were allowed to slip back into bed as soon as he had passed.

The sound of the sharp intaking of breath due to pain grew in intensity as he progressed through the dorm. More and more boys were suffering. The Dean was later to tell us that he called the procedure 'stoking the furnace', which he saw as a good description of the pain-filled sounds that he left in his wake. Two or three times a year over our first three years I remember the furnace being well and truly stoked.

Normally the Dean would call for boys to step out and admit to their misdeeds. Only on very rare occasions did he refuse to accept the result. It was a matter of honour to own up and save one's companions from punishment. There were a couple of fellows, however, who would lie on and pretend to be asleep even though they were guilty. They were certainly not too popular for their actions. We had to work out a rota system whereby a group of three would jump out of bed and claim to be responsible for actions of which they were not guilty.

There were quite a few boys in the college who came from County Derry. At one stage a priest who was taking a sermon during the retreat referred to this fact and told us a story he had heard concerning a couple of men from Derry.

One of the men was rather small but was considered very bright and was seen as a great credit to his people and his parish. His companion was very big and strong and not so bright but he acted as guardian for his friend. They were inseparable. If they were in a crowd and the big fellow thought that his companion was not getting enough of the conversation, he would demand silence and shout, "listen to what the 'Darry' man has to say or when

I'm finished with you, you won't be able to hear". At every opportunity he jumped to the defence of the 'Darry' man.

One day they were in a pub and at one stage the big fellow went out to the toilet. He came back into the bar a few minutes later to find his friend stretched on the floor. He looked around in an aggressive manner and demanded, "who hit the Darry man?"

An absolute giant of a man rose from the bar and confronted him. "I hit the Darry man", he said firmly, glaring into his face.

The guardian took a step backwards and looked at the huge man facing him and then he looked down at his friend still lying on the floor. "Be God", he said in a friendly way, "you must have hit him a quare thump".

The Derry boys saw this story as an awful insult to their county and complained bitterly about the cheek of the priest for telling such a story. They felt it was very unfair and as far as I could see it ruined the whole retreat for them.

CHAPTER 8
THE TALE OF A FRIENDLY COW

Special permission was necessary to go down town and it was only given to visit the doctor or the dentist. We were warned that to slip down to buy sweets or for any other reason would result in instant expulsion. In spite of this I heard of boys slipping into town and this was known as 'booling.' I never heard of anyone from our class who 'booled' but that does not mean that it did not happen.

Sunday afternoons provided a perfect opportunity for those who wished to bool. The morning had been taken up by a fairly long period of study and as a break after lunch we were taken for a walk if the weather allowed. One of the priests was in charge and he walked with some of the senior boys at the back of the long line of four hundred boys. It was impossible for him to see what was going on all along the line and so it was easy to slip into a shop if one had the money.

I never bothered to take advantage of these opportunities because I never had sufficient money. The walk usually wound its way across the city and along the Keady Road using the footpath that runs along the high wall that formed the boundary of the demesne belonging to the Church of Ireland Primate. The priest would then direct us to take one of the smaller side roads and make our way back by a circular route.

One Sunday when I was a senior boy, Fr. Curtin was in charge and Paddy McGuckin, Phil Stewart and I were his companions for the walk. Fr.Curtin, or Wee Baldy, as we called him, was our English teacher and was a very friendly and kindly character. The walk wound its way out into the country and we found ourselves at the end of a long lane. It was about three miles from the centre of town.

"There is no way out of here", said Fr. Curtin, "we are going to have to go back the way we came".

The entire school was milling about in a state of chaos.

"Look Father", I said, "if we climb over this gate and cross that field there is a lane at the other side and that will bring us back to the main road. It would be better than going back the same way".

"Oh God, look at here, Daly", the priest said, rubbing his sweating head, "that would be trespassing. The farmer would not like us going on to his land without permission". Fr. Curtin seldom failed to preface his words with 'look at here'.

"Och, don't worry about that, Father", Phil and Paddy assured him, "in this part of the country nobody worries about things like that. We come from the country and we know".

Fr. Curtin stood thinking for a minute or two, clearly in doubt about the wisdom of this suggestion. The walk had got completely out of order in the narrow lane. At last he made up his mind and called for order, which the senior boys helped him to restore.

"Look at here, we are going to cross this field", he announced, pointing to another gate at the far side, "and we will get out on to that other road and make our way back from there. The first years will go first and make sure that you keep in order and climb the gates carefully. On you go now". The boys were delighted with this new experience and it was surprisingly easy to organise the operation. In a few minutes the line stretched right across the field and the junior boys were already climbing over the other gate on to the road. An inquisitive cow came wandering towards us. Fr. Curtin was clearly alarmed.

"What kind of an animal is that?" he gasped. "I don't like the look of it".

"That's a wild looking bull", I lied. "That's the kind of animal you might find in a bullring in Spain, they tell me. You would need to watch that boy or he could gore you". Paddy and Phil looked at the old cow, which by now was nosing up beside us. They started to laugh. Fr. Curtin, however, had taken off and was running as fast as his legs would carry him towards the gate. There was total pandemonium.

"I know nothing at all about animals in the fields"!

It took a long time to get back to some semblance of order and start the journey back to town. The line was now noticeably shorter as numerous boys had taken the opportunity to escape and head for the shops in the city. As we eventually made our way through the narrow streets towards the college, large groups joined us from the alleys where they had been hiding. The day was henceforth referred to as 'booling Sunday'.

A few days later Fr. Curtin asked me to stay behind at the end of his English class.

"Daly", he said, in an offended tone, "did you clash on me and tell some of the priests that I lost control of the walk last Sunday?"

"I did not indeed, Father", I replied in an equally offended tone. "I never mentioned anything only to Phil and Paddy and I can guarantee you that they would not mention anything either. But Father, I am sorry for taking a hand out of you by telling you that the old cow was a bull. I thought you would have known that I was only joking".

"I know nothing about farm animals", he said, shaking his head. "But some blighter went and spilled the beans and old Gussy has been putting me through the grinder all week. There's some boys about this place who could not hold their own water".

I was dumbfounded. I would never have imagined that a member of staff would refer to the President in this way. And I was equally surprised that any student would think it worth his while to get Fr. Curtin into trouble. He was a real gentleman and a fine teacher and I loved all his English classes. He was now looking at me as though he were a wee bit puzzled. "Daly", he continued, "has anyone ever had a good conversation with you about the facts of life?"

This came completely out of the blue and it was the last thing on earth that I was expecting. "No, Father", I blurted out.

"Look at here, Daly, you need to know about the facts of life. Did your parents never mention anything about them to you?"

"No, Father", I assured him truthfully. It was a subject that was never mentioned in our house and anything I knew had been picked up by chance from others who seemed to know a lot more than I did.

"Well, Daly", the priest continued, looking at me in a serious way, "you are old enough to know about the facts of life. I have found out that you are an only child. I will keep you behind every Thursday after our English class and talk to you about them. By the way, Daly, it has come to my knowledge that you go about acting me for the amusement of your companions".

This really stumped me. I had picked up many of Fr. Curtin's favourite phrases over the years and I had got into the habit of trying to mimic him as best I could. But I never thought that he would find out about it. I could not think of a sensible thing to say.

"Look at here, Daly", he continued, certain now that he was correct, "in the next play I will give you the part of a girl. Now how funny do you think that is? Wouldn't you look lovely in a nice wee dress?"

He must have seen the look of utter horror on my face. He laughed. "There is a lovely wee cheeky girl in the next play I am thinking of doing and it is a part that was made for you. You will get all the acting you want".

"Father", I blurted out, "I could never play the part of a girl. I just could not do it Father".

"And why not, may I ask?"

"Father, I am no good at changing my voice. I could never make it sound like a girl speaking".

"That's very strange", he said in a puzzled tone and tapping his pen on the desk. "It puzzles me that you are so good at mimicking me and yet you are unwilling to take a main part in a play".

"I will take any part you want, Father, but I know I could never play the part of a girl. And I will never go about acting you again, Father".

"OK", he said, "we'll leave it there for now".

He kept his first promise, however, and every Thursday for the next few months he gave me a talk on the facts of life. I learned an awful lot from him in English class but I was no wiser after his course on the birds and the bees. I came to the conclusion that the poor man knew even less that I did myself. Each week was a repeat of the one before and never got beyond, "look at here, Daly, boys and girls are different and you have to get that into your head". I had known that much already and I was rather thankful for that difference.

One boy gained a notorious reputation for booling. His name was Tom Gallagher and although he was in the class above ours, I got to know him well. He was from Eglish, where his father was the schoolmaster so he was nearly a neighbour of ours at home. Tom maintained a constant supply of sweets, cigarettes, and fruit, which he sold at extortionate prices to students from all classes in the college. It was rumoured that he was making a fortune. I have no idea how he hid the produce but Gammy never found it.

"How do you manage to get down town without being caught, Tom?" I asked him one day.

Tom looked at me and winked. "You need to know when to go so that they will not see you", he answered with a knowing smile.

"And when would that be?" I enquired.

"If you knew that then you would be as wise as me", he replied. "That is something that I don't tell to anyone. If you want something, just you tell me and I'll have it for you in a day or two".

"I never have much money, Tom. Maybe you could see your way to give me a cut price deal. After all we live only a couple of miles from each other".

It would be impossible to describe the look of utter disgust on Tom's face. "If you don't have the money", he said sharply, "you get nothing from me. Do you think I risk expulsion for nothing?"

How exactly Tom avoided expulsion was a mystery, which puzzled everyone in the school. It was widely known that he 'booled' down town at least once a week and during some weeks many times. The authorities must have been aware of this and yet he never seemed to get into bother. It was a puzzle to which I never found an answer.

Expulsion was constantly held over our heads. It was seen as the greatest disgrace that could befall anyone and was to be avoided at all costs. It must have made keeping discipline a lot easier that it otherwise would have been. I can remember only one occasion when the penalty was used and two boys were expelled.

I think it was during my second year and the boys were two years senior to me. I was walking round the junior ring with Phil and Paddy and Arty as usual when Phil said, "did you hear that two lads are to expelled in the morning?"

"Did you hear what they are supposed to have done?" asked Paddy.

"Nobody from their year will tell me what their 'crime' was", replied Phil, "but they all agree that they have been punished in the wrong. The real villain has got off as usual but he is a great footballer and the authorities hope that he will help them to win the McRory cup next year".

"You don't mean to say that a good footballer can get off with anything?" asked Arty.

"Well, that's what it looks like", replied Phil. "I'm told that when Gammy calls on their dorm to own up to talking, your man lies on in bed and lets everyone else take the blame. But he's always the cause of the trouble".

There seemed to be general agreement amongst the students that this was so but I am not sure how justified it was.

We were told that the two boys would be leaving that morning at about ten o'clock. Our class happened to be in the study hall at the time and we were encouraged by the priest in charge to crowd round the windows and watch their walk of shame to the cars, which would take them home. We were aware that the same thing was happening all over the college and every possible window was being used for the same purpose. I remember the sombre atmosphere, which pervaded the whole school that morning. There was very little talk amongst us and I certainly felt an eerie sadness. It was meant to be a lesson on what could happen to anyone who broke the rules. I remember it with a feeling of disgust; I was revolted at the unfairness of it all. I am sure that most of the students who watched the scene had the same reaction.

CHAPTER 9
A CHANGE OF DIRECTION

As the first year progressed I found myself thinking more and more of becoming a priest. I suppose it was a very natural reaction because the priesthood was held up before us as a way of life far above all others. Priests were on a pedestal and their sacrifice for the sake of God was as close as one could get to perfection on this earth. This attitude towards the priesthood was prevalent in the Catholic community at large but was magnified for us by the clergy in the college. We were never allowed to forget that the college was a seminary and its main purpose was to produce priests for the diocese and for various orders working throughout the world. I imagine that there were very few boys who did not think of 'joining up' at some time during the course.

Students who came to the college with the idea of becoming a priest chose ancient Greek as one of their subjects. In my own case I had firmly set my face against such a course at first but the elation after the retreat changed all that. My conscience was now clear and I could think differently. I had chosen science, however, and that was somewhat of a problem.

I loved science and I got on very well with our teacher, Mr. Doherty, who was generally known as Johnny Neark. It was one of my best subjects and at the Christmas exams I had managed to get third place in class. A few weeks after Christmas I decided that I would ask to change to Greek. I shared my thoughts with Fergal O'Neill who was my best friend in the science class.

"Fergal", I said quietly as we worked, "I'm thinking of leaving this class and going over to Greek. What do you think of that?"

Fergal nearly dropped the test tube he was holding at the time.

"For God's sake, Arthur, is your head cut?" he asked in a loud voice, so that Mr. Doherty looked round sharply to see what was going on. We worked on until the teacher's attention was elsewhere.

"Your head must be cut", whispered Fergal. "You're at the top of the class and what in blazes would make you think of changing to bloody Greek? If I was as good as you at science I'd be counting my blooming blessings. Get your head right and forget about it".

At the break after class we walked round the junior ring together. Fergal was from Middletown, where his father was a teacher and he was to remain one of my best friends for the entire duration of our stay at the college.

"I have been thinking of becoming a priest Fergal",

I explained, "and Greek seems to be a good subject for that".

"We are more than half way through the year", said Fergal, "and you'd be starting from scratch. How do you hope to catch up?"

"It would not be easy, I know, Fergal", I replied thoughtfully, "but at the same time I think I might give it a try if Fr. Devine will take me into his class".

"I think your head is cut for sure now", Fergal said. "I know that Johnny Neark thinks the world of you and you are at the top of the class in a great subject. Definitely your head is cut and I think you need to get it straightened out".

That evening Fergal, Paddy, Phil, Arty and I were walking round the ring as usual.

"Did Arthur tell you all what he is thinking of doing?" Fergal asked the others.

"What's that?" they enquired in unison.

"He's thinking of leaving the science class and changing over to Greek", replied Fergal. "I think it's real madness. I have been telling him that his head is cut".

"Wait till I tell you something", said Paddy, looking at me with a scowl on his face. "Before I came here a man at home told me not to have anything to do with the Irish language. He said it was a load of gibberish. So I chose to join the French class. Then I found out that the Irish was a real language and as you all know I changed over. I heard all you boys starting to use the Irish and I realised that it was my own language.

Now that was after two months and I found out that I was already well behind and I've had to work like the devil to try to catch up. Now we're coming up to the Easter holidays so Arthur would be nearly a year behind. I think it would be clean madness. I do Greek and it's no picnic. Stay where you are Arthur if you're half wise".

Everyone agreed that I should stay with the science especially since I was doing well at it. "Wait till you see, boys", said Arty, "he'll change over in spite of us and he'll get his feet well burned".

A few days later I approached Fr. Devine.

"Father", I said, "I have been thinking of changing over from science to Greek. Would you take me into your class and would I have any chance of catching up with the rest of the boys?"

The young priest looked at me thoughtfully.

"And why do you want to change over?" he asked. "Are you not getting along with Mr. Doherty?"

"Oh I'm getting along fine with Mr. Doherty, Father", I said confidently, "but I was thinking of going for the church and Greek seems to be a good subject to have in that case".

Fr. Devine rubbed his hand through his hair and studied me for a long moment. "Greek is not essential for the priesthood", he replied, "but if you really want to change I'll give you some extra help during second study for the rest of the year. That does not mean that I think it's a good idea, but if you want to go ahead you will be welcome in my class. It's up to you".

I asked Fr. Devine to request the President to let me change over and in a few days word came through that my request had been granted. The lay staff had a rota for helping out at second study and it so happened that Johnny Doherty was on duty that evening. A couple of minutes after study started he came to my desk and tapped me on the shoulder. "Come down to the back", he said sharply, "I want to talk to you".

At the back of the study hall was a huge bookcase, which went right across the width of the hall and served as the school library. I stopped beside it with Mr. Doherty. He looked me straight in the eyes and it was easy to see that he was quite angry.

"So you have changed over to Greek", he snarled, "and you did not have the manners to even tell me that you had been thinking of doing that".

I got an awful shock. I had been so involved in trying to work out what was the right thing to do that I had never thought of consulting my teacher. "I'm very sorry, Sir", I gasped, "I have been thinking of the priesthood and I clean forgot to tell you".

"So you never thought of all the work I had put into you for the last seven months? And you have the makings of a fine scientist. I am very hurt and disappointed but I suppose you are well pleased with yourself and that's all that matters".

I felt really ashamed and disgusted with myself. I had been quite pleased with my own work in science and I had never thought of the work the teacher had been doing. It was difficult to know what to say.

"I am very sorry indeed, Sir", I stuttered, "I know that I was wrong and I'm sorry for that".

"Go back to your desk and study your flaming Greek", said Johnny through his teeth. "I want nothing more to do with you".

For the rest of my time in the college he totally ignored me. I was very hurt though I still think of him with a great deal of affection and respect. He was one of the finest teachers I have ever known.

I found myself in very deep water in the Greek class. Fr. Devine did his best to help out but he had to be fair to the rest of the class. He did take me out during second study for half an hour or so of tutoring two or three times a week and that helped. During these sessions I got an insight into his life.

"So you are thinking of becoming a priest, Arthur", he said one evening. "Have you any idea how hard this life is?"

I looked at him in amazement. I had never really considered that side of a priest's life. I had seen them in an aura of glory. The priest saw that his question had shocked me.

"How do you see my position here in the college?" he asked.

I thought this a strange question and I found it hard to know what to say. "You are good at your job, Father, and you get on well with the boys. Everyone is very fond of you and you seem to be happy", I stammered.

Father Devine sat looking at me for quite a while.

"And do you think that this is where I want to be?" He asked the question as though the obvious answer was 'no', but I could not think why that should be.

"Well, yes, Father, you always appear to be in good form and happy".

"I never wanted to teach and the same goes for Fr. Dougan. We both wanted to be away out on the missions in Africa or somewhere. But we were sent here and we have a vow of obedience. We have to do what we are told. The same goes for every priest in the school. Now what do you think of that? Do you fancy total obedience?"

I did not know what to answer and I looked down at the floor.

"Do you know at what time we get up in the morning?" was his next question.

I looked up at him in surprise. "I thought you got up at half past six", I said, "the same as the rest of us".

He lay back in his chair and laughed. "We get up at a quarter past five each morning", he replied. "We have over an hour's meditation done by the time you boys think of rising. How do you fancy that?"

"I do not fancy it at all, Father", I blurted out. He laughed and gave me a friendly punch. "I'm only telling you this so that you will not have a false idea of the life we lead. I just want you to know that it is no easy way of life".

CHAPTER 10
HOSPITAL

With Fr. Devine's help I struggled to catch up on the Greek and I seemed to be doing reasonably well until about five or six weeks after the Easter holidays. One morning I awoke feeling quite unwell and I asked Fr. Gallagher for permission to go and see the matron. To my surprise he glanced at me and told me to go quickly. "When you do go up there", he warned, "stay away from everyone else. Now do you hear what I say? Make sure you stay away from everyone else".

I was very puzzled by this warning and I felt like some sort of leper.

The matron was in charge of health matters in the school and had a small room with six beds in it, which we called the Infirmary. Some boys went to the ends of the earth to be confined there for a few days rest. There was a special diet as well and that was a big attraction. One boy in our class for instance, had a habit of eating soap now and again in order to make himself sick. For some reason the matron was always known as Julia.

There were about a dozen boys lined up outside

the door of the Infirmary and instead of joining the line I stood on my own on the other side of the narrow corridor. After a couple of minutes the matron appeared and walked quickly along the line glancing at each boy in turn. She turned to look at me and stopped. She took me by the shoulder and led me to the end of the little corridor.

"Go on son immediately, and get your pyjamas, a towel, your tooth brush and toothpaste and put them in a case", she ordered. "Come back here immediately when you have that done and do not go near anyone. I repeat, do not go near anyone. Go now and be as quick as you can".

By now I was completely convinced that I had contacted some dread disease that was a threat to the rest of humanity. It was really scary and I wondered why she was so precise about my night attire if I were only going to be in the Infirmary for a day or two.

When I got back to the Infirmary with my little bag all the boys had gone but the matron was standing at the door talking to a fairly tall man. He was wearing a white coat and had a stethoscope round his shoulders. I knew he was a doctor. Both he and the matron were wearing masks. They took me into the Infirmary and told me to get up on a couch.

"This is Doctor Woods", said the matron, when I had done as asked. "He wants to examine you but he will only be a minute or two."

The doctor first looked into my eyes using a torch,

which cast a strong, narrow beam of light. "I'm fairly sure that's what it is", he mumbled to the matron. "You were right to call me immediately".

I was now convinced that the disease was even worse that I had thought and I began to wonder if there was really any chance of life after death. In my mind's eye I could see a small coffin in a big hearse winding its way along the narrow lanes of Sessiagh with all the neighbours walking along behind. The doctor examined my chest and then he asked me to get down and sit on a chair. "Please cross your knees for me", he said.

I put one leg across the other as asked and was very surprised when he took a little hammer and hit me with it on the uppermost knee. To my utter surprise the bottom part of the leg shot upwards.

"That's fine", said the doctor, glancing at the matron. "Now my young man would you please cross the legs the other way round?" He hit the other knee with the hammer and again the leg shot outwards.

"The reflexes are fine as you can see", he said to the matron. Then he turned to me.

"What is your full name young man?" he asked, taking out a pen and note pad.

"Arthur Francis Daly, Doctor".

"And where do you come from Arthur?"

"Sessiamagaroll, Doctor".

"And could you tell me what part of the country that is in please?"

"It's outside Benburb Doctor".

"Have you got a phone at home by any chance?"

"No Doctor, no one in our townland has a phone. There is a phone in the village but no one in my family has ever used it as far as I can remember".

The doctor turned to the matron. "How are we going to get in touch with his parents?" he asked.

"We could send a telegram Doctor", she replied. "I can't think of any other way".

He turned back to me with a serious look on his face. "Now Arthur", he said softly, "you have got scarlet fever. Have you ever heard of that?"

"I think I have Doctor", I gasped, "but I know nothing at all about it".

"Well, it's very infectious", he said, "so you are going to have to go to hospital for a few weeks. Don't worry it is not too dangerous if it is treated correctly and you will be as good as ever in a short time. But we have to keep you away from other people for a while. There has been an outbreak of the disease and you will find a few others in the same ward so you will not be lonely. Now can you think of any way we can contact your parents quickly?"

I studied the problem for a minute or two while the doctor and the matron filled in some forms. At last the doctor looked up and asked if I had come up with any solution.

"I was thinking Doctor that if you could contact Doctor Garvin in Benburb, he might get news to my parents. We live about a mile from his house".

"That's a great idea, Arthur", he said with a big

smile. "I know Doctor George very well and I will get in touch with him this morning. And now we are going to take you downstairs where there is an ambulance waiting. It will take you across town to the Tower Hill Hospital. That is going to be your home for the next few weeks. And when you are feeling better in a week or so, they will feed you like a king. Come along now".

A few minutes took me to the hospital and I was brought upstairs to a small ward where there were six beds. To my amazement, five boys from the college were already there. They laughed when they saw me arriving. They were all from more senior classes and appeared to be quite happy to get a break from normal routine.

One of the boys I knew well because he had gone to Blackwatertown school and was the son of our local taxi driver. His name was Eamon Murphy. I was given the bed right beside him.

Christy Mallon from Dungannon was across the ward from me and although he was quite senior to me I had gotten to know him during the year. Pat Quinn from Armagh was laid up beside him and another senior boy called Stanley Harbinson had a bed in a little recess. I cannot recall now who the other fellow was but we soon became a very friendly group.

I got installed in the bed and from time to time nurses and doctors came and checked how I was getting on. I found out that the other fellows had been in the hospital for a couple of days already and it puzzled me that no word of their disappearance had swept through the college or at least I had not heard of it.

After a while a lovely lunch was brought in and everyone seemed ravenous but I found that I could not think of eating and the sight of the food revolted me. Everyone else tucked in and clearly enjoyed their meal. A nurse noticed that I was not eating and came over to me.

"What is wrong Arthur?" she asked. "Do you not like the food?"

"It looks and smells lovely Nurse", I replied, "but I feel sort of sick when I put it in my mouth".

"How are you feeling otherwise?" she asked.

"I feel sort of sore all over", I explained, "and my legs are sort of stiff. Is this part of the effects of the scarlet fever?"

"I'm not sure what is doing this to you", the nurse whispered, as she fixed the sheets round my bed, "I'll get the doctor to take a look at you".

As the day wore on I knew that I was getting worse by the hour. My whole body felt sore and stiff and the good humour of the other boys annoyed me. I was really scared because it appeared that this was not a normal effect of the fever as the others had not been affected in this way.

It was nearly teatime before a tall doctor and the nurse approached my bed. They pulled screens around and started to examine me. The doctor asked me all sorts of questions as he manipulated my legs and arms and tried to get reactions all over my body. Once more he tried the reflexes but this time there was little or no response. He talked to the nurse in whispers as though I were not there.

"I don't like the look of this at all. It looks very like the boy has rheumatic fever. What do you think nurse?"

The nurse nodded her head. "That's what I was thinking too, Doctor. It doesn't look good at all".

I was now really scared because I had heard of rheumatic fever and I had been told that people who caught it could be paralysed for life. I looked up at the doctor in a state of terror. "Do you really think that I have rheumatic fever, Doctor?" I gasped.

The doctor looked at me as though he had suddenly realised that I was a live human being. "Oh I'm sorry son", he answered, "I don't want to scare you but it has all the signs of it. I'll see you again in the morning and we'll take it from there". They pulled the screens back and went out.

The other patients fired questions at me from all directions but I buried my head in the pillow and did not want to talk to anyone. I remember very clearly that a cold sweat engulfed my body and I began to tremble in the bed.

A strange thing happened at this point. I began to pray. I prayed with an intensity that I could never have imagined and that I have never experienced since. I don't know how I prayed, whether it was in words or just in thought but the experience was one that I would remember for the rest of my life. I drifted off into a deep sleep and I remember nothing more of that evening.

I awoke the next morning when breakfast was being served and everyone else was already awake. I gazed around the ward and realised that my neck, which had been stiff and sore the night before was now totally normal. I tried the legs that I could not move the previous evening and they worked perfectly. Whatever the condition was it had disappeared in the night and there was not a thing wrong with me. I felt like screaming out loud for joy. The nurse came over to my bed.

"Well Arthur", she said in a concerned voice, "and how are we this morning?"

"I'm fine Nurse", I replied, "but I'm absolutely starving".

She looked at me as though she were seeing apparition!

"You're what?" she exclaimed, clearly astounded.

"I'm very hungry this morning Nurse and I can't wait till I get my breakfast".

"But you would not eat yesterday evening and we thought that you would not feel like eating this morning either. I don't understand this at all. I'll have to call the doctor".

"Can I have some breakfast first?" I pleaded.

She laughed. "I'm sorry", she said, "but I'll have to let the doctor see you first. If you can hold on for a few minutes we'll get you a special breakfast to celebrate your recovery".

Everyone else was tucking into breakfast and I thought I was never going to get a bite. The nurse returned with the doctor who had examined me the previous evening. He looked at me with disbelief clearly showing in his eyes.

"I'm told you are in great form this morning, young man", he said, "but I bet you can't get out of that bed on your own".

I threw back the clothes and jumped out of bed like an athlete and I even did a few steps of Irish dancing to show him that I was fine. "I could run back across town to the college this minute Doctor", I assured him, "if they'd only give me something to eat".

He made me sit down in a chair and he went through all the tests once more. "I don't understand this at all", he said to the nurse, "it looked so bad last night and now there's not a sign of it. And even the fever seems to have gone. I have never come across anything like this in my life".

They left the ward in deep conference with one another and obviously delighted with my condition. A couple of minutes later a girl came in with a huge fry on a tray with wee legs and placed it across me in the bed. She greeted me with a big smile. "I hear that we have a starving man this morning", she laughed. "If that is not enough give me a shout and I'll bring you another one".

I wolfed that lovely fry down as though I had not seen food for months and to be fair I had not seen food of that quality for quite a while. The rest of the boys could not believe the transformation. "What the hell has come over you?" said Eamon Murphy, who was in the bed beside me. "We all thought that we were going to have a grumpy devil or a silent nuisance in that bed. And this morning you are all bright and chirpy".

I cannot explain what happened. It may be that I was going to recover anyway and the condition of the previous evening was simply caused by the fever taking its course. The experience is as vivid with me today as it was all those years ago. I was astounded and I know that the medical people were even more astounded than I was.

A new patient arrived that afternoon. She was a young girl about the same age as I was and her name was Bríd Forde. Her father was one of our lay staff at the college and he was known as 'Buckey' Forde. He was a noted Irish scholar but he also taught French. Although I was never one of his pupils, he was always very friendly and helpful.

A bed had been set up for Bríd in a part of the ward that had been empty. It was positioned in such a way that she could pull a screen to give her some privacy but most of the time she kept it pulled back and acted as though she were perfectly at ease in our company. I was delighted because it was the first time that I had a chance to study a girl at close range and I found Bríd quite attractive. I began to think that changing from science to Greek had not been such a good idea after all.

After a few days everyone was feeling quite well, the food was very good compared to the diet at the college and everyone was very friendly. We all saw our confinement as a lucky break rather than a minor disaster. A couple of times each week Fr. Devine called and gave me some work to do in Greek. He was very thoughtful, helpful and did everything he possibly could to make sure that I could use the time to catch up with the rest of the class. It was only later that I realised that the poor man must have had to walk all the way to the hospital and back since none of the priests in the college had the use of a car. His visits were very pleasant indeed but I found it hard to do any work when he was gone and my progress was, therefore, stunted.

CHAPTER 11
THE NEW DEAN

I had come to see Fr. Devine as the ideal priest and when he was appointed Dean of discipline about three years later I thought that life in the college would be transformed and become a lot more pleasant for everyone. The very opposite happened, however. Very quickly he became moody, openly picked a few favourites in each class and tended to be vindictive. In the following year he had a nervous breakdown and had to leave the college. The job had broken him; he was no Gammy.

I remember one day in the fairly early part of his tenure as Dean when I was a fourth year. Four of us were kept back to do a job for one of the other teachers and we were pretty late going up to the dorm to tog out for football. The wooden mattress frames in the dorm all rested on angle-iron supports, which were fixed to the heads and bottoms of the beds. Someone had gone round every bed in the dorm and pushed the mattresses off their supports so that they lay at all sorts of crazy angles. We fixed our own beds back in place and proceeded to tog out.

We were about to leave for the football field when Fr. Devine came in. He was obviously in a foul mood.

"Did a bomb hit this place?" he enquired, looking round angrily.

"We had nothing to do with it", someone explained. "It was like this when we came up to tog out Father. We are just after fixing our own beds".

"A very likely story indeed", he said, glaring at each one of us in turn. "So none of you boys has the guts to own up to what you have done?"

I happened to be nearest to where he was standing at that moment.

"Honestly, Father", I said quietly, "the place was like this when we came in. None of us touched a thing except to put our own mattresses back in place".

"Oh, so I am meant to believe that innocent Mr. Smiler has never pushed a bed down in his life", he growled. I was surprised that he used one of my nicknames but the bitterness of his tone really annoyed me. I decided that honesty might be a good plan of action.

"I have pushed boys' beds down during the night Father, many a time", I answered.

"So you got out of bed and pushed some poor fellow's bed down just to annoy him?" he asked.

"Well Father, I didn't actually have to get out of bed".

He was gazing angrily down at me and the other boys were shaking their heads at me in warning.

They knew I was getting myself into a hole and I was still digging like mad.

"How did you push the beds down if you did not get out of bed?" He asked this question as though he thought I was telling him fairy stories.

"Father I had a bit of a brush shaft about three feet long and I used that".

"Where is it now?"

I reached under the mattress and produced it. He grabbed it and held it out in front of him.

"So you go to bed at night armed and ready to wreck the dorm and wake up boys who are sleeping. And today you decided to wreck every bed in the dorm".

I knew now that there was no hope of convincing the priest that we were innocent on this occasion. I remembered my father's old warning that it was usually better to keep one's ears open and one's mouth shut but it was too late.

"Honestly, Father, none of us touched a bed in the dorm today".

"Oh, I see," he hissed, "so all these beds flew up into the air and came down like this on their own. You boys wait there until I come back". He rushed out of the dorm slamming the door behind him.

He came back a couple of minutes later carrying a long thin cane and administered six strokes on each hand to all four of us. He was very red in the face and looked flustered. "That was for your actions in the dorm here", he said when finished. "Now you are each going to get six more on the bottom for telling me a pack of lies".

Football shorts are not the best protection one could have against a cane and we were certainly very sore by the time he had finished. "Now you are all going down to the chapel", he said, "and you are going to kneel there and ask pardon for your actions. Go now and if I find one of you sitting up in the next hour, you won't want to sit for some time".

I found that in the chapel there was no problem carrying out his wishes. Kneeling was not very comfortable but sitting was impossible and I found praying to be much the same.

The boys came back from football and the news of what had happened spread like wildfire. One of our classmates, a boy called Gerry Eastwood, went up to Fr. Devine immediately. "Father", he said, "I want to tell you that I did all the beds in the dorm. The other boys never touched a bed today".

Fr. Devine looked at Gerry with a big friendly smile and laughed. "You're very honest, Gerry", he said, "but there's no need to worry about it. If they didn't do it today it will make up for the times when they got away with things that they did do. On you go about your business".

Gerry was one of the boys whom Fr. Devine had picked out as one of his favourites and he went out of his way to show it at all times, much to Gerry's annoyance. Fr. Gallagher could be equally harsh at times but everyone accepted that, and forgot about it. In Fr. Devine's case it created deep and lasting resentment. I always think of it as an example of how an impossible job ruined an admirable man.

CHAPTER 12
HOLIDAYS

The weeks in the hospital passed quickly and in the middle of June we were told that we could go home without going back to college. We were getting an extra fortnight added to the long summer holidays. Needless to say we were delighted though I tended to regret parting company with the young girl with whom I had spent many hours playing Ludo and draughts, or simply chatting. She was discharged from the hospital at the same time. My mother arrived with Tommy Murphy in his taxi and his son, Eamon, and I travelled home together.

Once again I was struck by how small the rooms in our house were and by the warmth and friendliness of the place. I remember too, working in the front garden and being astounded by the strong smell of the plants around me, especially of the lush nettles as I cut them with my father's scythe. The oil lamp was not lit until nearly bedtime because of the long summer evenings but I did enjoy sitting in the kitchen and chatting to my parents in the kindly light of the fire. I never told them about the very different life that I had found seven miles away in Armagh and they never asked.

This may seem strange but I think it was because one never told tales out of school in those days. It was taken for granted in our community that if a youngster came home and told his parents that he had been punished in school, they were likely to give double the dose on the spot. It was not that I was trying to hide anything; it was just that I did not feel any necessity to discuss college life. I imagine that my parents thought that in Armagh I had a life of luxury leading to a career free from toil and care. I got the impression that the neighbours too thought I was in a very privileged position.

A few days after I came home I went round to Tommy Curran who lived in the townland of Drumay, a couple of miles away. I knew that he had acres of strawberries and he would need help to pull them when they were ripe. I was hoping for a job. Tommy greeted me as though he had known me very well all my life.

"Ach God but we're right and lucky to see you", he said, throwing his head back and laughing out loud. It was a mannerism for which he was well known and his laughter could often be heard over quite a distance. "I suppose you have come round to share some of that great learning that you are getting in that big, fancy school that they have sent you to", he continued. "Pat and me hardly ever went to school and we could do with a bit of education at this time of our lives for we know damn all".

Tommy and my uncle Pat, were great friends and I knew that they were always out for a bit of fun and would try to take a hand out of anyone who was daft enough to fall into their traps. I looked up at Tommy's smiling face and I could see that I would have to be very careful in all that I said and did.

"If you were a wee while in that school Tommy", I said, "you would be in a quare way to get back here to the land and the farming. And I know one thing for dead sure. If a fellow wanted a good education he could certainly get it from you and Pat".

Tommy looked at me for a second and once again he threw his head back and looked up at the sky and his peals of laughter echoed and re-echoed from the surrounding hills. I waited until he had finished laughing and then I said, "I am going to have a lot of free time in the next few weeks Tommy, and I was wondering if you could do with a bit of a hand at the pulling of the strawberries".

He looked at me, serious now. "Be God, I could do with a hand", he said, "and if you're anything like your father, you wouldn't be a bad man to have about the place. Would you be any good at the hay?"

"I've worked at hay at home with Da", I replied, "so I know a wee bit about it. I did a bit of turning and I was supposed to be good at lapping when it was needed. My main job was to do all the building of the cocks as he did the pitching".

"The strawberries won't be really ripe for a week or more", Tommy said. "I was waiting for Pat to come to turn the hay on the back hill when you arrived on the street. If you would like to throw the coat off, we'll get started in half an hour or so. Would that suit you?"

"Oh that would be great Tommy", I answered, well pleased that I had got a job.

"We'll start you on three pounds a week", Tommy continued, "and if you can hold your place with the rest of us then we'll raise it to four. Now, sure that is not too bad? The only thing is that when the strawberries come in you might have to work till nine or ten at night. Until then we'll stop around six".

"That's fine", I replied. I was delighted because I knew that my father was getting about five pounds a week and it was reckoned to be very good wages.

Uncle Pat arrived a few minutes later and looked as though he were very surprised to see me. "What the hell are you doing here?" he asked as though he thought I was in the wrong place entirely. "I thought that the only time you came to this part of the country was when you needed a turkey tramped or when you were selling tickets for the clergy. Oh, be God, I know what it is. You have come to educate the ignorant".

The two men went into howls of laughter and I had to join them.

"The lad's going to work with us for the rest of the summer", Tommy informed Pat, "and I hope you are going to leave the cub alone".

They both laughed heartily and I knew that this was a big joke between them because they were always trying to take a hand out of whoever happened to be near them. The fact that I was Pat's nephew would not save me from his tricks. Tommy produced three rakes and we headed off for the back hill to turn the hay. They put me between them and explained that I would have to keep up with them.

It was a great crop of hay and it lay deep and heavy in the swathes. I found it very hard work turning the swathes over and keeping up with the two men. They were both in their forties at the time and well used to heavy work. We were not long started when Tommy looked at me sideways and asked, "did you ever hear of a place called the Dew Drop Inn?"

I noticed uncle Pat putting a bit more effort into his work and giving an uncomfortable cough.

"I did not, Tommy", I replied while wrestling with the rake.

"Och, be God here, Boy, sure you're not educated at all. I can't get over this at all, at all. Are you sure they never told you about the Dew Drop Inn? They tell me it's a place where a man might get anything he wants".

Pat's rake was now bouncing off the hay and he was growling to himself with each pull he made upon it. I knew that Tommy was leading me where I did not want to go but there was nothing I could do about it. Tommy was laughing quietly and turning the hay with ease.

"They tell me that there's men around this part of the country and they can't be kept away from the Dew Drop Inn and it's not drink they're after. They tell me that they'd even walk home in their bare feet from it, even on a damp, wet night". In his usual manner he threw back his head and laughed heartily and loudly.

Pat had been so energetic in his efforts that by this time he had gained three or four yards on us. After a few minutes he stopped, turned the rake upside down and slapped the back of it into the ground. He pushed his hat back on his head slowly while staring at me and holding the rake in his left hand.

"Could you tell me this Arthur", he asked, "did they teach you anything at all about camels in that school in Armagh?"

I worked away and considered this strange question, which seemed to have no connection with what had gone on before. I knew that the two men were using me to taunt each other. I worked on without answering and Pat resumed his work as we came abreast of him.

"It's a tarra altogether", he said, glancing sideways at me, "that you know damn all about camels. Dammit wouldn't you think it's the kind of thing everybody should know about. Did you never hear about them in the school in Blackwater?"

"Well Pat", I said, feeling really foolish, "they live in the desert and they are very bad tempered as far as I know". Pat gave a howl of satisfied laughter and Tommy gave a low growl. I knew I had put my foot in it and yet I could not think of anything else I might have said.

"Be God here boy, you might be right there", laughed Pat. "I'd say a man might be well advised to keep well away from them when they're in bad temper. I wonder now, would they bite you at all?"

Without taking time to think, I blurted out, "the first thing they would do would be spit at you".

Pat stopped, pulled off his hat to wipe his face and gave a loud guffaw of a laugh. "Be God, I always knew that a man should keep well away from an animal like that. Did you know there was one of them living here in Drumay?"

I suddenly realised that I had heard somewhere that Tommy was going with a girl called Mary Campbell and that they might be getting married. I thought carefully before I answered Pat.

"I don't think, Pat", I said quietly, "that there's such a thing as bad temper in this townland". Once again Tommy's loud laugh rang out across the hills. We continued with the work.

"Tell me this boy", said Pat after a few minutes. "Did you ever learn anything about limekilns? Now they tell me that is a subject that a man should be well versed on".

I knew that I was being led into another trap but I could not think of any method of avoiding it. After a long pause I replied. "All I know about them Pat, is that lime is burned in them".

Pat stopped, leant on his rake and gazed at me intently.

"And would you happen to know any place around

this part of the country where a man might find a limekiln?"

Reluctantly I answered, "there's a limekiln on the Knappagh Road a couple of miles outside Armagh, Pat".

"Well, when you were near that limekiln did you ever feel a great heat coming from it?"

I had been at the limekiln when Da had taken me with him to a bullet score, or a road bowls match, as it is often called nowadays. I knew that the kiln had not been used for many years. "Och, sure you know as well as I do that it has not been used for ages, Pat", I murmured.

Pat stopped, laid his rake against his body, took off his hat and scratched his head as though faced with a great puzzle. He gazed at me intently. "Well, could you tell me why a man would leave this townland and go the whole way to that limekiln on a dark night in the dead of winter?" he asked. "And mind you this man had to walk the whole way home for some boy stole the valve out of the front wheel of his bicycle. Now what do you think of that?"

This time I was so intrigued with the question that I answered before giving myself time to think. "Well, whatever that man was looking for, it wasn't heat, Pat", I replied.

Pat took the rake and battered the hay in front of him with it. He jumped up and down while doing so and roared with laughter. On the other side of me Tommy was growling like an angry dog. I knew that I had said exactly what Pat wanted me to say and I was angry with myself for being so stupid. Pat continued to laugh for two or three minutes and then he turned to me once more.

"Well, would you have any idea why a man would take a woman out of this townland, and ride on two bicycles the whole way to that limekiln with her? Would you not think that a woman must have no heat in her at all when a man has to take her to a limekiln to court her? Would you not think that he would be better courting her at the side of the fire at home? Now, could a smart bit of a lad like yourself solve that wee bit of a puzzle for me? Be God, here, if they were not after a bit of heat, what could they have been after?"

The questions has been asked with long pauses between them and I was pretty sure that this was as much for Tommy's sake as it was for mine. I didn't answer because I could not think of anything reasonably sensible to say and I knew that no matter what I did say it would only lead me into deeper trouble. I stayed silent and tried to put all my attention into turning the hay.

"Damn you anyway, Pat Dawley, would you leave the lad alone?" said Tommy at last. "Now, that's enough of your smart talk for one day".

"Be God, here boy", said Pat, "haven't things come to a bad end when a man can't have an innocent wee talk with his own nephew about the things that the lad might be able to help him with. Dammit, here boy but the neighbours round here have got very thin skinned altogether. It's not a bit of wonder that they have to go for miles for a bit of heat and I doubt that's what he was after no matter what you say".

I noticed that Pat worked for the rest of the day as though he had got a new lease of energy. Every few minutes he laughed quietly to himself in obvious satisfaction. Neither man spoke much as we continued with the work. There were times when I thought I was going to have to drop out but I managed to keep going. By dinnertime, or lunchtime as many people would say, we had the hay turned and I breathed a sigh of relief.

"Right lad", said Tommy, "you kept your place with us well there. Come on and we'll get a drop of tay and then Pat has a field to turn up at his house".

Tommy's father, old Tom, was in the house and had the kettle boiled. He was a very friendly man and had all sorts of interesting stories to tell about the days of his youth. That day he told me how his father and my great grandfather had walked all the way to the Hill of Tara to hear Daniel O'Connell speaking. The only food they could afford was a couple of potatoes in their pockets. When they got there, a fierce storm arose and the meeting was cancelled and they had to walk all the way back home again. He assured me that life had been tough in those days. After turning all that hay, I was thinking to myself that it wasn't exactly easy at the present time either.

Tommy took a loaf and cut it in four. He threw a

piece to each of us together with a banana. "Stick a bit of butter on that and chew at it", he said with a friendly laugh. "There's no women about this house to give you wee thin slices that are no good to any working man. Women have this country destroyed".

The rough meal was delicious. Our hunger satisfied, we headed of to Pat's field to turn his hay too. The crop was not just so heavy and he produced three pitchforks with which to do the job. I found this a much easier way of working and I was able to keep up easily. The men had eased off too and stopped from time to time to lean on their forks and have a rest. I learned a lot that afternoon about what the neighbours were doing and what their ancestors had done in years gone by. The two men never ceased talking. It was nearly five o'clock by the time we had finished.

"That's enough for the day", Tommy said to me. "That's not a bad day's work for the start. We'll see you sometime around ten o'clock or so in the morning".

The first ten days of my employment were spent at the hay and doing odd jobs about the house. Then the first strawberries were ripe. Most people found it hard and unpleasant work crawling in the drills from morning until night, pulling strawberries into punnets or twelve pound chips. I did not mind it at all and I found I could easily keep up with the best pullers in the field and at least produce chip for chip. Tommy told me that he was satisfied that I was worth four pounds a week and I was delighted.

I worked with Tommy until the end of August and a few days later I had to go back to the college in Armagh. After the fruit picking was finished the plants had to be cleaned. It meant digging every drill with a digging fork and removing the weeds. I had earned more that half the money needed for my board in the college and my mother was both relieved and delighted. "That takes a big burden off my shoulders", she said, "but it means that you have had no holiday at all. I hope it will not have a bad effect on your work in the college".

I doubt very much if it made a difference.

CHAPTER 13
FRYING PAN OR FIRE

We returned to the college in September for the start of our second year and I found that little had changed. Our dorm was now on the first floor of the block rather that at the top but otherwise it was exactly the same. Gammy was still on the prowl. The boys gathered round me, eager to find out what had happened when I was in hospital. They were all a bit envious of the fact that I had managed to get an extended summer holiday.

Classes started and I got a bit of a shock to find that the few weeks in hospital had made a marked difference. It was noticeable that while I had been away the rest of the class had made quite a bit of progress. I knew that I had a job on my hands trying to catch up. Fr. Gallagher stopped me on the second day coming out of lunch.

"I suppose you noticed", he said, "that the time you were off has made a lot of difference in your class work?"

"I did indeed, Father", I replied. "I find that I am quite a bit behind in everything".

"Don't worry too much about it", he said softly, "if you work that wee bit harder you'll soon catch up, I'm sure. Is there any particular class where you find you have lost a lot of ground?"

"I noticed Father, that in Irish, which was my favourite subject some of the boys have made fantastic progress. They are able to talk with Mr. O'Boyle very easily and I think I am now far behind them. I can see the change especially with boys who have been to the Gaeltacht during the summer".

The big priest looked down at me, smiling. "Well," he said, "that is hardly due to the fact that you lost a few weeks in hospital. Next year you will have to try to get to Donegal for a few weeks yourself. It's my own county and it's a grand place to spend a week or two in the summer. Sure anybody would know that a county that reared a fine man like myself, must be a wonderful place. Seriously though, don't worry too much; if you keep the head down for a couple of months I have no doubt that you will make up for lost time. Good luck now and I'll be keeping a close eye on you".

A day or so later we had our first Greek class of the year and I really got a shock. I had been expecting Fr. Devine to continue from the first year but in walked Fr. Kenny the Vice Principal. He was a very fair and well-liked priest and an excellent teacher but he made no allowance for the fact that I was a total novice at his subject.

Fr. Kenny gave a lot of work to be done during

study time and he expected very high standards. Everyone soon learned to look carefully at the exercise books as he carried them into the next class. Some were closed and some were open. The owners of the open ones had to go for punishment to him before lunch as their work had not been to his liking.

Fr. Kenny had a really horrible job. He had to punish all boys from every class in the school whose work had not been up to standard or who had misbehaved in class. He held the post of Dean of Studies and no one else was allowed to administer punishment for schoolwork or misbehaviour in class. It meant that every day there was a long queue of boys lined up on the steps outside the study hall waiting to be punished. Most of the time it meant that around two hundred boys got either two or four slaps of his strap. It has amazed me ever since that the authorities were so heartless and unthinking as to burden any one man with such a horrible task.

There was one very strange thing about Fr. Kenny's punishment. A boy would stand up and hold his hands out as directed and the priest would administer a number of slaps. I have often seen boys walk off with smiles on their faces. The strap seemed to have no great effect. But half way down the stairs from the study hall they would suddenly bend over and push each hand under the opposite armpit. The strap had a delayed action. I don't know why it worked that way, or if Fr. Kenny realised it, but it never seemed to fail.

As time went by I found that my exercise was always open in the Greek class and I did not look forward to visiting Fr. Kenny in the study hall almost every day. The first time it happened I tried to explain my situation to him. "Father", I said, "I only started Greek a few weeks before the summer holidays and then I was in hospital. I have had no chance to catch up with the rest of the class".

He stopped for a moment and looked me in the eyes. "Are you telling me that you think that is my fault?" he asked.

"No Father, but I thought maybe you did not know that I have only been doing Greek for a few weeks".

"Did anyone force you to change over to Greek or did you do it of your own accord?"

"Oh, I did it of my own accord, Father. No one suggested that I should do it".

"Fine, so you know it is not my fault that you are producing such poor work. My decisions are based on the standard of your work and not on your life history. Hold out your hand".

After a few such visits I considered my situation carefully. "To hell with this for a game", I said to myself, "I'm going to have to find a way out of this plight that I've got myself into. The only thing I can do is work my head off at the Greek. Nobody else is going to help me out so I'll have to do it myself".

Up until that time it had been my practice to get most of my work done in first study and to spend quite a bit of second study reading stories or working at the Irish. I changed over and spent every spare minute struggling with the Greek. It was tough going and at times I felt like giving up as my exercise books continued to be returned open at the start of each lesson. Gradually, however, over the next few months, this happened less and less and towards the end of the year, hardly ever.

One day, just before the Easter holidays, Fr. Kenny asked me to see him after class.

"How do you feel that you have been getting on with the Greek?" he asked with just the trace of a smile.

"It has been getting a wee bit easier, Father", I assured him, "but there were times in the early part of the year when it nearly drove me mad".

"You must have been trying very hard", he continued, "you have caught up with most of the boys and you are away ahead of quite a few. I know that must have taken a lot of endeavour. I felt that I had to congratulate you".

"Thank you very much, Father", I replied with satisfaction.

"I suppose you thought I was some sort of monster at the start of the year when I punished you nearly every day?" he continued. As he spoke he gazed steadily at me with searching eyes, but there was a wee trace of a smile still on his face. There was something about him that made everyone feel at ease in the presence of a good friend even when he was dishing out punishment.

"I soon decided Father, that it was a choice between getting punished after every Greek class or working my head off to catch up. As you said it was my own choice to change to Greek and I decided to work like the devil. I have to admit though that it has not been easy, Father".

He hit me a friendly punch on the shoulder. "I'm proud of you", he said with a grin. "Not many boys would have had the grit to work their way through it. I felt that it was the only way I could help you though it may have seemed cruel at the time. Keep up the good work".

At the end of third year we sat the Junior Certificate examination. To my great surprise, I managed to get quite a few distinctions and a couple of credits. Greek was at the head of the list with three hundred and ninety marks out of four hundred. I have often wondered since what would have happened had I stayed with science.

CHAPTER 14
GAELTACHT

During the Easter holidays in our second year, Fr. Moore, our curate, stopped me one day as I was coming out of chapel. "Have you ever thought of going to the Gaeltacht, Arthur?" he asked.

I looked at him in surprise and I wondered why he was asking such a question. I knew that the priest had taken a special interest in me when I passed the entrance exam for the college. It was partly I think because I had been one of his altar boys and partly because he had been a classmate of my father's at school in Eglish, a generation previously.

It would be true to say that the great majority of his parishioners had a very high opinion of him and felt that they were very lucky to have such a gifted and capable man in their midst. Fr. Moore did nothing at all to alter their admiration for him and in fact he fostered it. His attitude of great self-belief gave some people the idea that he was 'stuck-up' or arrogant and his manner of speaking in a very polished fashion added to this perception.

My father had explained to me that when Peter

Moore had been at school he suffered from a very bad speech impediment. As a clerical student he had received a long course of speech therapy in Dublin and had conquered the impediment but could not speak in what one might term a natural fashion. It made him sound very high-brow and sophisticated, which could seem out of place in a country parish. He stood studying me after he had asked the question.

"I would have loved to go Father", I said, "but I have to work during the summer and I could not afford to go right in the middle of the strawberry season. We are not very well off, you know".

"Are you absolutely certain that you could not afford to take a fortnight off work?" he asked.

"I might be able to do that Father but I still could not afford the money for my keep. I have to help my mother out with the money I get for working in the summer holidays. It's not easy for her to find the money for my fees".

He put a kindly hand on my shoulder. "I have a scholarship to give away", he said, "and there is no one else for it. It will cover all your costs except the travel and pocket money. A couple of weeks in Rannafast would do your Irish a world of good. Talk it over with your parents and give me a call in the next couple of days if you want to take up the scholarship".

That night my father was sitting reading in the light of the little oil lamp and my mother was knitting at the opposite side of the fire. From time to time, Da read bits of news out loud and they discussed these quietly. I pulled a chair up to the fire between them.

"I was talking to Fr. Moore today", I informed them.

My father glanced up from his paper. "I suppose you might take it into your head sometime in the next week to tell us what he was talking about", he said. "I suppose he is looking for a raise in his dues?"

"He never mentioned the dues at all". I replied.

Da looked across at Ma and shook his head. "Living in Armagh has put this cub of ours to hell altogether", he said. "People from the county are always very hard to understand". They both laughed. Da always referred to Armagh as 'the county' almost as though it were the only one in Ireland. I sat gazing into the fire and waited until I felt that I had their attention.

"He says he has a scholarship for the Gaeltacht in the summer, and if I want it, it's mine. It would mean taking a fortnight in Donegal and that would be a fortnight I would lose at work with Tommy Curran. He asked me to talk it over with you both".

"There's damn all to talk over about it", said Da. "If it is going to help you with your work in the college go ahead and take it. What do you say Sarah?"

My mother gazed into the fire with a serious look on her face. "Right enough, Mick", she said thoughtfully, "a couple of weeks talking Irish would be a big help I'm sure, but the few pounds Arthur got at the strawberries was very handy last year. The loss of a fortnight would make a bit of a difference and there has not been a great price for the eggs this last while".

"Difference be damned", growled Da, "if that's all there is to it, I'll give you the extra ten pounds or whatever it is myself and I'll give the lad whatever money he needs to go".

He turned to me as he rose to go to bed. "Go to Donegal", he said. "I'm damned but you would think that we were ready for the poorhouse the way your mother talks. As far as I know none of the Dawleys was ever in the poorhouse in the bad days and I've never heard of any of the Bloomers being there either. We're hardly going to start now. To hell with poverty; I'm away to bed".

He stomped off talking to himself and my mother looked at me and laughed. "You have to know how to handle your father", she said. "He can always come up with a few extra pounds if you take him the right way".

That summer I worked as usual with Tommy Curran but I had warned him that I would have to leave in the middle of August.

"I suppose you're going on one of them fancy big holidays", he said, "a poor man like me can hardly get out of my own townland".

"I feel real sorry for you, Tommy", I said sarcastically. "I'm going up to Donegal for a couple of weeks to try to learn a bit of Irish".

"Well you are welcome to work here till it's time to

go", he said. "Be God here boy, by the time you come back with all that Irish there's nobody about this part of the country will be able to know what the hell you are talking about. There was a very smart man told me one time that boys that can talk Irish have a quare way with the women. By God I say, there'll be no holding of you at all, at all". He threw back his head and gave his usual raucous laugh.

The middle of August came and it was time to go to Donegal. My mother packed my things in a small case and I strapped it to the carrier of my bike and rode into Dungannon, feeling excited at the prospect of this new adventure. I knew a man in lower Scotch Street who worked at bikes and I left my machine in his care. It was only a very short distance from his shop to the train station. It was the first time I had ever been there.

A couple of boys from The Moy were already at the station. One was Gerry Twomey and the other was a boy called Tom Reilly from near Dungannon. I was delighted to see them because I was feeling a bit lonely and unsure what to do or where to go. "Go up to the desk at once", ordered Gerry, "the train will be going in a couple of minutes. They won't wait on you if you haven't got your ticket".

I really enjoyed the journey to Derry city. It was very pleasant chatting to the boys and looking out at the countryside as it flashed past. I don't remember anything of the city but maybe that is because a ramshackle Lough Swilly bus was waiting at the station to take us on the journey right across county Donegal. We arrived in Rannafast late in the afternoon.

I had been used to small and twisting lanes at home but Rannafast was different. The roads were even narrower and they had sharp corners every few yards. There were bumps like humped backed bridges every few yards as well. The bottom of the old bus scraped on the road surface as it passed over the bumps. There were huge rocks everywhere as far as the eye could see with little thatched houses dotted between them. I thought it was like a scene out of fairyland.

"How does anyone manage to get a living in a place like this?" I asked Gerry.

He gazed around thoughtfully. "They are on the edge of the sea", he replied, "and I suppose they fish a lot. They all have wee tiny fields in between the rocks and they grow crops there. As far as I know they are all very poor".

The bus stopped in front of a fairly big building called Coláiste Bríd. (St. Bridget's college.) The driver told us to take our luggage and make our way inside. We found ourselves in a fairly large hall, not unlike the gym in the college in Armagh. There were crowds of young people milling about everywhere.

"My father tells me that this place was started by Fr. Larry Murray", Gerry informed us. "He used to be in the Moy parish, you know".

I looked at Gerry in surprise. "There's no such

place as the Moy parish", I said. "It's Clonfeacle parish and The Moy is only part of it. People on our side of the parish believe that the Moy people are trying to steal the name of the parish. We all think that they are stuck up and want everything".

"Well whatever you want to call it", said Gerry, "my Da tells me that Fr. Murray used to be a curate in it. It seems that he was a great man for the Irish".

"I heard my mother talking about him", I said. "She told me that he used to ride a motor bike and when he came to our townland there was a bit of a row going on between a couple of the neighbours. He remarked to her that when a man came to the townland of Sessiagh, he should make sure to have a good bag of stones with him".

A stout, red-faced man called for order in Irish and welcomed us to the Gaeltacht. "There should not be one word of English spoken in this sacred place", he said slowly in Gaeilge. I did not understand every word but he spoke slowly and clearly and I got his general meaning. "My name is Mr. McKeown and I am in charge here for this fortnight. If anyone is caught speaking English", he continued, "he will be sent home on the bus first thing the next morning".

He went on to allocate the houses in which we would be stopping. I was delighted to find that Tom and Gerry had been given the same house as myself. It was called 'teach Aodhi Mhichi Aodhi.' (the house of Hugh, son of Michael, son of Hugh) As soon as it was called out and we had identified ourselves, a small, rather fat woman with a big friendly smile came over to us. "I am your bean an tí", (*woman of the house or landlady*) she said, speaking slowly, "follow me and I'll show you how to get to the house".

We took our things and followed her. As well as the three of us there were five boys from Derry city in the group.

Instead of using the road the woman led us down a narrow path amongst rushes and rocks. It led down to a lake, which was behind the college and she informed us that it was called Lough Bríd. As she led the way we were chatting quietly to each other. She stopped. "You must speak only in Gaeilge," she said rather angrily. "I will not have boys in my house using a foreign tongue. If you want to go home and speak English, that's all right by me". The people of Rannafast got students on condition that only Irish was spoken. They were keen to keep the rule because the extra money was precious at that time.

It was the longest speech that I had ever heard in Irish. It was spoken slowly and firmly. There was no doubting its meaning. The path wound its way round the lough and then headed out across a rocky tract of land. At the far end of the lough the woman warned us to be very careful, as we had to jump across a deep drain and there was only one spot where it was safe to do so. If we jumped anywhere else we would find ourselves in very deep and dangerous water.

This crossing place led to us being involved in an interesting incident in the second week of our stay.

There was a ceilidh every second night in the big hall and as soon as it was over we were supposed to go straight home. The three of us, however, walked a group of girls to their house, which was not far from the college and quite close to the path, which would take us home. We were standing chatting in the moonlight outside the house. None of the conversation was in Gaeilge and at times it was rather loud.

Suddenly, to our great surprise, McKeown appeared from behind a rock about a hundred yards away. We knew that the girls were safe because they were at their own house but we were in deep trouble. "You don't know our names", hissed Gerry, speaking to the girls, and we took to our heels down the path, with McKeown in hot pursuit. We had just jumped the drain as the moon came out from behind a cloud. McKeown saw us on the far side of the drain and decided to take a shortcut. We were about sixty or seventy yards away from him when we heard a splash and a howl of surprise.

"Help me, help me", he roared in Gaeilge with only his head showing above the water in the moonlight. We stopped and gazed back to the pool where he was trapped.

"We'd better go back and try to get him out", I said to the other two. "He might drown".

"It wouldn't be any great loss", said Gerry to Tom.

"We can't let him lose his life", answered Tom, "come on and we'll see if we can get him out".

We went back to the drain and found him attempting to get a grip on the rocks and trying to pull himself out. "Help me to get out", he pleaded, looking up at us in the moonlight.

We reached down and let him grasp our hands and with a lot of trouble he managed to slither up the side of the drain and reach dry land. He stood dripping in the moonlight as he studied us.

"You were talking in English back at that house", he said, pointing a finger at each of us in turn. "You should be sent home in the morning. Do you understand that?" He spoke very slowly and made the Irish very simple and we got the message.

"It was very good of you to come back and help me", he continued, "and this time we will let you off. You may have saved my life. But you are still in the wrong so don't be too proud of yourselves. If I find you speaking English again you won't get another chance. Go on back to your house now".

He took a few steps back from the drain and it was obvious that he meant to jump it.

"Stop", we yelled in unison.

"What's wrong now?" he asked.

Between us we managed to explain to him that he was in the wrong place and that he would end up back in the drain. We pointed out the place where it was safe to cross and having jumped it he went off shivering, and clearly in quite a bit of distress.

The house was a tiny thatched cottage and we had a room with nothing in it but beds. There were two sets of two tiered bunks, a couple of single beds and a double bed. The room was so crowded that it was a struggle to move between the beds. "You will have to decide where you want to sleep", said the bean an tí, pointing to the beds when we first arrived. It was difficult enough to work out what she meant.

"I know what we can do", said one of the Derry boys. "We'll write numbers on pieces of paper and have a raffle. That will give each of us a number. We will then number the beds and have a second raffle. Whoever pulls the number of a bed will have that bed for the fortnight".

The bean an tí had been standing in the doorway during this conversation and it had to be carried out in Irish. It took a long time and there was a lot of English mixed in with the Irish. The lady shook her head and muttered something about how poor our Irish was. It ended up that Gerry and I had to share the double bed.

During our stay the woman took endless patience during meals to teach us about the things on the table and around the house. She talked incessantly. I found that I could understand her better as time went on but I still found it difficult enough. Her husband was a different matter altogether.

He was recognised as one of the storytellers of the area and at night he would sit in his chair by the fire and tell us simple tales. At least that is what I think he meant to do. But he spoke in a very low voice and seemed to mumble through his lips at breakneck speed. I was lucky if I managed to hear an odd word or phrase that I could recognise. I marvelled that the woman had no bother at all understanding him and I felt downhearted because I felt that this language was beyond me. None of the other boys could understand him either but that did not seem to worry them.

"Can you understand the fear an tí at all?" I asked Brendan Duddy, one of the Derry boys as we were walking towards the college one morning. He looked at me as though he thought I was a little crazy.

"Not a bloody word", he laughed, "the auld idiot might as well be speaking Chinese. But who the hell cares? It's only a bundle of rubbish that he is talking anyway".

"They tell me that he is one of the best Irish speakers in the place", I said, "and it annoys me that I haven't a clue what he is talking about".

Brendan kicked a stone out of his way as we walked along and didn't answer immediately. "You must be damned easily annoyed", he said. "Do you not know that we are here for a bit of a holiday? It would worry me a lot more if I couldn't understand the girls after the ceilidhs".

"You have a good point there, Brendan", I agreed. But it still annoyed me that I found this great speaker so incomprehensible.

The fortnight was really enjoyable and the time flashed past. By the time we boarded the bus for home I felt that I had learned very little and was no better at Irish than before I had gone. When we resumed classes in Armagh the next year, however, I was amazed at how easy I found the Irish compared with boys who had not been to the Gaeltacht. While in Rannafast I felt that I was not learning at all yet on going back to class I discovered that I had learned a lot without knowing it.

CHAPTER 15
NEW VISIONS

A couple of days before it was time to go back to college I was giving Da a hand to put a barbed wire fence round the hay stacks. "You know Da", I said slowly and quietly as I knew he might have done, "I have been thinking".

He stopped, put the hammer that he had been using on top of a post, leant on the post, and looked at me.

"Well, that's a tarra to man", he said with a snort, "I thought that you and that Jordan fellow were so busy running the country after girls that you'd have no time to think. Would this be some sort of a miracle?"

It was difficult to talk to Da seriously when he was in this mood. He was now standing studying me with a wide grin on his face.

"You and Tommy have never missed a dance in the Brantry this long time", he said, "and as far as I can hear you both have a full time job leaving girls home. A man should maybe do a lot of thinking when he's on a job like that. They tell me that there's some quare tight bits of young women round that part of the country. A fellow would not be cold in the long evenings if he was in company like that". He lifted the hammer, hit the top of the post a good thump with it and gave a roar of a laugh. "Well maybe you might get round to telling me what you were thinking about sometime before the end of the year", he said.

"You know the way I have been working with Tommy Curran this last couple of years at the strawberries, Da?" I said.

He looked up and his brow was furrowed with puzzlement. "Wouldn't I need to be damned stupid and blind and deaf as well not to know that?" he asked. I knew he was being crooked for the sake of being crooked. I worked on at the fence and said nothing. He worked on for a minute or so too and then asked, "and what was it that you were thinking about?"

"I was thinking Da, that if we broke up a bit of the top field here and put in an acre or so of strawberries, I would have plenty of work to do at home without going to the neighbours".

"Pull that wire a wee bit tighter", he said, and drove a steeple in to hold it. He hung the hammer on the wire and folded his arms over the top of the post and gazed at me. His steel blue eyes were steady and he seemed to be looking into the very depths of my being. He stood like that for most of a minute.

"It would take a lot of work to look after a cut of strawberries like that", he said thoughtfully, "and sure you will be away most of the time".

"I would have the long summer holidays", I answered, "and that is when most of the work is needed. I could get a bit done at Easter too".

"That sounds all right standing here on a good dry day like this", he replied, "but there will be lots of days when it's pouring out of the heavens and you would not be able to do a thing. On the good days you would have to be up with me in the mornings and you would have to work till black dark at night. That would not be easy for a boy that has been running the country all night and doing his best to court every girl in two or three counties. Be God, here I say, those women up in the Brantry might find themselves trying to court a bit of an old rag doll".

Nothing more was said on the subject but when I came home at Christmas I discovered that about an acre of ground had been planted in strawberries. I was puzzled as to how he had found time to do all the work. He rode seven miles on a bike to Dungannon every morning, he worked as a labourer all day on a building site and he rode home again in the evenings. I was standing admiring his work when he came up behind me.

"You will have all the work you want there boy for the next few years", he said quietly. "I was wondering who those lassies round Eglish and the Brantry will find to take your place. Dammit, I say, maybe Tommy will have to look after them all on his own. But then the Jordans already have a couple of acres of strawberries so he might not be so sprightly himself".

Da had been referring to the fact that Tommy and I had been going to ceilis, which were being run in a Gaelic Athletic Association hall. The hall had been built in the townland of Cadain, which is part of the Brantry district, and at that time the dances were very popular. They were organised and supervised by a man called John McCann and he did an excellent job.

I am not sure what perception my father had of what transpired either during or after the ceilis. He gave me the impression that he thought I knew all there was to know about the birds and the bees even though the subject had never been mentioned in our house either by him or my mother. In truth leaving a girl home from a ceili meant a bit of chat on the way and perhaps a short cuddle and a quick kiss before we parted company. I really thought that I was being quite adventurous.

That summer the Jordans had a great crop of strawberries and they had about a dozen young people working with them at the pulling of the fruit. They were nearly all girls from The Donnelly Hill area near Benburb. One night, in the middle of the pulling season there was a big ceili in the Brantry and all the girls were there and of course Tommy and I were there as well.

It so happened that a big crowd of us were coming home together on bicycles. I was with one of the girls at the front of the group going down a fairly steep hill. I can't remember why but I reached across and grabbed the handlebar of her bike. We both swerved and the two front wheels locked together. We landed on the road in a tangle with the machines, and the crowd coming behind could not avoid us and piled on top of us. Everyone was trying to free themselves from the mass of bikes and people and chains and oil. Nobody was really hurt but bikes and clothes fared badly in the mess.

We all ended up in a mess of oil and chains and damaged bicycles with clothes ruined and suffering from all sort of minor injuries.

For the next week a sort of mini war raged at Jordans. The strawberry pullers blamed Tommy for the pile-up and demanded that his mother, Julia, pay them compensation for ruined nylons, bent wheels, chains, and in some cases entire bicycles. Julia pointed out angrily that she could not be responsible for what happened to people in the middle of the night but there was an uneasy atmosphere until the strawberry season was over. It amazed me that nobody blamed me for what happened but maybe they thought there was less chance of being compensated had they done so.

"That Tommy fellow will be the death of me yet", I heard Julia telling my mother a day or so later. "He's never out of bother and I don't know what he'll be at next. There will be a bad end to these two boys and the goings on round that Donnelly Hill. There's some quare cute blades up there I can tell you. There could be a bad end to the whole thing".

"Och, now Julia", answered Ma, "sure the whole lot of them seem to have been in it and Tommy's no more to blame than the rest. Our fellow came home with his clothes destroyed and the front wheel of his bicycle all bent. He was away off to Dick Wilson the next morning to get it fixed before his Da or me could get a good look at it".

"I don't know what will be the end of the two of them", replied Julia. "My heart is sore listening to all those girls looking for money. I feel sorry for them in a way but I can't buy nylons and clothes to cover the half of the County Armagh".

"Don't you worry about that", said Ma earnestly. "Sure girls are always getting boys into trouble and they deserve all they get".

Julia simply nodded thoughtfully in agreement.

That summer Tommy and I got into a row, which resulted from a pure accident although nobody would believe us. At that time a young man called Pat was working more or less full-time at Jordans. He was rather small and not as worldly wise as most people. He could read and write and was not a bad worker if carefully directed. He was what is called in Irish, 'duine le Dia.' (God's special person) He was continually complaining to our parents that Tommy and I were playing tricks on him; most of the time I have to admit his complaints were justified.

Beside Jordan's spring well there was a little house, which was used as a dairy. A fairly narrow path ran between it and a bigger shed and on the other side of the bigger shed was Jordan's front street. Tom, Tommy's father, was sick and was spending a few days in bed. He had asked Tommy to clear some dirt and rubbish that was lying to one side of the dairy and I was giving him a hand.

There had been wet weather and the rubbish was soaking. We had cleared most of it when we came upon an old tyre from a bicycle wheel, which had been thrown away long before. Tommy pulled the old tyre out from the rest of the rubbish, the inside of it full of dirt and dripping wet. He drew back his arm and threw the old tyre over the top of the big shed in front of us in order, I think, to demonstrate his undoubted skill in throwing all sorts of things. A second or two later there was a howl of anger and a frenzied string of curses from the other side of the shed. The old tyre had landed round poor Pat's neck.

We came round the shed to see what had happened but by the time we reached the street Pat was pounding on Tom's bedroom window, the old tyre still hanging round his neck. His face and clothes were covered in dirt and he was raging.

"Come out here Tom", he was yelling, "till you see what this wee bastard that you have reared has done on me now".

We could see movement behind the curtains in Tom's room. Tommy gave me a dig in the ribs and hissed through the side of his mouth, "come on Boy, it would be far healthier for us to be a right bit away from here when our man comes out". He took to his heels and I followed him simply because I did not know what else to do. We ran as fast as our legs would carry us until we were three or four fields away from the street and out of sight from the house. I ran up to Tommy as soon as he stopped.

"What the hell is wrong with you?", I demanded, "sure it wasn't your fault that the tyre landed round Pat's neck. You had no way of knowing he was on the street and in the right place to get hit. It was a pure accident".

Tommy looked at me as though he thought I was mad. "Surely you're not daft enough to think that our man would believe that it was an accident?" he asked. "He would have had my two lugs well warmed before I was able to get a word out of my mouth.

There would have been no talking to him. It is far healthier for us to be well away from the house for an hour or so".

"I happened to hear our man and your Da talking the other day", continued Tommy, "and they were on about all the stories we told them and expected them to believe. Your Da said that the last thing anybody could expect to hear from either of us would be the truth and our man said he was dead right. Haven't I always told you never to trust your bloody parents?"

"Come out here this minute Tom, till you see what this wee bastard that you have reared has done on me now".

He was now standing gazing up at a field near the fort and when I followed his gaze, I saw a calf grazing in the middle of a field of corn. The summer was well through and the corn was up to the animal's belly.

"There's a quare bit of luck", said Tommy. "It's a grand job that that calf decided to break out just when we needed him to".

"How do you make that out?" I asked.

He shook his head to indicate that he thought I must be dead stupid. "We'll go and get that calf out of the corn", he explained, "and we'll make as much noise as we can when we're doing it. We'll let the whole country know that we're doing a fine job. They can't say much to us when we're saving the corn".

We made our way up to where the calf was, and as we guided him back towards the hole in the hedge where he had entered, we roared and shouted at him at the top of our voices even though he walked quietly back towards the place where he had entered. Looking down, I could see Julia standing in the middle of the street looking up towards us. I could also see Tom's form in the shadow of the doorway and Pat standing beside him, obviously talking to him. We got the calf out and fenced the hole as best we could.

"Be God", said Tommy, "I can tell you it was a great job that I saw that calf at the right time. They can't say very much to us when we have done such a good job".

"I have a feeling", I objected, "that they will know why we were making so much noise. They're not stupid you know".

We walked at a slow pace down to the house and just before we reached the street Tommy decided that he needed to go to the toilet. I arrived back on the street alone. Julia had disappeared but Tom was standing in the doorway leaning against the jamb with his heavy coat wrapped around him, even though it was a glorious day.

"That must have been a damned awkward kind of a calf", he remarked to me as I came within earshot. "It's a good job there weren't five or six of them or you two boys would have needed a pipe band with you to get them out".

I ignored the sarcasm of his remark as best I could. "He was in the middle of that field of nearly ripe corn and he was tramping it all down, Tom", I answered, as though he needed an explanation. "Tommy saw him in the corn and we got him out as quickly as we could. We got some thorn bushes and ditched the hole as best we could. I don't think anything could get through it now".

"Dammit", said Tom thoughtfully, "I don't know what we would do if we hadn't got you two boys when things go wrong. Where did our fellow go anyway? Is he away to see if any other calves have broken out?"

"He just stopped to go to the toilet", I explained. "He'll only be a minute".

"Tell me", asked Tom, "which of you hit poor Pat with that old dirty tyre?"

"That was a real fluke, Tom", I assured him. "We found the old tyre in the middle of the rubbish at the side of the dairy and Tommy fired it over the boiler shed. There was no way he could have known that Pat or anybody else was on the street".

Tom gazed at me, starting to light his pipe. "Isn't it very strange", he said slowly between puffs of smoke, "that poor Pat always seems to be in the right place for something to happen to him when you two boys are about?"

I could not think of any sensible answer to this question and at that moment Tommy arrived back. He obviously thought that I was not doing a very good job convincing his father.

"Wasn't it quare and lucky, Da", he asked, "that we saw that white headed calf in the corn before he had the whole field ruined?"

At that moment Julia came out of the barn with a white bucket in her hand. She stopped and studied us. "Maybe you could tell me", she said, "who it was lucky for?"

Tom gave a titter of a laugh and Tommy had a look of consternation on his face. I decided that it was my turn to handle the situation.

"Surely, Mrs Jordan", I asked, "it was lucky that we saw that calf before he had a whole lot of damage done?"

"And it was far luckier for you two boys that he

happened to break out at the right time", she said scornfully. "Now the two of you go and clear up that mess that you have left at the side of the dairy. And don't be throwing anything else. You'd never know who might happen to be standing where it might land."

We went back to our work, but having put a couple of forkfuls of dirt into the wheelbarrow Tommy stopped and looked earnestly at me. "Do you see now", he asked, "what I have been trying to tell you? When you tell them the truth they never bloody believe you. Is it any wonder that we keep telling them a bundle of lies? They have nobody to blame for it only themselves".

At about this time Tommy and I were given the job of putting up posters for our local football club and this meant that we had to travel all round the district in Tommy's van. We had about half of the job completed one evening when we became aware that a couple of cars were following us but keeping some distance behind us.

"That must be the bloody B-men", said Tommy, "I wonder if we could give them the slip".

He drove very fast on the narrow roads, which we knew well and slowly the cars fell further behind. At one stage we could see them on a road, which we had just left as we travelled on a parallel road in the opposite direction.

"I could get away from them if we hadn't all these other posters to put up", said Tommy. "Do you think we should give it up for the night and head for home?"

"You're the driver", I replied. "I can't see that we have been doing any harm and I don't think they could say much to us. If you think we'd be better to go home, however, that's fine with me".

"To hell with it", he growled, "I'll see if we can't get away from them altogether and still put up the posters".

For the next half hour we had a car chase at ridiculous speeds around the local roads. Eventually we pulled in to Tullymore hall to put up a poster there and we had barely got out of the van when the cars screamed to a stop beside us.

Men with rifles piled out of the cars and took up positions in a semi circle resting on one knee and aiming the rifles at us. I could clearly hear the safety catches being released and for a moment I thought we were going to be shot on the spot.

"Hands above your heads", roared one man who seemed to be in charge. "Stand against that wall and don't move or we'll open fire. Get those feet well apart and keep the hands high".

The leader walked over to Tommy at last and pulled the posters from his hands. Without really looking at them he asked, "would you boys be working for the IRA now?"

"We're putting up a few posters for the football club", replied Tommy. "I didn't know that was a big crime in this country".

"The way you were driving for the last half hour and more would indicate that you have been up to no good", snapped the man. "Keep the arms up and the feet apart and stand upright against that wall. You and you", he said, pointing to two of his men, "leave down your rifles and do a body search".

The men did as ordered and one of them went to search Tommy while the other came to me. There was not a sound until Tommy's searcher reached his private parts. Suddenly Tommy's strong voice broke the silence, "you can be dead sure, ye boy ye, that's not gelignite anyway".

The tension was broken. The men had to laugh and then they packed up and went on their way.

CHAPTER 16
STRANGE HAPPENINGS

We went back to the college for our third year to discover that we had been put in Blessed Oliver's dorm, which was in the oldest part of the building. It was on the first floor of the building and ran all the way above the main corridor. I suppose most people would describe it as quaint. It was divided into little cubicles, which had wooden partitions separating them but they were open to the middle corridor. Each section held four beds, two on each side of the corridor. The ceiling was very low and arched and had a huge black pipe attached to it running the full length of the dorm. It was very different from the big open modern dormitories I had been used to but I preferred it and I think most boys did too.

We had just settled in on our first night when Gammy appeared and called for silence. "I want everybody to stand in the central corridor at the end of his bed", he commanded. "Now you boys might think that you have the ideal situation for all sorts of carry on in this dorm", he said as he started to saunter up the middle corridor between us. "If you do think that", he continued, "then you are in for a shock. As you know my room is just beside the door and I will be on the look out for mischief all night and every night. If I hear any noise I never ask people to stand out and own up in this dorm. I simply punish the whole dorm. I stoke the furnace as one might say. So if you talk or carry on you will be responsible for getting every one of your classmates punished. It's up to you".

By the time he had finished speaking he had nearly reached the end of the dorm furthest from the door. He turned and sauntered back down in silence. Just before he reached the door he stopped, turned round, swished his cane, and said, "it's up to you. Have a happy year". During the year he stoked the furnace rather well a couple of times.

Beside me, on my side of the corridor, was a boy called John Foley. He came from south Armagh, was very friendly but had strange ways with him at times. He had a habit of lying on top of the bedclothes some nights even in the coldest part of winter. In Greek class he had a habit of handing up work, partly in Greek, partly in Latin, partly in Irish with a bit of English mixed in. The result was that on nearly every day of the year his book was open and he had to report to Fr. Kenny for punishment. Across the corridor were Paddy McGuckin and Peter Taggart, both of whom were determined to go on for the priesthood. Peter was to become a priest and serve in the Archdiocese of Armagh for many years.

His untimely death in the recent past deprived us of a person who as boy and man had been a real gentleman, and a man of very considerable intellect.

On the second night of the annual retreat I noticed John tying two or three of his ties together and making sure that they were firmly fixed. I was very puzzled by this but I had kept the silence and I did not ask him what he was doing. I knelt down at the bedside to say my night prayers.

A couple of minutes later I heard a strange gurgling sound to my left and above me. I looked round to see John hanging from the big round pipe, his face already red and swollen, and in places going a very deep purple. "Quick Boys, give me a hand here", I gasped to Peter and Paddy. "John is in trouble".

Together we lifted him by the legs and then I got up on his bed and tried to loosen the ties. They were so tightly fastened that they would not budge. I leapt down, got a penknife from my jacket, and jumping up again tried to cut them. Luckily the knife was quite sharp and they slowly gave way. Together we lowered John down and laid him on his bed.

By now boys from other sections had gathered round and were peering at John. For a few moments it looked as though we had been too late because his face remained very swollen and discoloured and he showed little signs of life. Gradually, however, normal colour returned to his cheeks and he began to splutter. He opened his eyes and looked up at the ring of eager faces peering down at him.

"Where am I?" he asked. "What happened?"

"You tied yourself up to that pipe", I answered. "You were nearly away with it only we managed to cut you down. Do you think we should get some of the staff in on this?" I asked the others. "It looks serious to me".

Most of the watching boys nodded but John shook his head violently without rising in the bed. "Don't clash on me for God's sake", he begged. "I was only fooling about and I fell off the bed. Gammy is liable to kill me if he finds out. Or I will be expelled and then Da will definitely have my life. I'm fine".

We all looked at each other in stunned silence. Some of the group were still shaking their heads slowly as though to say that they thought we should definitely get some of the priests and tell them what had happened. At last Paddy said, "We'd better make our minds up quickly about what we are going to do or Gammy will be in and he'll take the arses off every one of us".

"I think we'd be better to go and get him anyway", said Peter.

John raised himself up on his elbows. "Please don't tell Gammy or anybody else on me?" he begged again. "Get back to your own beds and leave me alone".

Everyone turned and made their way slowly back to their own beds clearly unsure that we were doing the right thing. At that moment the door burst open and Gammy bounced into the dorm. "There's something going on in this dorm", he announced and strutted slowly, menacingly, and silently along the corridor and looking carefully into each section. He reached our cubicle and seemed to sense that it had been the centre of the disturbance.

"Were you boys having a feast?" he enquired, "and in the middle of the retreat too".

"No Father", we answered in unison.

He looked intently at John with a puzzled frown on his face. "What have you been up to Foley?" he demanded.

"I haven't been up to anything, Father", John assured him. The priest then knelt down and looked under John's bed and finding nothing there he examined the spaces under the other three beds. He arose, shaking his head, clearly sure that the wool was being pulled over his eyes. Finally his gaze fixed on my bed and the spot where John's ruined ties protruded from the side of it. He reached over, grabbed the ties and held them up to the light.

"Are these your ties, Daly?" he asked.

"No Father", I replied. "They are John's ties".

He held them very near to my face. "Have you taken to destroying other people's property?" he asked.

I was now in a really tight spot. I could not deny that I had cut the ties and yet I knew that I had not really ruined them without good cause. I did not answer.

"Bend over the end of your bed at once", he commanded. "I'll teach you not to destroy things that don't belong to you".

I was making my way to the end of the bed when John intervened.

"Arthur had to cut the ties, Father", he said very quietly.

Gammy spun round and glared at him. "I knew you were up to something, Foley", he growled. "And why exactly did Arthur have to cut your ties? It all seems very strange to me, but then anything to do with you always seems strange to me".

"I had tied them together and tied them round my neck and they were choking me", explained John.

Gammy shook his head and rubbed his hand slowly through his hair, gazing intently down at John all the time. "You know, Foley", he said softly, "your explanation is so really stupid that there is just the slightest possibility that it might be true".

He suddenly spun round and startled Paddy and Peter. "Is this true?" he demanded.

"It is Father", they replied together.

He then turned back to me where I was still standing as ordered at the end of my bed. "Why did you cut John's ties?" he asked as though he never heard any explanation.

"I thought he was really choking, Father".

"And why didn't you tell me that at the start?" he asked, peering into my face.

Once more I was lost for an answer and again I remained silent.

"Do you think you deserve six on that backside of yours?" he asked.

"I don't know Father", I mumbled, feeling very silly.

"There is an awful lot going on here that I am not being told about", announced the Dean, speaking to all in the immediate vicinity. "I suppose, Peter", he said, "that you have nothing to add to what I have already been told".

"No Father", replied Peter quietly.

"Get into bed the whole lot of you", said the Dean as he walked away. "One day you will have a far greater judge to face than I am and I hope all of you are ready for that".

He walked purposefully down to the door and switched off the light. His voice then filled the dorm, "if I hear one sound from this area I'll stoke the furnaces as they have never been stoked before".

I lay on my back gazing up at the form of the big black pipe in the darkness. There was not a sound in the dorm except the occasional snore coming from fellows who had fallen asleep. I could not get to sleep because I felt uneasy about the whole episode and I was nearly certain that I had done the wrong thing. I looked over at John and I was fairly sure that he was not sleeping either. I slipped very silently out of bed and went over to him.

"What the hell were you up to anyway, John?" I whispered into his ear.

He squirmed. "I was just fooling about and I made a mistake", he whispered back. "Only for you I might have been a goner".

"It was a damned foolish way to be fooling about", I hissed quietly into his ear. "I never heard of anybody trying on something like that in my life".

"Get back to bed", growled John with venom, "or you'll get the whole dorm into trouble. I'm going to sleep".

He turned his face to the wall and pretended to be asleep. I had no option but to slip back into bed. I had just settled beneath the bedclothes and was lying on my side looking at John, when I heard the door of the dorm opening and the Dean's footsteps approaching along the corridor. I pretended to be asleep but kept my eyes open to such an extent that I was able to see vaguely in the semi darkness.

The Dean's shadow slowed as he approached our cubicle and then he stopped and looked at each of us in turn. He stood there apparently thinking for a couple of minutes and then turned and walked slowly back the way he had come. When He reached the end of the dorm, however, instead of going out through the door, he turned and prowled very slowly back along the corridor. Again he stopped at our cubicle and stood for a moment or two. Twice more he did the same thing and I sensed that the man was worried. Finally he disappeared out of the door.

I turned on to my back and lay looking up at the shadow of the big pipe again. My eyelids became very heavy and as I was about to fall asleep I imagined I saw a human form dangling from the pipe. I jumped up in terror and gave a shriek of horror.

"What's wrong now?" gasped Paddy, slipping out of bed and coming over to me.

"I just had a kind of nightmare", I assured him. "It's nothing. Get back to your bed or Gammy will come in and do the whole lot of us".

"Are we not going to get any sleep tonight at all?" mumbled Paddy angrily. "Maybe we're not going to get any sleep for the rest of the year".

Paddy was scarcely back in bed when the door burst open once more and I could hear the Dean slipping along the corridor. Again he stopped at our section but everyone pretended to be fast asleep and unaware of his presence. Finally he turned and left the dorm quietly and soon we did not have to pretend any more. We fell over to sleep at last.

Years later I heard a rumour that John had committed suicide and it brought the events of that night very clearly back to mind. I have wondered ever since if I did the right thing in not telling the Dean the full story of what had taken place. I have wondered if our code of honour may have stood in the way of getting real help for a troubled mind.

CHAPTER 17
DANCES GALORE

Our third year ended with the Junior Certificate Examination, which was second in importance only to the Senior Certificate, which would come at the end of five years. In my case I did surprisingly well, and came home to enjoy the long summer holidays of 1951. It was a couple of months, which I spent working at strawberries by day and going to dances at night. That year there was certainly no shortage of either fruit or dances.

The Government of Northern Ireland had decided that everyone should have a secondary education and that the school leaving age should be raised to fifteen years. It meant that new schools had to be built in towns all over the country and this posed a very big problem for the Catholic authorities. They did not trust the Government, and would not accept any of the schemes by means of which they could have had the full cost of building the new schools entirely covered. They insisted that they would have to have full control and ownership of their own schools and this meant that they had to find money to pay for one third of the cost. A new secondary school was to be built in Dungannon and eight or nine surrounding parishes had to contribute to the cost of its construction. It was a huge burden to impose on parishes and the priests in charge of them.

Guest teas, whist drives and tombola were some of the methods used to raise money in the local parishes. There was a frenzy of activity and excitement. Women were invited to put up a table in the parochial hall and then invite ten or twelve of their relations and friends to a guest tea. Since nearly all the women in the parish were expected to organise a table it was not always easy to find enough people to invite. Each guest was expected to contribute generously to the event but the women had to bear the full cost of the food and other expenses. My mother decided that she could not afford such outlay and only went as a guest to our neighbours' tables.

Very quickly a fierce rivalry arose amongst the female hosts, not only about the amount of money raised but also regarding the grandeur of each table. It was obvious that women were looking askance at other tables to see how their own matched up and with each successive guest tea the quality of table cloths, of cutlery, of china and crystal reached new heights. Whilst the ladies grumbled that the whole thing had become ridiculous, the spirit of competition only increased.

Our parish of Clonfeacle has always been divided into two sections, one centred on the village of

The Moy and the other taking in the villages and Blackwatertown and Benburb. The people of The Moy were regarded in our side of the parish as being very stuck up and thinking of themselves as superior to the rest of us. Our curate, Father Peter Moore used this fact to stoke the fires of rivalry to danger point. Speaking in The Moy he would tell the congregation, "the ladies over in the other side of the parish had a really marvellous guest tea last week, and the money raised has reached new heights. We really have an outstanding group of ladies over there and they are an example not just in this area but to the rest of the diocese".

In the our chapel he made sure to praise the Moy ladies to the skies and assure the people that, "the work being done by the ladies over in Moy could not be matched anywhere". People came out of the church grumbling that 'he had only eyes for the 'big hands' round The Moy' but the next event showed that everyone was determined that their side of the parish would not be outdone.

The main source of money was, however, dances, which were run in the parochial halls and which were very popular and attracted great crowds. The popularity and profitability of the dances encouraged the organisers to go further and carnivals were run, which included football tournaments as well as big dances in giant marquees. In that summer at the end of my third year, there were carnivals in many surrounding parishes and a big attraction was the marquee, which had been erected in Assumpta Manor in Dungannon. Buses were hired all over the country to bring people to it and the crowds were immense. There were attractions that week in many other places such as The Moy and Armagh. We were spoiled for choice and Tommy and I saw it as our duty to attend as many events as possible, even though we had to work long days at the fruit picking or the cleaning of the crop.

One night Tommy met a girl and arranged to walk her home. "I'll only be a very short time", he assured me, "and you can keep the bicycles at the entrance to the houses on the Donaghmore Road. I definitely will not keep you too long".

It was a lovely moonlit night with patches of light cloud, which from time to time shaded the bright light of the moon. I was quite happy standing at the entrance to the little estate admiring the surrounding countryside. I was there only ten or fifteen minutes when I heard a commotion somewhere deep within the little group of houses. As I tried to make out what had happened I could see a dark shadow approaching in the shade of overhanging trees. It seemed to rise upward every few yards as it came towards me, and I wondered what on earth it could be. Eventually I recognised Tommy running as hard as he could go and jumping over the fences between the gardens. He rushed up to where I was standing, grabbed his bicycle, and jumped on to it.

"Come on, and ride like hell", he yelled over his

shoulder. He was already riding as fast as he could and I could see no alternative but to follow him. He continued riding at breakneck speed until we were about half way home and I had no opportunity to ask what had taken place. I had bother enough trying to keep up with him. Eventually he stopped, threw his bike on a bank at the side of the road and sat down on the grass. I followed his example. We were both out of breath and lathered in sweat. We sat there for a few minutes in silence.

"Under God, Tommy", I asked at last, "what the hell happened? Why were we in such a hurry?"

He did not answer immediately but sat looking at me and using a handkerchief to wipe sweat from his face.

"I talked that lassie into taking me in and making a cup of tea", he said slowly.

I sat waiting for further explanation but he stayed silent. "And what has a cup of tea to do with rushing home like this?" I enquired. "I'm half dead and we have a big day's work to do tomorrow".

"I was taking the tea at the table in the kitchen", Tommy said slowly. "I heard her old boy coming down the corridor from the bedroom and I went out through the window into the back garden. Did you not hear the noise?"

I could hardly believe what I was hearing. "I heard it surely", I gasped, "but I can't understand why you had to get out, Tommy. Sure taking a cup of tea is no great crime".

Tommy gazed at me as though he thought I was absolutely crazy. "I wasn't going to wait to find out if it was a crime or not", he said. "I got up on the chair, and I jumped into the back garden. I never did any real harm at all".

"God, Tommy", I said earnestly, "that poor girl will have some explaining to do. She will have some job trying to explain what sort of boy left her home and then jumped out of the window at this time of night. That man is liable to go stone mad".

I could see concern on Tommy's face for the first time as he sat there in the moonlight. "You would hardly believe it", he whispered, "but do you know I never thought of that. Right enough she'll have some job trying to explain to her Da, about the kind of boy that left her home from the dance. I suppose they will think that I have just got out of the asylum. There's nothing more we can do about it, so come on and we'll get home right away. It's nearly day light and we'll be in some shape for a day's work tomorrow".

I never heard any more about the incident although I have often wondered what happened in that house after Tommy had left. We avoided going back to Dungannon for the rest of the week but this made little difference since there was no shortage of other places to choose from.

On Saturday morning of that week I was due to go to Rannafast in Donegal, even though I had slept less in the past ten days or so, than would have been normal for one night. I set out for Dungannon on my bicycle and left it with my friend in Scotch Street. I was feeling very tired and sleepy as I made my way down to the station but I was delighted to find Michael Byrne from The Moy waiting on the train. Michael had joined us in Armagh after a couple of years in St. Patrick's Academy in Dungannon and he had three of his companions of earlier days with him. I got my ticket and we boarded the train and found a compartment to ourselves. The next thing I remember is Michael shaking me in Rannafast.

"Damn you, would you wake up", he hissed into my ear.

"What's wrong?" I mumbled. "Where are we?"

"In Rannafast", he snarled through gritted teeth. "Damn you would you keep quiet, we're supposed to be speaking Irish".

"How in hell's blazes did I get here?" I asked.

Michael shook his head to show that he was disgusted with me. "You fell asleep as soon as you sat down in the train", he whispered, looking around to be sure that no one could hear. "You're some companion to have on a long journey. We had to carry you from the train in Derry and put you on the bus. You were out to the world and felt like an old sack of potatoes. Damn you would you wake up. We're not going to carry you down to the house. We're in teach Mhic Arbhaigh".

At that moment a young girl of about seventeen came over to us and addressed us in beautiful Gaeilge. "I am Sarah McGarvey", she said, "and my mother has sent me to take you down to our house. It's only a wee bit down the road and there's six of you staying with us for the next fortnight". Not only had she beautiful Irish, but she was very attractive and very friendly. I began to wake up fairly quickly.

We got our things together and Sarah led us down the road to the house, which was only about four hundred yards from the college and right on the side of the main road. It was called the main road in Rannafast but it was really a rather narrow track, little more that the width of a horse's cart and very bumpy. Mrs McGarvey met us on the front street with a big smile and welcomed us into the house where she already had a cup of tea ready for us. Another girl, who looked a bit like Sarah but was, if anything, even more beautiful, introduced herself as Maire, Sarah's sister. I quickly came to the conclusion that this would be a holiday worth waking up for.

Mrs McGarvey enquired where we came from and then allocated our rooms. Since Michael and I knew each other we were put in a small room at the back of the house with two single beds. The other four boys were from south Derry and they were pleased to share the front room, which was quite big. The tallest of the Derry boys was called Jim Kane and he announced in a friendly, if slightly threatening way, that the Derry boys would have to get one over on the Tyrone boys.

We were getting ready for bed when Michael slapped his knee and hissed, "we're going to have to watch ourselves with those smart guys in the front room. They are out to get us and we had better make sure to get them first".

"They seem very friendly sort of fellows", I said in surprise. "They were very helpful when we were coming down here to the house".

Michael sighed deeply. "You must be still half asleep", he said, "and you had better wake up quickly. What the hell were you doing that you could sleep through that long journey. It was pouring all the way across Donegal and some of the boys were saying that you were lucky to be out to the world. There was one very attractive wee lassie and she said that you looked lovely when you were sleeping and she would like to take you home with her".

"She mightn't be so fond of me when she sees me awake", I said rubbing my tired eyes. "Before we came here I was at a dance every night for about ten days and then I had to work at the strawberries from dawn until it was time to go out again. I hardly saw a bed for a fortnight and I'm still dead tired. I'm going to sleep".

The next morning the rain had cleared and the sun blazed out of a clear blue sky. Mrs McGarvey assured us that we were lucky because a long spell of good weather was forecast and we would have a great holiday. She warned us to speak Irish all the time and she and the two girls made it easy for us. I really felt that I learned a lot of the language in the first few days and I felt quite confident and pleased with myself.

Three or four days later a couple of the Derry boys and I were sitting at the front of the house talking to the two girls. They were telling us about their life in this remote place and how they were planning to go to Dungloe that night to a dance. At that point they obviously wished to discuss private affairs between themselves and their language changed completely. I was shocked. I was hardly able to catch one syllable of what they were saying and the total conversation was incomprehensible. It taught me how difficult it is to really learn a new language.

The next day we were free in the afternoon. Michael and I came home and found nobody about the house. The family had gone shopping in Letterkenny and would not be home until much later. The Derry boys had gone exploring with some friends of theirs. We had the place to ourselves.

"This is a great chance to get one over on those Derry boys", said Michael. "I think we should make French beds for them and put in some of those big nettles that are growing at the back of the house. If we are careful they'll never know that the beds were touched and they'll get some shock".

"What are French beds?" I asked, "I have never heard of them in my life".

"You go and pull a good bunch of nettles and bring them into the front room and I'll soon show you", he replied with a knowing smile.

Michael told me to keep a watch lest some of the Derry boys return and while I was doing this he showed me how to fold the top sheet so that it formed a sort of pocket half way down each bed. Before he replaced the rest of the bedclothes he carefully inserted the nettles in the pocket and then fixed the beds so that they looked as though they had never been touched.

"Don't you think that is a fine job?" he asked as he stood back and surveyed his handiwork.

"It is in one way", I replied, "but by God I wouldn't fancy being the poor crayturs that stick their bare feet down there at bedtime. And I'd say they will surely be out for vengeance before we go home".

Michael laughed. "Come on out of here before they come back", he said in urgent tones. "We'd be as well to make our way up to the college and stay there for a while and pretend that we were never back at the house. But we'll have to go by the paths over the bogs in case we meet some of them on the roads".

We used a series of footpaths well away from the road and came to the college by a roundabout route. We joined in with a few people who were still there and a couple of the Derry boys happened to be in the group. After a half an hour or so we all walked back to the house chatting away in a very friendly manner. Everyone else had returned by the time we got back and the tea was on the table. There was no ceili that night so we spent the evening playing board games and talking to the two sisters. At eleven o'clock Mrs Garvey made a cup of tea and announced that it was time for bed.

Michael and I went to our own room and got ready for bed quickly. We then sat on the edge of our beds waiting for uproar from the front room. "It was dead lucky the way things turned out this evening", whispered Michael. "The way we were able to join the other two boys and walk home with them left us above suspicion. Wait till you hear the hullabaloo". He looked at his watch and we sat waiting.

Twenty minutes went past and there was not a sound except for the faint tones of the family conversing in the kitchen. I looked at my watch and it was just after half past eleven. "To hell with this", I said to an obviously disappointed Michael, "they have caught on and cleared the beds. I tired and I'm going to sleep".

Michael shook his head in puzzlement and disappointment. "I can't understand it at all", he said, rolling into bed. "I can't see how the hell they would have discovered that the beds had been set".

At that moment there were howls and yells of anguish and loud curses from the front room; none of them were in Irish. Michael jumped up in his bed and rubbed his hands and chuckled to himself quietly. "I knew it would work", he said, smiling broadly. "The trap was far too well set for the mice to get out of it. Damn it all, but those boys will have warm feet tonight".

We could hear Mrs McGarvey and the two girls going into the room but the conversation which followed was far too faint for us to make out what was being said. We lay listening for a while and whispering congratulations to each other and at last we fell asleep.

Breakfast the next morning was perfectly normal and no one said a word about the night before. It was as though nothing had ever happened. All six of us walked up to the college together and Jim Kane was the essence of good company, friendship and conversation. The main topic of conversation was about how easy it was to learn Irish when we had two native speakers like Sarah and Maire. We agreed too that we had probably the best house in Rannafast.

"I tell you", said Jim, "we are dead lucky to get that house and we're more than lucky to have been put in the same house. Even though you two boys are from Tyrone, I really enjoy your company and I know these other three Derry men feel the same".

As soon as possible, I got Michael on his own. "I'm dead worried Michael", I said. "Those Derry boys are up to something. They are far too friendly and I don't like the way they have never said a word about what happened. And it's funny that Mrs McGarvey did not give out to us".

Michael sat studying me for a moment. "I know we will have to watch out", he said thoughtfully. "But what the hell can they do for they know well we'll be watching out? I don't know about you but they damned well aren't going to catch me".

Wednesday of the second week came and nothing had happened. We had a half day, and the Derry boys announced that they had made friends with a man who had a car and that they were going for a couple of hours to Dungloe. We were left in the house on our own.

"Would you like to take a walk down to Annagry?" asked Michael. "It's only a bit over a mile and I wouldn't mind seeing round the place. It's only a very small village, but at least it would be a bit different".

"That's great", I assured him. "I had intended going to see it before going home. We have plenty of time and we can take it easy in that boiling heat".

We informed Mrs McGarvey of what we intended to do. A great big smile came over her face and she told us that she didn't mind at all and we could take all the time we wanted. Tea would not be ready until six o'clock or maybe a little later. A thought flashed through my mind that there was something peculiar in her attitude but I put it to the back of my mind as ridiculous. We set out and dandered slowly down to the little hamlet.

I remember Annagry on that afternoon for one reason. We got talking to an old man who was very hard to understand but I was very interested in him because of his way of life. He lived in a one-roomed house at the edge of the village and his sole companion was a big blue cow. He lived in one side of the big room and the cow had the other half! He explained that when the cow dung and bedding got too high on one side they changed over. He did not clean the place out until the dung was about three feet deep. I would not have believed him except that when we were there the cow's side was already a foot and a half higher than the place where he had his table, chair and bed. He said that the change over was due!

We spent about an hour and a half examining the village and chatting to anyone who would chat to us. It was very warm indeed and by the time we decided to walk back we were feeling tired and a bit sore. It was the sort of heat that sucked the energy out of one's body. We reached the end of the road and turned towards the house and were really surprised to see the Derry boys approaching from the opposite direction. We met on the front street.

"Are you boys just back?" asked Jim Kane in a very surprised tone. "We have been away to Dungloe and it's miles away and a fairly big place. What the hell were you doing in a wee place like Annagry?"

"Ach, this boy was talking for a long time to an old fellow who lived with a cow", replied Michael. "I thought for a while that he was going to stay with him altogether. It looked for a while like he might take up residence with the cow. God, I'm dead beat. I'm going to take a rest".

"I'm dead tired too", I added, "that heat would kill the devil".

I noticed a pleased smirk on Jim's face as we headed for our room but I paid little attention to it. I was too keen to get a chance to lie down. Michael opened our room door and took a flying leap, turning in the air to land on his back. There was a dull thud. "Oh Jesus, I'm killed", roared Michael from the bed, his face contorted in obvious agony. Slowly he put his hands round to his back and squirmed in discomfort. He then felt the back of his head. "Jesus there's a lump on the back of my head the size of an orange", he roared. "I'm going to kill somebody for this".

I stood there like a statue for a minute or so. Then I bent down and felt my bed. It was all hard lumps and when I pulled the clothes back it was filled from top to bottom with big stones. Even the pillow was filled with stones but the clothes had been put back so carefully that it had looked perfectly normal when we came through the door. I heard some titters behind me and turned to find the Derry boys and the three McGarveys all admiring their handiwork, their faces encased in satisfied smiles. Poor Michael was still groaning and cursing on his bed and swearing that somebody was going to pay for what had happened to him. It was one of those times when I felt I had been far luckier that I deserved to be.

Mrs McGarvey moved past me into the room and stood beside Michael, looking down at him. "I hope you're not hurt really", she said softly. "Nobody could have foreseen that you would take such an athletic leap onto the bed".

Michael straightened himself up until he was sitting on the side of the bed, still muttering curses and groans under his breath. He looked up at Mrs McGarvey. "That's the way I always go to bed", he growled. "I'm a bit sore but I'll be better in the morning and some people had better watch out".

"Now, I want this to be the end of the playacting", said Mrs McGarvey firmly. "I want everyone to help carry all these stones outside and we'll fix the beds. Michael can be excused because he has come out badly in all of this. Come on now, and we'll get everything tidied and then it will be tea time".

It took a few minutes to get all the stones outside and the beds newly made. There was a lot of chat during tea about the rivalry between Tyrone and Derry but Michael took no part in it. He sat quietly nursing his sore places. That night as we were going to bed he glared at me and said, "you are the luckiest frigger I ever met in my life. Why the hell couldn't you have come into the room first? There's definitely somebody going to pay dearly for this".

We reached the end of the fortnight, however, and nothing more happened.

CHAPTER 18
A CALL TO ORDER

At the start of our fourth year in Armagh it was explained that we were now senior grade students and would be treated as such. We were expected to take on a more mature role, totally different from the children in the junior classes. In reality though, very little changed. Fr. Devine had become Dean and Fr. Gallagher had departed for foreign fields. I was delighted at first to find my old friend in this new role. I expected to experience a much more human approach. I soon discovered, however, that he was totally unpredictable and could be vindictive. I was not one of those on whom he consistently chose to vent his spite but his unfairness cast a dark cloud over the whole college.

We were all a bit shocked to find that our Greek teacher had been changed again and we now had Fr. Doherty. He was a small man, probably in his late thirties, and was always very pleasant, kind and helpful.

For some reason, which I can't explain, I found it difficult to learn with him and by the end of the year

I felt that I was slipping behind in the subject.

The other big change was that we had Mr. O'Riordan, one of the lay staff, for mathematics. Bill O'Riordan was a genius, and was pitted against a computer at one stage. Apparently he won the contest easily. He was a true gentleman but he was very nervous and had a habit of eating the corners of his textbook as he taught from it. He found anything to do with mathematics so easy himself that he raced through the course at breakneck speed. The very bright boys kept up with him but I found myself struggling. Towards the end of that year I felt quite downhearted about my chances of doing well in the senior.

A sports tournament was arranged at the end of September. I was practising for the high jump one evening at a jumping pit, which had been set up in the middle of the junior ring. Everything was going quite well until I came down on my right ankle and twisted it very badly. It was very sore and I found it difficult to walk. I was sent to the doctor. He told me I had chipped the bone badly and it would take three or four months to heal. It not only meant that I could not take part in the sports but it ruled out football in the evenings. I hated having to limp round the field in the company of a few fellows who hated football and avoided it at all costs. It was certainly not my year.

A girl whom I had met at the ceilis in the Brantry started to write to me about once a month. It was quite pleasant to hear from the world outside but

I knew that sooner or later her letters would be stopped and I might well be in trouble. As expected the letters suddenly stopped before Christmas and I was fairly sure that one or more of the censors had them in their possession.

I was settling down in second study one night when Fr. Devine came in and tapped me on the shoulder. "The President wants to have a word with you down in his office", he whispered. "Go down immediately and make sure you knock the door before entering". He left me to go down the stairs on my own and went over to talk to Mr. Hicks, who was on duty. As I made my way down to the 'holy of holies,' I knew that I was in fairly deep bother.

I pushed through the heavy wooden doors into the dimly lit foyer and made my way over to the President's door. I knocked and his sharp voice told me to enter. I opened the door in trepidation and slipped into his office. "Close the door behind you", he said curtly, "and take a seat on that chair". He was sitting in a deep leather armchair on the right hand side of the fireplace in which a lovely coal fire burned and he had pointed to a wooden chair on the other side of the fire. I closed the door and took my place gingerly. I noticed that he was reading a book and that he had an envelope as a marker. I suspected that the envelope was addressed to me and contained my confiscated letter.

He left down the book on the arm of his chair and sat studying me for a long time. At least it seemed a long time in the tense silence. "I believe", he said slowly and apparently thoughtfully, "that you have been thinking that you have a vocation to the priesthood and that you intend entering at the end of your time here".

It was the last thing in the world that I expected him to say and my mind went into a whirl. "To tell you the truth Father", I began, but got no further. The President jumped up and glared down at me, apparently very angry. "And what else do you think you might dare to come in here and tell me? Did you mean to come in here and tell me a bundle of lies?" he demanded in a harsh voice.

His whole manner, and the tone of his voice, startled me. It was probably meant to scare the life out of me but it had the totally opposite effect. Instead of the fear and trepidation I had felt coming into the office, I now felt cool and calm but I did not want him to sense that. I did my best to appear shattered. "If you want to hear a bundle of lies then that is what you will hear", I thought to myself.

"No Father", I answered quietly and softly. "I did not intend to tell you a bundle of lies".

He sat down again and lay back in his chair, studying me all the time. "And do you still intend to go on for the priesthood?" he asked.

"I do Father", I lied, "I have been thinking of going to the missions".

"And have you any Order or place in mind to where you might think of going?"

"Well Father, there is the Servite Priory in Benburb and I know them quite well".

"I remember you changed over to Greek a few years ago", he said. "You don't need Greek for most of the Orders. Would you think of going to Maynooth?"

"I had thought of it Father, but I don't think my results will be good enough at the end of next year".

He straightened up quickly and glared at me again. "Are you suggesting that Orders are some sort of second rate type of priesthood?" he demanded. I realised that he was suggesting that my remarks were a slander against his own Order.

"No Father", I said, "but I have been told that a Maynooth student needs a state exhibition to go there, and I have no chance of getting that".

He leaned forward and looked intently into my eyes. "And if you did get a state exhibition, would you then think of going to Maynooth?"

"No Father, I would still go for the Orders".

Once again he sat studying me. He lay back in his chair once more and in an apparently friendly tone asked, "and how have you been spending your time during the holidays?"

"We have over an acre of strawberries, Father and they have to be cleaned and then when the fruit is ripe they have to be pulled".

"What time do you start in the mornings?" he asked.

"If the day is good Father, I would usually start before seven o'clock".

"At what time would you finish?"

"I would work until nearly dark Father".

He sat upright suddenly and again he glared into my eyes. "So if you are so fully occupied, when do you get time to go and meet girls?"

I knew the question was meant to be the springing of a trap and I answered casually as though it were the most natural question in the world. "Oh, my friend and I go to ceilis in a place called the Brantry Father. We meet lots of girls there".

I could see he was not happy with my answer and he looked a little puzzled. "Do you leave girls out from the dances?" he asked, still glaring at me.

"I have walked one or two girls to their houses Father".

"Why?" he barked.

"Well Father, it's something that all the fellows do and sometimes the girls are quite interesting to talk to".

"Have you ever kissed a girl?"

"I have kissed one or two girls good night, Father".

"Why?"

"I suppose because it is the normal thing to do Father".

"Does it ever go any further than that?" He was now staring steadily into my face, as though he expected to the answer to be yes. It annoyed me that in this case I felt that I had to tell him the truth.

"No Father, it has never gone any further that a quick kiss".

"Humph", he growled lowly. "Have any of these girl friends of yours ever written to you?"

"One girl has written to me a few times and I have written back to her".

"Who did you give the letters to, to post?" he snarled. I knew that this was a tricky situation, because if I told him the truth, I would be putting a day-boy in a lot of trouble. I had to think quickly.

"I didn't give them to anybody, Father, I slipped them into a post box during the Sunday walk".

"Do girls sit on your knee in the intervals between the dances?"

"No, Father, the man in charge never allows girls to sit on boys' knees at any time".

"Why?"

"Well Father, I never asked him, but he is very strict and we all know that both the boy and the girl will be sent home if the girl sits on the boy's knee".

"Who is this man?"

"His name is John McCann, Father, and he comes from the Brantry".

"Humph", he muttered again and sat back comfortably in his chair once more. "If you are so keen on going to the priesthood", he asked, "why are you so keen on leaving girls home from dances?"

"My father insists that I get to know girls a wee bit Father. He says I am an only child and have never had a chance to meet girls. He says that if I don't get to know a few girls I would be like a man with one eye." I was really pleased with this answer because my father had never said any such thing.

The President remained lying back in his chair and rubbed his chin thoughtfully. "So you only go out with girls because other fellows do it and because your father had told you to?"

Suddenly I did not think that my answer had been so wise and I knew I was in a fix. I looked back at him but could not think of a reasonable answer.

"Why have you asked to take up ancient history?" he asked. I was delighted because I felt that I was now on much safer ground.

"I have always loved history Father, and the teacher in the primary school used to tell us great stories about the Romans. Since I am doing Greek I have already learned a bit about Greek civilization and it would be an extra subject".

"Are you so good at all your other subjects that you can afford time to give to this new subject?"

"I thought I would give it a try Father".

"How many girls have been writing to you?" The question, and sudden change of subject again, must have been meant to catch me out.

"Only one Father", I answered, which was true.

"Are you going to continue to correspond with her?"

"No Father. We have stopped writing to each other".

"Why are you so keen on going to dances?" The question was posed in an almost friendly tone and I was suspicious of it.

"There have been lots of dances organised by the parish lately and Father Moore is always urging everyone to attend. He has an awful lot of money to raise and dances seem to be the only method he has of raising it".

"You still think that you might have a vocation?" he asked slowly. "Do you not think that going to dances might put it in danger?"

I looked at him in genuine surprise. "I would think Father, that if a vocation can't survive a dance, then it is not much of a vocation".

He shook his head and lifted his book again. "Go on back up to study", he ordered. "If I have to bring you back to this office again it will be to expel you. Get a move on now".

"Thank you Father", I said softly, and slipped out of the office.

About a fortnight later, Fr. Dougan stopped me at the end of his Latin class. "I was out in your part of the country last Sunday", he said, "I took a trip out to the Brantry on the bicycle. I noticed a building on the side of the road with a door like a big horseshoe. Is that a blacksmith's forge".

"It is Father," I answered, "it's Donnelly's forge and the family are well known all over the country".

"Who built the wee hall on up the road?" he asked.

"That's the G.A.A. hall Father, and as far as I know a few of the locals built it some years ago".

"Fr. Sheridan asked me to go out and do a bit of

investigation", he said, looking sideways at me with a smile. "I think you were talking to him one night and he felt that you were telling him fairy tales. He was very suspicious about what you had told him about how John McCann runs the dances. I was talking to some of the locals, and I found out that every word you had said about the man was true. I was delighted to be able to report back to him confirming what you had told him".

"John does a great job Father", I said.

"Right Arthur," said Fr. Dougan, "try and work a bit harder at the Latin because I noticed that you have been slipping of late. Maybe keeping up with all these dances has been getting in your way".

"Right Father", I said. "Thank you very much".

CHAPTER 19
TO READ OR NOT TO READ?

A couple of months later I had an even more difficult confrontation with the President. Fr. Curtin picked about six of his best readers from his English class to read in the priests' refectory in the mornings. Each reader was on duty for a week and it was regarded as a very desirable job because the reader was rewarded with a full fry when the priests had finished their breakfast and had left the room.

The priests' refectory was a fairly small room in the old part of the building and they sat round a long table to take their breakfast in silence. Fr. Sheridan sat at the top of the table and appeared to me to keep very strict discipline during the meal. There was a small alcove in the wall opposite the door and the reader sat in this and read for about twenty minutes or so while the priests were eating. The President decided what text should be read. Apart from the reader's voice there was not a sound in the room except the noise of knives and forks scraping on plates.

I had read a couple of times in the early part of the year and everything had gone without a hitch. Just before Easter I was on for my last session that year. The book chosen was '*The Siege of the Alcazar*', which told the story of the Spanish Civil War from the point of view of the Christian forces under General Franco.

The week went well until Thursday. That morning I felt very strange going up the stairs to the priests' ref and when I started to read, the letters of the text seemed to jump about all over the page. The first couple of paragraphs were difficult enough but then it got worse. I felt rather sick. I came to a word, which I could not see and I made an attempt to pronounce it.

"Stop", roared the President.

I stopped and looked down at him. He seemed to be far away in a mist and moving from side to side. "What was that last word, Boy?" he barked.

I made another attempt to pronounce the word but I could hardly see the page never mind the text. "Pronounce that word correctly", ordered Fr. Sheridan, "if you cannot read a simple word like that you have no call to be reading here".

I began to panic. I couldn't see the page and I did not know what to do.

"Read that section over again", roared Fr. Sheridan. "I want to hear each word clearly".

I tried once more but now the text was a drifting in a fog. I was beginning to feel very sick and my head was aching.

"Read Boy," barked the President once more.

Fr. Doherty intervened at this juncture. "Father Sheridan, that is hardly fair", he said. "There is obviously something wrong with Arthur this morning. He is usually an excellent reader".

Fr. Sheridan jumped up, scattering his chair behind him. "You", he said, pointing to Fr. Doherty, "go up there and read in his place. And you", he said, pointing up to me, "go to his place and eat that breakfast".

Very slowly, Fr. Doherty got up and made his way over to my alcove. Someone retrieved the President's chair and he sat down. I rose and staggered down to where Fr. Doherty had been sitting. I stood behind his chair and took out my handkerchief to wipe my face. Fr. Doherty began reading where I had left off.

"Stop", roared Fr. Sheridan once more, sitting bolt upright on his chair. He glared across at me. "Didn't I tell you to sit down and eat that breakfast, Boy", he yelled. "Do what you are told immediately".

I sat down and lifted the knife and fork but I was now feeling hopelessly ill and my head was splitting. I could hardly see at all now.

"Read on", ordered the President, looking up angrily at Fr. Doherty. The priest had read about a paragraph, when Fr. Sheridan roared, "Stop" once more. He was glaring across at me but I could only see him in a haze.

"Didn't I tell you to eat that breakfast, Boy", he yelled. "Are you not going to do what you are told? Do you want to be expelled?"

At this point Fr. Dougan rose from his seat and came over to me. "There is clearly something very far wrong with Arthur, this morning, Fr. Sheridan", he said firmly. "I am going to take him up to the matron to see what is the matter. Come on Arthur", he said to me, helping me to get up, "we'll go and see if we can get you some help".

Fr. Dougan led me towards the door without another word. "I don't want to see you back here again, Boy", roared Fr. Sheridan, but he did not try to stop us.

The matron examined me and told me that she thought I had an attack of migraine.

"Have you ever had it before?" she asked.

"I don't ever remember having anything like this Matron," I mumbled.

"Lie down on that bed", she said, "and I will close the curtains over. If you lie there in the dark you will probably be fine in a couple of hours. But you may find that you will have other attacks from time to time in the future. It's not dangerous but it can be very unpleasant".

It was the first time I had experienced an attack of migraine but the matron's forecast proved to be very accurate indeed. For many years I was subject to attacks of varying degrees of intensity and it proved to be a most unpleasant condition indeed. That morning, almost as soon as the matron had gone, I fell into a deep sleep, which lasted for some two hours. I awoke to find the pain and discomfort completely gone and I got up to make my way down to class. The matron met me in the corridor outside the Infirmary.

"Oh", said she with a big smile, "so the patient is back with us again. Are you feeling better now?"

"I'm feeling fine Matron", I assured her.

"You must be hungry", she said, "if you wait there for a wee while, I'll get you something to eat".

I glanced at my watch. "It will not be long now till lunch time Matron", I said, "I can wait until then".

She looked at me smiling broadly. "I'm giving you a choice", she said. "You can stay up here and have a lovely big fry or you can go down to lunch. It's up to you".

"That's not much of a choice Matron", I replied eagerly. "I'll wait here if you don't mind".

She was true to her word. I had the best meal I had tasted for a long time.

I made it my business to find Fr. Doherty and thank him for standing up for me and I apologised for getting him into trouble. "Never mind", he said, "it was the right thing to do but things happen in the priesthood that you would hardly believe. At the same time I'm delighted that you had the courtesy to come and talk to me. By the way I'm worried about your Greek. You will have to work a lot harder".

"I know that Father", I replied. "It just seems to be getting more difficult".

I then searched out Fr. Dougan and thanked him for taking me out of the ref and up to the matron. "I am glad you did not get into trouble like Fr. Doherty", I added.

Fr. Dougan looked at me and I could see kindness

and gentleness in his eyes but for once there was no smile on his face. "Arthur", he said softly, "things are not always what they seem to be. Or maybe I should say you don't always see the whole picture. Now go on back to class and the best of luck".

On the Thursday evening Fr. Curtin came to me. "I will have to get somebody else to read in the morning", he said. "You made a real mess of things this morning and the President will not allow you back".

"I feel fine now Father", I assured him, "I will be ready to read in the morning. It is not likely that I will take another bout of that migraine".

"No", he said firmly, "I'll have to get someone else".

I was very unhappy. I thought it was unfair to say I had messed up and I wanted to show them that I could read as well as anyone else. There was nothing I could do about the last day of that week but I decided that I would find a way of getting another chance in spite of them. At the start of each of the following weeks I approached the boy designated to read and asked him if he would take a day or two off and let me take his place. He would have to pretend to be sick.

They all looked at me as though I had gone mad. "Do you think I am going to give up my chance of a fry and let you take it?" each one enquired. "It's the big fry you are after, isn't it?"

"I'm not really that interested in the fry", I assured them. "I have a special reason for wanting to read".

No one would believe me but I kept on trying and at last one boy asked me how I would reward him if he let me take his place. "What will you give me if I give up my place for you?" he asked.

"What do you want?" I asked.

"What about two pounds?" he said with a sly laugh.

Two pounds was an awful lot of money to me and he must have seen the look of shock and agony on my face. He started to shake with laughter. "Oh, so you are not so keen on getting a fry when you have to pay for it", he said.

"I don't give a damn about the fry", I stated firmly, "but I would love to get the chance to go in there and read. I'll give you a pound and I'll smuggle out the fry for you to eat if you want it".

"How are you going to smuggle the fry out?" he demanded. "And how would I get a chance to eat it? Give me two pounds and I'll be sick for one day and you can read for me".

I thought for a moment. "I'll give you thirty bob", I offered.

"No", he said firmly. "It's two pounds or nothing".

"Right", I said with a heavy heart, "but I want you to show me exactly where you left off in the book. There's a copy of it in the library upstairs".

The deal was made and that night during second study I managed to get a loan of the book and I read the next section over and over again until I had it nearly off by heart. The next morning I slipped into the alcove and had started reading before Fr. Sheridan thought of looking up. I was sure of the text and I put a very special effort into reading with expression and dramatisation. He did not stop me but when the breakfast was over he called me up to him.

"What are you doing here?" he demanded. "I told you not to come back".

"Oh, I didn't know that, Father", I said.

"The final words I said to you when you were here last", he said, "were that I did not want to see you here again. Maybe you only hear the things which you want to hear. Perhaps you could explain to me how is it that you didn't hear me?"

"Oh Father, that morning I had a bad migraine and I was very sick", I explained confidently. "I could not see and I suppose I was not hearing too well either. I'm sorry about that".

"Why are you here this morning?" he asked with an edge to his voice.

"Big Frank was sick Father," I said, "and he asked me to take his place".

"Humph", he murmured. Then he looked up at me and tapped me on the chest with his finger. "You read excellently this morning", he said. "It's the best bit of reading with meaning that I have heard for a long time. So you will read for the rest of this week and you will read all of next week and maybe I will get you to read the following week as well. I will tell Fr. Curtin what I have decided. What do you think of that?"

I was stunned and I could not help staring down at him in amazement.

"Well what do you think of that?" he repeated.

"Some of the boys will kill me Father. They are always very keen to read because they get a nice fry. They'll kill me". I was thinking ahead and almost forgot that I was speaking to the President.

"Humph", he murmured again. "When I decide something", he said, "it's the law within this building. You will be reading for the next fortnight at least. Go and sit down and take your breakfast there".

Frank did not appear until after lunch and he explained that he had convinced the matron that he was not well and had got a couple of hours lying in the Infirmary. "And how did you get on?" he asked.

"I am afraid to tell you Frank", I said. "I got on nearly too well".

"What do you mean by that?" he asked, clearly puzzled.

"Fr. Sheridan has ordered me to read for the next fortnight. I didn't mean that to happen. I'm sorry".

"You're sorry be damned", growled Frank and I could see anger in his eyes. "You made sure you got right value for your money. That was a real dirty one to pull on me, when I was doing you a good turn. The other boys will have it in for me too".

"Honestly Frank", I said, "I did not mean it to happen. The President spoke to me at the end of the reading and told me what he had decided and he said that was the law. It was the last thing in the world I was expecting, Frank".

"It's very strange that you were so keen to take my place if you are so sorry", said Frank angrily. "It was a real dirty one".

I could not convince Frank that I had not set out to play a trick on him and even though we had always been good friends he did not speak to me for over a month. My next problem was with Fr. Curtin. He came up to me in the main hall after supper.

"Have you set out to get me into trouble with Fr. Sheridan?" he asked angrily. "A few weeks ago you let me down and he ate the ears off me for sending you to read in the first place. And now he has told me that you will be reading for the next fortnight and that has messed up all my schedules. Look at here, Daly, have you set out to make trouble for me?"

"I have not indeed Father", I protested.

"Look at here, Daly, how come you were reading this morning anyway?" he asked.

"Big Frank was not feeling well and he got me to take his place", I explained.

"How very convenient", he snapped. "Look at here, Daly, you are well worth keeping a sharp eye on. You have got me into hot water".

"I'm sorry, Father", was all I could think of saying and he stomped off in bad temper, muttering to himself.

My classmates whose turn had been usurped, were very unfriendly for a few weeks but eventually they forgot about the whole thing. I could never get the strange escapade out of my mind however. It gave me an insight into the strange lives of the priests that I would not have believed if I had not experienced it personally.

CHAPTER 20
A CARDINAL ERROR

Our fourth year had just started when quite a few of the boys in my class took up making model aeroplanes as a hobby. The authorities saw it as a beneficial way to spend some of our spare time and they put a room at our disposal where we could work and store our materials. I was not particularly interested in aeroplanes but it was the nearest I was likely to get to woodwork and I joined in to partake in the comradeship. I was amazed to discover the properties of balsa wood and I quite liked working with it, but the relaxed company and the conversations were the greatest attractions for me.

Some of the boys were able to get very advanced kits for their planes and small petrol engines could be fitted to some of the more advanced planes. These were pretty expensive models, far beyond anything I could possibly afford. I managed to buy a fairly basic kit for a Lancaster Bomber, which was driven by a twisted piece of elastic and even that was almost beyond my means. It contained a fairly heavy circle of wood behind the cockpit and many of my friends advised me to give up on it because they were sure that I would never manage to get it to fly.

A boy called Frank McGirr, from Bangor, was the first to finish his model mainly because he had worked on it all during the summer holidays. It was a fighter plane with a petrol engine, which was started by spinning the propeller with one's finger. It was about the middle of October I think, when Frank declared that the job was finished and his masterpiece was ready to take flight. News spread, and one evening, just after football a big crowd gathered on the junior ring to witness the historic event.

The plane was controlled by double cords, which were perhaps fifty yards in length. Frank explained that it would be very simple to operate and he could get it to do all sorts of acrobatics as it flew in circles around him. He appointed one of his friends to hold the lines as he spun the propeller to start the engine.

It took quite a while before the engine showed any sign of starting and boys who had experience of mechanical things gathered round to give advice. At last the engine fired and almost took the plane out of Frank's hand. He roared at his friend to keep the lines tight and holding the plane above his head he prepared for take-off. The little plane began a steady climb puffing out quite a trail of black smoke. The boy holding the lines was attempting to get it to level out when the lines came adrift and the plane set out in a slow circle over Banbrook Hill on its own. It disappeared behind a row of houses and that was the last we ever saw of it.

Fr. Doherty took Frank with him to try and discover where it had gone. They searched through all the streets in the Banbrook area but they could not find any signs of it. Stories came back later that it had flown through someone's window smashing the glass and that there would be a law case. Another story was that it had hit a woman on the head while she was waiting for a bus on the Mall. No trace was ever found of it. It was a disappointing start for the budding pilots.

Arty McAnerney built the biggest and most beautiful of all the planes and he had also got the most sophisticated engine. A couple of weeks after Frank's disaster, Arty's masterpiece was ready for flight and while he started the engine he left me holding the lines. The engine fired at the first attempt and I found myself trying to get the plane to do what I wanted it to do. Arty arrived at a run and relieved me of the controls.

For a minute or two he let it fly in circles making it climb and descend and the assembled crowd, gasped in amazement at how adept he was. He managed to get it to do loops and finally he brought it in to a perfect landing. It was probably the most successful of all the models, which were built during the few months that the craze lasted.

In my own case, I eventually got my model finished before Easter but my first few attempts at getting it to fly were unsuccessful. The elastic was not able to lift the fairly heavy little plane. I found stronger and stronger elastic and eventually it took off and flew about thirty yards before diving into the ground. Everybody said that it was a minor miracle that it had flown any distance at all.

A few days later I got much stronger piece of elastic and made sure that it was wound as tightly as possible. I let it off and to the amazement of everyone including myself, it climbed in a wide circle and disappeared over a hedge. It ended up near the top of a tall tree in the Cardinal's garden, which was next door to the college grounds. Our caretaker Tommy McGinn, was watching. He came over to me.

"Go to my shed at the back of the school", he said. "You will see a ladder there and you can take it and get your plane back. I will tell the Dean that I have allowed you to do that".

"Are you sure Tommy", I queried, "that the Dean will allow that? Are you sure that we will not get into trouble for going out of bounds?"

Tommy looked sternly into my face. "I've done the Dean a few good turns of late", he said, "and he owes me one. Go on now and fetch the ladder and get your wee plane".

A couple of boys came with me and we got the ladder and carried it into the Cardinal's garden and propped it against the tree. I climbed up gingerly for it was probably well over twenty feet to where the plane was resting. I was just about to reach out to retrieve it when I heard a strange voice at the bottom of the ladder. I looked down to see a figure in crimson helping to hold the ladder. No less a figure than Cardinal John D'Alton had come out to see what was going on. I nearly fell off the ladder.

I held the plane in one hand as I slowly and carefully descended. I was wondering how I was supposed to address the Cardinal. The words 'Your Grace", came into my mind but I was not sure that it was correct. A few seconds took me to the bottom of the ladder and I found myself looking into the kindly eyes of the Cardinal. I could see that he was amused.

"I did not know", he said with a gentle smile, "that pilots were supposed to land their planes in trees. Should I get a runway made for you here on my lawn?"

"I'm very sorry, Your Grace", I replied. "I never expected it to fly at all, never mind get all the way to the top of your tree".

The Cardinal was still smiling broadly as he took the little model out of my hand. "Isn't it very light?" he remarked thoughtfully. "What kind of timber is it made from?"

"That's balsa wood, Your Grace", we answered in unison.

He looked at each of us in turn and then asked, "do any of you know where that comes from? In what part of the world does it grow?"

Brian Hackett decided to answer first. "I think it comes from the tropics", he said, "but I'm not sure which country it grows in".

"Well there is a wee job for all of you", continued the Cardinal. "I suggest that you all make it your business in the next couple of days to find out where the wood grows".

He then looked at me again. "What is this stuff that you have as a skin on it?" he asked, rubbing his hands all over it.

I explained that it was a kind of light material and that it had to be painted with a liquid called dope in order to make it hard.

"Does that not make the whole structure warp?" he enquired.

"It would", we explained together. "It has to be fixed to a frame until the dope dries and sets",

"What is your name young man?" he asked, looking at Brian.

"I'm Brian Hackett", Brian replied.

"And where do you come from Brian?"

"I come from Coalisland, Your Grace."

He then looked at Hugh Flannigan who was the other member of the group.

"Do you come from Coalisland too?" he asked.

"No, I come from the county Fermanagh", Hugh answered.

"And your name is?"

"I'm Hugh Flannagan, Your Grace".

Finally he looked at me again. "And what would the pilot of this mighty machine be called?" he asked with an engaging smile.

"I'm Arthur Daly, Your Grace".

"And where do you come from, Arthur?"

"I live about a mile outside Benburb in a townland called Sessiagh", I told him.

"So you would know the Servite Priory there", he said.

"Yes, Your Grace", I replied. "I go there for midnight Mass with my parents".

"That's great", he said. "I have really enjoyed meeting you boys. It's not often I get a chance to talk to boys like you. I'm glad that your plane landed in my tree. Is there anything that you would like to ask me?"

We were all silent for a moment and then Hugh spoke up. "Do you like being Cardinal, Your Grace?"

He punched Hugh lightly on the chest. "That is a great question", he said looking quite serious for a moment. "It's a very big responsibility, but yes, I suppose I do quite like it. It gives me a chance to meet lots of people".

He then looked at Brian and me, clearly expecting another question. "This is not a question, Your Grace", I said, "but I would like to thank you for the big banquet you gave us all in our first year".

"So would we", chimed in the other two. "It was the best meal we have ever had".

"Well, isn't that lovely", said the Cardinal. "I'm glad that you all enjoyed it and it's lovely to see that you have the courtesy to thank me even though I do not need thanks. Have any of you ever been in the County Mayo?"

None of us had and he shook his head somewhat sadly. "You have never been in my county", he said slowly and thoughtfully. "You must make it your business to go there as soon as you can. It's a lovely place. Maybe your parents will agree to take you there on holiday if you are very good".

At that moment Fr. Devine came walking across the lawn to us. "Have these boys been giving you bother, Your Eminence?" he asked.

"Not at all, Father", the Cardinal replied. "It has been a real joy to talk to them and I only wish I had the chance to meet students like them more often. I'll have to be off now because I have an engagement and the driver is waiting".

He handed the plane back to me. "You might make a good pilot some day, Arthur", he said in his quiet friendly way. "In the meantime, don't forget the little task I gave you".

He turned and walked across the lawn to the waiting car and we were left in the presence of the Dean. He took the plane out of my hand and examined it.

"You must have made a good job of this when it can fly so well", he said in thoughtful tone.

"I never meant it to fly over here Father", I said. "In fact I never expected it to fly at all. That round piece of wood behind the cockpit is too heavy. I don't think it is balsa at all".

Father Devine turned the plane over a few times in his hands, examining it carefully.

214

"I have to go down south in the summer to visit my brother who has a wee boy of eight", he said. "I know he would love a toy like that to play with. Would there be any chance of you boys making him something like this?"

I broke in before anyone could speak. "Take that one with you, Father", I said. "I would love you to give it to your nephew".

"I did not mean it like that", said the obviously embarrassed Dean. "I can't take your model after all the work you have put into it",

"I have got a lot of satisfaction out of making it", I told him. "I'm not really interested in planes and I would be delighted if you took it for the wee fellow. Please take it Father".

"I have one nearly finished too", said Brian. "He can have that as well, because I am not interested in planes either and it's a whole lot better than that one".

Father Devine was clearly unsure what to do. We started to walk together back towards the college. Finally he put his hand on my shoulder and said, "That is very generous indeed. I know my nephew will have great fun with it".

"It's not generous at all, Father", I replied, looking up at him. "You were very good to me when I was in hospital and it's the only chance I will ever get to thank you".

"Right", he said, "now you boys hurry up and get ready for study".

CHAPTER 21
OUR NEW CURATE

The year ended and when I came home for the summer holidays our strawberries needed a lot of work but were looking very promising, which excited my mother greatly. She took no interest in them until she saw red berries beginning to appear and then she would stay in the field from morning until night. She took over as supervisor and handled all money matters.

All over the country carnivals were organised once again and that year a new assistant curate had arrived in our parish. His name was Fr. Tom Fee, or Tomás O'Fiaich, as he preferred to be called. He was newly ordained and he was full of energy and enthusiasm that inspired everyone he met. In the middle of the summer he was in charge of a big carnival and football tournament, centred on Blackwatertown, or Portmór as he taught us to call it.

I arrived down at the village to attend the festivities and I was astounded to see the whole place festooned with flags and bunting. Bands were waiting to parade from the bridge over the river at the bottom of the village to the schools and football fields at the top. I left my bicycle against the wall of the bridge and was about to join some of my friends to partake in the march when the new curate came bouncing over to me.

"Art", he said, speaking in Gaelic, "I am glad to see you here because I have a job for you and no one else is going to get doing it".

I was astounded because I had only met him for a very short time a few weeks before and I wondered how he had remembered my name. Really surprised, I asked him what the job was. He walked over to the other side of the bridge and came back carrying a pole about ten feet long with a big flag wrapped round the top of it. He unfolded the flag and I saw that it was a huge Irish tricolour.

"I am giving you the honour of leading the parade up through the village". he said. "I want you to carry that flag with dignity and pride and hold it a wee bit higher when you are passing the police barracks. Only a Gaelic speaker can be honoured with that task".

He took me by the arm, led me to the middle of the road, and made sure that I was holding the flag to his satisfaction. He then organised the bands in formation and we began the march up through the village. As we passed the police barracks I did as I was told and held the flag that wee bit higher. I have no idea if the police were watching or not but no one said a word.

The incident raised great excitement because it was

forbidden to fly the tricolour in public at that time. A man called Liam Kelly was sentenced to six months in jail for doing so at about the same time. I have often wondered since what would have happened if the police had intervened.

The carnival was a huge success and the enthusiasm of Fr. Fee seemed to affect everyone in the parish. He had a gift for making everyone believe that he was their friend and people loved being in his company. It was obvious that he really loved the people and got great satisfaction from being with them.

Many years later, I happened to remark to a friend who was a few years older than me about what had happened on that day and about the remarkable effect Fr. Fee had. He glared at me and I could see a cold anger in his eyes. "I hate the very thought of that man", he snarled.

"I cannot believe that", I said. "I can't believe that anyone would feel that way about Cardinal O'Fiaich. I thought everyone loved him".

James spat out through the side of his mouth. "I was getting the best court ever I got in my life one night", he hissed. "That damned man came with a blackthorn stick and beat us out of the car. I never forgot him nor forgave him for it".

Everything that summer was most enjoyable because of the energy and enthusiasm, which the curate inspired. People who would not normally take part were anxious to work and to be in the presence of this extraordinary cleric. There was a warmth in his eyes and he met people with a huge smile, which convinced them that he really cared for them. Everyone felt that he was a lifelong friend and it was almost impossible to believe that we had only met him a few short weeks before. I happened to be in Armagh one day and I met Mr. Ó Riordan, who was one of my teachers and I told him about how excited everyone was in our parish.

"Oh Tom Fee", he said, "I know him very well. He is the only genius I have ever met in all the years I have been teaching in the college. He was phenomenal. He chose to study languages and history but he was brilliant in mathematics too. That man could have chosen any career and he would have been its brightest spark. Did you know that he is one of the leading scientific historians in Europe?"

"I really don't know very much about him, Mr. Ó Riordan", I answered. "I know he is great at the Gaelic but I have never heard of a scientific historian".

"It's a new way of looking at history through the study of sources", he said. "He is leading the way in that field. But I am sure that you will not have him for too long out in Clonfeacle. He is destined for higher things".

I felt a little crestfallen. "I hope you are wrong, Mr. Ó Riordan. I said.

"I don't think I am", he replied, as he went on about his business. Mr. Ó Riordan was right of course and the young priest soon moved on. It was almost exactly twenty-five years later until I met him again. That was at a Gaelic speakers' reception for him in Armagh when he was appointed Archbishop. I remember that night vividly because he walked up to me, shook my hand and said, "hello, Art, it's great to see you again". There was no hesitation, no need to think. It was the greatest example extraordinary powers of memory that I have ever experienced.

Sean Skeffington, who would only have been a child when Fr Fee was in our parish, was with me that night and I introduced him to the new Archbishop. "I don't know you Sean", he said and then he talked on about other things. I was aware that while he was carrying on a conversation with us he was thinking about something else. A minute or so later he grabbed Sean by the arm and said, "I have you now. When I was in the parish your uncle Peter Foley, was working on the river and you had another uncle who worked in Dungannon".

"That's right", agreed Sean, totally amazed.

Fr. Fee made it clear that he preferred working on our side of the parish, while Fr. Moore gave the impression that he was much more at home in the Moy. Since the carnival in Blackwatertown was such a success, Fr. Moore decided that he would have to organise a really big event in the Moy and perhaps take some of the wind out of the new curate's sails. He chose to run one of his operatic concerts in the Moy hall with some of the leading artists in the country. He was known far and wide for his ability to bring the very best opera stars from Dublin and even

London, to a little hall in the middle of the country, and had been repeating this feat for years.

On this occasion, however, the concert was a complete flop. The hall was only about one third full and many of those who were there did not appreciate the excellence of the singers and musicians. They had come out of loyalty to Fr. Moore, or in some cases simply by accident. Big Jamie was there somewhat the worse for drink.

One of the artistes wore a very skimpy, low-cut frock and when she came forward to take a bow Jamie expressed his admiration for the various parts of her figure in a loud and inappropriate manner. Fr. Moore had been sitting in the wings and he rushed out, jumped across the footlights and strode purposefully down to where Jamie was sitting. He grabbed him by the collar and tried to pull him out of his seat. It was like trying to move the rock of Gibralter.

"Lord, but you are a great wee man altogether Father", said Jamie, in a friendly tone. "Isn't it a terrible pity that you never grew any bigger?"

"Get out of this hall at once", hissed Fr. Moore.

"You're all right, Father, you're all right", muttered Jamie in a brotherly way, putting his arm round Fr. Moore's shoulder. "I'm all right here. It's warm and comfortable, and sure there's nobody hurting us. Lord, but you are a great wee man, Father".

The priest was livid. A few of his helpers came to his aid and, with a lot of bother, they managed to get Jamie out of the hall.

The next Sunday Fr. Moore announced that the concert had cost a fortune due to the fact that the people had not appreciated the wonderful feast that had been made available to them.

"I thought that over the years I had managed to give people a taste for the really worthwhile things in life", he said. "I brought the very best artists to this parish, people who would be at the top of the bill in any big hall in any great city in the world. And only a handful of people had the grace to come to the concert. As a result, I am going to take up a collection next Sunday to defray expenses. I will expect all of you to be very generous".

At that time the collection was taken up in a shallow wooden bowl with a long handle with which the collector could reach to the middle of each pew. Fr. Moore collected the money personally, stopping here and there to say a special word of thanks to someone whom he considered had been very generous. He eventually reached the middle of the gallery where Jamie was seated near the end of a seat. As the ladle was passing him Jamie dropped a half crown into the bowl.

The priest stopped, brought the bowl back towards him, lifted the coin and handed it back to Jamie. "There is no need for you to contribute to this collection this morning, James", he said loudly. "I have very good reason to remember that you were present at the concert last Sunday night".

He tried to push the ladle along the seat once more,

but Jamie grabbed it with one hand and dropped the half crown back into it with the other. "Och, to hell with poverty, Father", he said, speaking just as loudly as Fr. Moore had done. "Shite, sure it'll thicken it up a wee bit for you".

The whole congregation burst into howls of laughter and the frustrated priest had to admit defeat.

CHAPTER 22
THE FINAL STRAIGHT

It was the last Saturday of the summer holiday and I had spent the day finishing work on a window for a barn, which my father had built at the end of the house. We had made a head for the window in concrete but when I went to put it in place I found that I could scarcely move it. Lifting it one end at a time, I managed to manoeuvre it close to the wall and then I began to raise it by placing bricks under it, again one end at a time. It was slow and tedious work but eventually I managed to manoeuvre it up to where the bottom of the window was. It still had about three and a half feet to go and it was very unsteady. My father arrived home and studied my work.

"That bit of a head must be a damnable weight", he said. "It looks right and dangerous perched on those piles of bricks. It could fall over and break somebody's leg".

"It's not that light", I assured him, standing well back from it.

"Take a bit of mortar and put a trowelful on the wall on each side of the window", he said slowly.

"We'll see if we can't get it up to its place before the end of next week".

I did as I was told and by the time I had finished he had made a scaffold with a couple of planks on two barrels and had placed a ladder against the wall so that it nearly touched the end of the planks. He walked over to where the head was still resting, bent and put his shoulder under the middle of it, and then walked over to the ladder with it. He walked up the ladder, stepped onto his scaffold and placed the head exactly where it was supposed to be. He came down smiling. I don't think I ever felt so small or foolish in all my life.

"That's not a bad job at all", he said casually, looking up at it. "Put the spirit level on it till we see if is anywhere near the thing". It was perfect.

"You'll be heading back to Armagh on Sunday evening", he said, looking at me thoughtfully. "This is your last year and I was just wondering if you had any idea what job you might get".

It was the first time that anyone in my family had asked me about my future and it took me by surprise. As I saw things, there were very few jobs open to me and I had more or less made up my mind that the only place I could go was to the Civil Service. My father was now leaning on the scaffold and gazing into my eyes.

"I don't know, Da", I answered. "The only job that I had been thinking of was the Civil Service. They tell me that the pay is not too bad".

"I don't know much about jobs that need the learning", he said thoughtfully. "You will have to spend the rest of your life in whatever job you choose and you would need to be sure that you will be satisfied in it. It's not like me. I can move from job to job because I'm only a labourer. But those higher sort of jobs are different".

I did not know what to say. I had thought very little about what I wanted to do and I was not looking forward to my final year because I felt that I would not get good results and, therefore, my choices would be very limited. I did not even have any idea of how to apply for jobs. Perhaps the fact that I was an only child from an isolated rural townland was to my disadvantage. My father put his hand into his pocket and took out twenty pounds, which he handed to me. I looked at it, stunned.

"You've worked hard all summer", he said, "and I know that you have given all the money to Ma. Don't tell her that I gave you this. You will need extra money in the last year, for you are a young man now".

"I can't take all this Da", I stammered. "It's a wee fortune".

"Stick it in your pocket", he said, walking into the house. "And mind to keep your mouth shut about it".

Big decisions faced us when we went back to college. The Senior Certificate had been changed so that there were now two levels, Advanced and

Ordinary. We were advised that one could score much higher in Advanced but it was also much easier to fail. Some people were told not to attempt Advanced Level. It was a complete surprise to us and we had to choose our courses very quickly. There must have been lots of preparation made for the change but the first we heard of it was on that Monday morning. We were brought to the study hall to make our decisions.

Fr. Dougan was one of the priests in charge that morning and he moved round the hall, talking to boys who seemed to need help. He came to my desk, pushed me over on the seat and sat down beside me.

"Have you decided to do any Advanced subjects?" he asked.

"I was thinking of doing Irish Father", I whispered.

"That should be fine", he replied. "Mr. O'Boyle has a good word on you. What other subjects might you try?"

"I was thinking of having a go at the English and the history Father", I said.

"That sounds good thinking to me", he said very softly. "And what about the other subjects?"

"Oh, I'd leave them alone at Ordinary Level, Father", I said. "As you know I'm not doing that well at the Latin and the Greek's even worse. And I'm finding it tough at the maths too".

"I think you have made sensible choices", he replied. "And did I hear that you are doing Ancient History on your own?"

"That's right Father", I agreed. "But a lot of it comes into the Latin and the Greek and then I do modern history, so it's only a matter of reading".

"Grand, he said rising, "but if you feel you need any help with the Ancient History let me know and I'll see if I can help. Good luck now and I'm expecting lots of work at the Latin".

I cannot say I enjoyed my senior year. I knew that I was falling further and further behind in both Greek and Latin and into the bargain my ankle continued to annoy me, and greatly hindered my participation at football. Someone told me of a saint who had talked about the 'black night of the soul', and to some extent I felt that I knew what he meant. Relief came from an unexpected quarter.

Religious education was a compulsory subject throughout the school, even in the final year, though there was no public examination in it. We got a great surprise when, for our first lesson, in walked Fr. Hederman. We had seen him about the college but he was the Purser and had a full time job looking after the finances. I was unaware of anyone who had spoken to him in previous years and I was pretty sure that he did not teach.

Fr. Hederman took a completely different and novel approach to teaching religion. He told us about a place where he had spent lots of Sunday mornings in London. It was called Speakers' Corner in Hyde Park. He described how all sorts of people would get up on a soapbox and discuss their pet subject. They would be heckled by the crowd and had to be very skilled debaters, otherwise they would be laughed out of the place. He explained that each week he would like to have a voluntary speaker who would defend a point of view, while the rest of the class acted as hecklers. It meant, for instance, that whereas we had always heard about Communism from a Catholic viewpoint, a speaker would have to study it from Communist propaganda and literature, and then try to defend it. Almost everyone in the class hated the idea, but I loved it.

I was one of the first to get up on the soapbox and I had to pretend to be Martin Luther and defend the actions I had taken against the Church. I spent a lot of time preparing and reading books, which Fr. Hederman suggested. It was a great success and I really enjoyed the banter and the arguments with my classmates. Fr. Hederman congratulated me and said that it sounded as though I was Luther himself, convinced of every word I had said. I had really caught the bug.

One of the rules was that if someone did not want to defend a position he could appoint a substitute in his place. I found myself eagerly taking the places of half the boys in the class. I was having a ball, but the amount of time that I spent preparing different standpoints was at the expense of crucial study. After a few weeks Fr. Hederman asked me to come and see him in his office.

"You obviously really love a good argument", he

said in his soft friendly way. "You have a real flair for it but I'm worried that you are spending far too much time preparing the defence of all the different points of view. This is your final year, you know, and other things must be going to the wall. I feel that I have to call a halt and forbid you to take anyone else's place from now on".

"Och, Father", I protested, "I have enjoyed it all and I have learned a lot too".

"I know that", he said with an understanding smile. "But it would be unreasonable of me to let you go on because your other subjects must be suffering. We are half way through the year and you have only a very short time to go. You will have time for all the fun later but now you must concentrate on your work".

I was very disappointed but I knew the priest was right. From that point on, I had to be a good heckler and defend the Catholic point of view. That was not nearly so entertaining. To this day I look back on Fr. Hederman with a great deal of affection. In his quiet, thoughtful way, he was the nearest thing to a real saint that I have ever encountered.

A few boys joined our class that year from the class that had already done the final exams. They had not got the results that they wanted and wished to repeat. One of them was Sean McCallion, a great handballer who had coached me in earlier years and who had been the instigation of me winning many a fry. I was delighted to see Sean coming into our class.

In the dorm that year, Sean's bed was at the end of a row. We soon discovered that he had a habit of sleep walking or rather sleep leaping. At least Sean claimed that was the problem but I have a deep suspicion that it was an act and he was fully awake. At any rate he would get up about three o'clock in the morning and leap from one bed to the next until he had completed a full circuit of the dorm. The problem was that he was not stepping on the beds but on the bodies of the boys sleeping therein and usually on the very tender parts of those bodies!

He was extremely athletic and landing on various parts of bodies did not put him off balance in the least. He went bounding onward, leaving startled howls of tortured pain in his wake. It was bad enough for someone like myself, who slept on his side, but those who lay on their backs had a far more unforgettable and unpleasant experience. The dorm would suddenly erupt with cries of pain and anger.

The Dean that year was a new priest called Fr. Corkery and things reached a stage where he was in our dorm nearly every night, trying to pacify boys who in their suffering were threatening to end Sean's life in no uncertain terms. Fr. Corkery tried all sorts of solutions.

He tied a rope across the bed in the hope that Sean could not get out but Sean managed to slip underneath it, no matter how carefully it was tied. He tried tying ropes at the side of the bed from the top to the bottom but Sean merely stepped over them.

At one stage, the Dean fixed a mobile blackboard firmly along the side of the bed but the sleepwalker managed to get round it. In the end Sean was given a small room of his own and everyone breathed a sigh of relief.

Fr. Corkery was probably the most handsome man I have ever known. He was tall and slender, with a mop of wavy golden hair and fine features. Stories abounded that when he took a service from time to time in the cathedral, young women fought each other in order to get places near the pulpit. It was said that the authorities had to stop appointing him to parish duties because of the constant vicious fights. As Dean, he was reasonable and helpful and I don't think he ever used a cane. Yet he proved to be efficient and successful in an almost impossible position.

CHAPTER 23
VAGUE FUTURE PLANS

In the middle of the Easter term, I glanced sideways from my desk in the study hall one evening during second study and noticed Paddy McGuckin filling in a very impressive looking form.

"What are you at there, Paddy?" I whispered from the side of my mouth.

Paddy looked carefully over his shoulder and put his fingers over his lips to warn me to be quiet. Mr. Hicks, or The Hawk, as we called him was on duty and was bearing down on us. Gerry Hicks was a real gentleman, a great scholar and a great teacher. He had a habit of wandering the study hall with his neck bent forward and a very intent and determined look on his face that earned him his nickname. It was almost impossible to escape his attention. Paddy let him wander a few yards towards the front of the hall and then he hissed, "I'll tell you outside". Mr. Hicks spun round but even though he was quick, he was not quick enough and by the time his eyes glared at us we were both working assiduously.

As soon as study was over, I collared Paddy and

asked, "what was that form you were filling in? It looked very important".

Paddy stuck his hands deep into his pockets, looked down at the floor as we walked along and at last answered. "That was a form for the King's Scholarship. If I get enough marks in the Senior examination it will let me go to teacher training".

I gasped, hardly able to believe what I was hearing.

"But Paddy", I stuttered, "I thought you were dead keen to go on for the priesthood. Why are you filling in a form for teaching?"

Paddy rubbed his chin thoughtfully. "I do still want to go to Maynooth", he said. "But if things do not work out, or if I change my mind, it gives me another road to go. You know as well as I do that it is not easy to work out if you have a vocation or not. Have you not applied for anything yourself?"

"I was thinking of going for the Civil Service", I replied, "but I don't know where to get the forms".

"All the forms are in Fr. Kelly's office", replied Paddy. "I thought everybody knew that".

"How the blazes could everybody know that if we have never been told", I answered in exasperation. "Who told you where to get them?"

"I was talking to an old teacher at home during the last holidays", Paddy explained. "He told me that the teaching was a right handy sort of a job and while the money's not great it's not too bad either. He advised me to apply and warned me that the forms had to be in before Easter. I asked the Fr. Corkery about the forms and he told me that they would be in this week and that is how I happened to fill one in. It takes quare high marks to get to the training college, however, and that is why we have boys repeating a year to try to get there".

I walked along beside him thinking for a few moments. "Dammit, here Paddy", I muttered, "maybe I should get a form and fill it in too. It might be a real wild goose chase for I'm not doing well in a lot of subjects. But sure it won't cost anything to give it a try".

"Whatever you like", said Paddy, "but don't tell them that I told you where to get the form".

The next morning I knocked on Fr. Kelly's door and to my surprise a hard voice ordered me to "enter".

I opened the door and got a shock. The President was sitting behind the desk. I was amazed because we all believed that he never left the 'holy of holies'.

He looked at me with a hard glint in his eye. "Yes, Boy?" he asked.

"Father, I was looking for forms to apply for teacher training and for the Civil Service", I answered.

He continued gazing intently at me with the same hard look in his eye.

"I thought you were intent on entering the priesthood", he barked. "Am I right in thinking that you have changed your mind?"

"Not at all Father", I lied, "but sometimes it is

not easy to know if I have a vocation or not and I thought that it might be as well to have another road to go".

"How did you know where the forms were?" he demanded harshly.

"I was talking to an old teacher of mine during the holidays", I replied meekly, "and he advised me to apply for a few things. He said it was never wise to put all one's eggs in one basket".

"Humph", muttered Fr. Sheridan. He lifted two forms from separate piles on the desk and handed them to me.

"Here are the forms you asked for", he said curtly, "get out".

"Thank you very much indeed Father", I said, "I am very grateful for your kindness".

"Humph", he growled as I was closing the door behind me. It proved to be the last words that we would ever speak to each other.

It has always amazed me that we were given no guidance at all about applying for jobs. We were informed of the many Orders of the church, which we might join, but beyond that, nothing. It may well be that being an only child from a rural area I was in a worse position, in that regard, than boys who lived in a town or even in a village. I had never seriously spoken to a doctor or teacher in my life. I had never ever seen or met an architect, a journalist, nor any person connected with the law. I suppose I knew vaguely that such professions existed but it had never occurred to me that I might have a chance of joining one of them. It was a stroke of sheer luck that I now held two application forms in my hands.

The month of May that year was one of the hottest that I can remember. The temperature in the exam halls was sweltering and most people kept a tissue or handkerchief on their desks during the tests in order to wipe the sweat away. This was in spite of every window and door in the place being propped wide open.

The first big surprise I got was in the Latin exam. For the first time in a long time I found myself faced with a piece of Latin, which seemed to me to be very easy to translate and then the passage of English which had to be rendered in Latin looked simple as well. I was a bit worried though, because I always believed that it was never good to feel that any exam was easy.

Immediately the exam was over, I sought out Phil Stewart and we sauntered round the senior ring together.

"What did you think of that Latin test, Phil?" I asked, hoping that he would have found it easy.

"I thought it was difficult enough", answered Phil. "None of the translations were straightforward. I made a reasonable stab at both sections but I wouldn't be too sure of the results".

My heart fell like a stone. Phil was one of the best students in our class at Latin, and indeed in most things. I felt that I must have totally misunderstood the whole thing and made a mess of it. Phil looked at me in a puzzled fashion.

"What did you think of it yourself?" he asked.

"I felt that it was not too bad. In fact I felt that it was a lot easier than most of the pieces of translation we have been doing in class. I must have made a muck of it".

"Maybe you just got a bit that suited you", said Phil, but I sensed that he too was doubtful. Much the same thing happened with the Greek and I was really downhearted. I knew that I had not done myself justice in Irish, because I had tried to tell a ridiculous story using pieces of Irish that I had learnt from native speakers and it had not worked. There did not seem to be any light in the tunnel as the end approached. The Ancient History was a day later than all the rest and this meant that I had to stay on with two or three other boys who had decided to attempt the subject.

On the afternoon of the day on which the class was breaking up for the last time, I was dandering round the college grounds with one of the boys who had been my constant companion for the past five years. We talked of the many things that had happened during our time in Armagh.

"You know", I said to him, "I do not think I could have survived all the tough times but for the friendship and comradeship of my friends here in the college".

He looked at me sideways and spat on the ground.

"You know what I'm going to tell you?" he answered. "I have never trusted any of you effers".

I walked away from him saddened, and went to the study hall to prepare for the Ancient History examination the following morning. It was a useless exercise because I could not concentrate on the text. I felt so utterly depressed that I could have wept. A friend's words had put a terrible blight on my last days in the college.

CHAPTER 24
DOUBTFUL SURPRISES

The exams over, I was home in early June to find that there was a lot of work to do cleaning the strawberries before the berries ripened. It was a slow and tedious task for one had to be careful not to ruin the fruit by covering them with soil. But when the fruit ripened there was a great crop and my mother was delighted. She was out in the field directing operations from early morning until late at night.

My father had a week or two off at the Twelfth of July and he took the opportunity to finish replacing the windows at the front of the house with bigger steel framed ones. He only helped out with the strawberries when we really needed him as he wanted to get the windows finished before he had to go back to work in Dungannon.

A young man called Eugene Daly, a cousin of our neighbour Tommy Jordan, had bought a van and set himself up in business collecting strawberries and bringing them to the market or into the jam factories. His van was not very reliable and he was always worried that it would let him down.

One day Eugene and I were loading our fruit into the van at the front door and my father was working away at the top window, apparently taking no notice of us at all. We were nearly finished when there was a tremendous bang and the whole van shook. I got an awful shock, but poor Eugene went deathly white and I thought he was going to faint. He forgot where he was and straightened up and banged his head off the roof of the van. He looked at me with fear-filled eyes. "Oh hell's blazes", he cried, "the whole damned van is finished this time. That must have been the bloody engine, which has blown up. What the hell am I going to do now?" (That of course is a printable version of what he said.)

"I don't know Eugene", I said, getting out and walking round the side of the van to the front. There was no sign of any damage nor anything being wrong. Eugene followed me and gazed at the bonnet. "I don't understand this at all", he muttered, "I expected to see the whole bloody bonnet hanging from one of the trees. It must have been one of the damned tyres that exploded".

We walked round the van together and examined all the wheels but they looked perfectly normal. We could not find anything wrong. Eugene stood back from his van, looking at it suspiciously and scratching his head in wonder. "It must have been the whole inside of the engine that blew up", he said at last. "Maybe I forgot to put water in it".

"I don't understand how that would happen,

Eugene", I said thoughtfully, "surely if the engine was going to blow up it would have done so while it was going. It has been sitting there for nearly an hour while we loaded the strawberries. Why would it blow up when it is cooled down?"

"Och, dammit all, I don't know what the hell happened to it", said Eugene angrily. He got into the van and gingerly turned the key to see if the engine would start. It started immediately and seemed to be running smoothly. Eugene put it into gear and drove it slowly a few yards up the street. He stopped and reversed a couple of yards. He stopped, switched off the engine, and sat behind the wheel thinking.

I was standing about the middle of the van when Eugene began to move it and as the back end passed me, I noticed a black patch of something that looked like smoke on the street, about the place where the middle of the van had been a few moments before. I glanced up to where my father was apparently working away on his scaffold and I could see his shoulders shaking. I realised that he was having a great laugh to himself. I suspected that the bang had not originated from anything to do with the van.

I walked up to where Eugene was still sitting behind the wheel, still a deathly white colour. "I think you can go ahead, Eugene", I said, "the van seems to be fine".

Eugene looked at me with a vague fear showing in his eyes. "This old van has the curse of God on it", he muttered. "I've never had a day's peace since

I bought the damned thing. There's some yokes like that you know".

He put the van into gear and moved off slowly and it was obvious that he was waiting for something dreadful to happen. I turned round to see my father watching the van disappear round the corner of the lane with a broad smile on his face. I walked over to the scaffold and looked up at him.

"That was a real dirty trick you played, Da", I said. "Poor Eugene had no call for a fright like that".

He looked down at me pretending to be surprised and angry. "What the hell are you raving about?" he demanded.

"You put some sort of explosive under the van when we were carrying strawberries up from the field", I said confidently. "The evidence is there in the middle of the street".

He looked down at me and laughed. "Sure it was only a detonator", he said. "It wasn't going to do any harm, and it needed something to wake you two boys up".

"Well I don't think it was one bit funny", I said in an angry tone. "It could have caused poor Eugene to have a heart attack, and he's away to the factory all worried". I stomped off down to the field to resume work on the strawberries. Half an hour later, Da came walking slowly down the field to me. "I suppose that was a daft kind of trick I played", he said awkwardly. "Right enough, the bang could done Eugene harm".

I stopped work, and stood up and looked him in

the eyes. It was the first time in my life that I had ever heard him admit to being in the wrong. In fact I had trouble thinking of a time when I had known him to be in the wrong. I laughed in spite of myself.

"Where did you get the detonator?" I asked.

"I had it from the time I worked in the quarry, he said. "It was my job to work with them all the time".

"How did you manage to time it?" I asked.

He shook his head in exasperation at my ignorance. "We always had to time them when we set the explosive", he explained. "If you didn't get the timing right, you could have had a hundred tons of stone on top of your head before you had time to get out of the road".

"It felt that something like that had landed on top of the van", I answered.

The results of the exams were due to come out in the middle of August and I felt that I'd prefer to be a fair distance from home when that happened. Once more I took up the opportunity of a scholarship and went back to Rannafast. I was now in the top class and I found it very interesting. The weather was fine as well and the first few days proved enjoyable. Once more I was in McGarvey's house and my companion in the back room was a boy from Country Down called Jim Doherty. We quickly became firm friends.

There was a big ceili on our second night at the college and the star attraction proved to be a girl from County Louth called Deirdre O'Callaghan. She was not very tall, probably not more than five feet in height, but she was certainly built as a girl ought to be built! Her face was constantly encased in a captivating smile and she was very friendly. She did a few exhibition dances and in all my life I had never seen anything so beautiful. I met her in a few of the dances and like everyone else I was entranced with her.

I walked home from the ceili with Jim and I noticed that he was less talkative than usual. At last he said thoughtfully as though he were thinking to himself, "Lord but that is some dame, that O'Callaghan girl. I would give my right hand to have a chance of going out with her. I saw you dancing with her too. What did you think?"

"She is certainly a lovely girl", I agreed. "Sure all the boys in the hall were keen on her".

"Do you think I should ask her for a date?" Jim asked the question as though he wanted assurance.

"Well, Jim", I replied, "I don't know of any other way you will find out if she's interested in you or not. Why don't you ask her tomorrow and see what she says?"

"Right, he announced firmly. "I'll see her tomorrow afternoon and I'll ask her. At the worst, she can only say no".

The next day at teatime, Jim was very quiet and looked a bit disappointed. As soon as tea was over I managed to get him alone outside the house. "Did Deirdre turn you down, Jim?", I asked. "You look a bit down in the mouth".

"You could say that, he replied in a flat tone. "She seems to have a notion of someone else".

"That doesn't surprise me", I said. "She has the choice of the whole college as far as I can see".

Jim looked straight into my eyes and glared at me. "She says that if you are interested, she'd love to meet you at the post office at lunch time tomorrow. She says you have a lovely smile, you lucky dog".

"She what?" I asked, flabbergasted and delighted at the same time.

"She's dead keen on you", he replied, "I never stood a chance, so if you want to meet her, be at the post office at lunch time tomorrow. The best of luck to both of you".

I sat down on the wee wall at the front of the house in a daze. I could never have imagined that this girl would pick me out of all the others and I was over the moon. I could not wait until lunchtime next day. I sat there for a long time in a heavenly daze. I was still sitting there when a boy came riding up on a bicycle. He stopped.

"Is there an Arthur Daly living in this house?" he asked.

"That's me", I told him, "totally surprised and a wee bit worried".

"Here is a telegram for you", he said, handing me an orange envelope. "You have to sign for it and it's urgent".

I had a sudden feeling of dread. I wondered if something had happened to my father at work, or if my mother was ill because she was never very robust. I tore open the envelope to find the message:

"Come home at once. Interview for teacher training on Friday. Mother".

I could not believe what I was reading and I sat staring at the words for ages. It was fantastic news that I had never expected but it came at the cost of my not being able to meet Deirdre next day. It was now Wednesday evening and I had to be on the bus at nine o'clock in the morning. Jim came along and sat down beside me, offering me a piece of chocolate.

"What's wrong now?" he enquired. "You look as though you have seen a ghost or got an awful shock. It can't be as bad as that".

"I have to be in Belfast on Friday for an interview at St.Marys, Jim", I said. "I'll have to be on the bus first thing in the morning".

"God. That's great. Congratulations", said Jim. "Surely that is what you wanted, is it not?"

"I never expected to get offered that at all", I said. "I thought I would have been lucky to get into the Civil Service. It's great surely but do you see how one thing is offered to me and another snatched away. I won't be able to meet Deirdre tomorrow. I don't feel too good about that".

"Ach, sure you were only going to have next week together anyway", said Jim. "You go off on the bus and I'll try to keep her company in your place. I don't mind doing a wee job like that for a friend".

He got up and went into the house laughing.

I explained to Mrs McGarvey that I would have to leave and then I got my things ready for the morning. Jim and I talked far into the night, with the result that I nearly slept in next morning. But by nine o'clock I found myself sitting on a bus heading across Donegal towards Derry and the train for home.

CHAPTER 25
INTO THE UNKNOWN

By the time I arrived home it was well on in the afternoon. My mother was feeding a few hens in the front garden as I left my bicycle against the wall of the house. She rushed over to me, obviously quite annoyed. I knew that she had been worrying all day lest I miss the interview, and as usual she had been terrified that some accident might happen on the journey home.

"It took you some time to think of coming home", she said angrily. "Did you not get my telegram telling you to come home at once?"

"I did surely, Mammy", I replied gently. "I have been on the road since nine o'clock this morning. There were a lot of delays in getting to Derry and then I had to wait on a train for a long time. When I got to Dungannon, the man at the bicycle shop was away and the girl would not let me get my bike so I had to wait until he came back. I could not have got back any quicker".

"Come on in and get a bite to eat", she sighed, exasperated. "You might have told us that you had done so well in the exams and not have had me praying all summer for you and worrying myself sick. You had no call to go away to that Rannafast this summer anyway. You have to be in Belfast for two o'clock tomorrow. I have been worried sick all afternoon for I thought something had happened to you on the road".

It was easy to see that she was still annoyed as she placed my dinner of potatoes, cabbages and bacon on the table. As I was about to sit down at the table, my father arrived home from work.

"This boy has just arrived on the street before you, Mick", she said, "I thought that something must have happened to him on the road and I have been worrying my heart out all day". She placed his dinner on the table too, as she was explaining her problems to him.

"Och, sure he's here now and the thing is all right", Da answered calmly. "You seem to have done right and well in the exams", he said to me, giving me a slap on the back.

"I have not had a chance to look at the letters and see how I have done, Da", I replied. "Where are they anyway, Ma?"

"They're over there on the dresser", she replied. "Where do you think they would be?"

The first letter I opened was from the Education Authority giving me the results of the test. To my utter astonishment, I had got good distinctions in almost all my subjects and Latin and Greek were at the top of the list. The only slight disappointment was in Irish, where I had only got a credit but since it was at advanced level it was equal to a distinction at ordinary level too. But since Irish had been my best and favourite subject I should have expected it to be at the top of the list.

I was sitting gazing at the paper totally stunned by the fact that my initial feeling about the test had been very accurate. My mother sat down beside my father at this point and said, "Tommy Coalter was asking how Arthur had done when he called with the bread this morning and I showed him the results. He says that those results would take Arthur into any department of the University that he would care to choose".

"Did you apply to go to the University?" Da asked.

"I did not", I replied. "I knew nothing about how to apply for things and it was only a chance in a million that I applied for the teacher training".

"It's a wonder you would not have tried to find out about all the different things that would be open to you, when you knew that the exam was so important", said Da quietly.

"I didn't expect to do well at all", I answered. "Wait a minute till I see what is in these other two letters".

The first was from St. Mary's Training College, asking me to attend for interview in the College on the following day, and congratulating me on the results. The second was from the Civil Service people, also congratulating me, and asking me to inform them as soon as possible as to which branch I would prefer to enter. There was a fairly long list of different options. I sat studying the papers for quite a few minutes.

"Well, what are you going to do?" asked Da.

"I'll go to the interview tomorrow", I answered, "but there are some great offers here in the Civil Service and they seem very keen to have me. The only thing is that I would be far away from home. The other side of the coin is that I would be earning money immediately".

"Surely to God you would have more sense than to go into the Civil Service, when you can go for teaching", cried my mother. "What would take you away overseas when you can get a good job here in your own country. For God's sake Mick, talk a bit of sense into him".

"It's all right Sarah", said Da quietly, "it's never a bad job to look at all the different offers. I never believed in jumping in before you take a good look. How do you intend to get to Belfast tomorrow?" he asked.

"I'll ride into Dungannon on the bicycle in the morning", I replied. "I'll take the train and that will leave me in the middle of the city".

"Do you know where you are going from there?" he asked.

"There was a boy from Belfast in the house in Rannafast", I told him. "He told me to turn left outside the station and go to the Grosvenor Road. He said it was between two big picture houses and only about a hundred yards or so from the station. He said I could take a trolley bus up the road to the Springfield Road lights. I have to get off there and go left again for a few hundred yards and the college will be on the right hand side of the road. He says that I can't possibly go wrong".

"That sounds fine to me", said Da thoughtfully, "but be careful, for it's not easy for someone who has never been in the city in his life. Make sure to ask the conductor on the bus to warn you about the right place to get off. The only time I have ever been in Belfast myself was the time you were born".

"Did you go on the train?" I asked.

"Indeed I did not", said Da. "I went on the bicycle for there was no money to spend on trains at that time. I was lucky to have a bicycle and all I got to eat was a couple of bits of bread that I put in my pocket. There was no money in the country at that time and no work".

"It must have taken you a quare while to cycle the whole road to Belfast". I said in astonishment.

"I would have taken me about three and a half hours", said Da thoughtfully. "But sure at that time I was only thirty years of age and there was not a man in the country could keep up with me. But by the time I spent a couple of hours with your Ma here and then rode back home, the whole day was gone. There was a man Oiney Mallon lived down in Mossmore just before that time and every so often he would take a notion of heading off no matter how much needed to be done at home. He walked to Belfast and spent a couple of days wandering round the city. When he had seen all he wanted to see, he walked back home again. The neighbours all gathered into the house when he came home, to hear what Belfast was like".

We sat round the fire and discussed the new situation until Da announced that he was tired and was going to bed. My mother insisted that I have a good wash and got my clothes ready for the morning. There was very little getting ready to do, because she had my suit pressed, my shirt ironed, and she had even polished my shoes. She insisted that I would have gone out with them like man who had been ploughing in wet weather.

CHAPTER 26
SHYING AT THE BUSES

Next morning I set off on my bicycle to catch the half past eleven train. Luckily it was a lovely morning and I rode into Dungannon at a very leisurely pace. I considered what sort of meeting might be before me. It was common knowledge that there was intense competition for places and I expected to face a pretty unpleasant half hour or so. I had never even heard of an interview in my life before and I felt pretty uneasy. I spent quite a bit of time trying to think up answers to awkward questions, but eventually gave up. I decided to do my best and if that was not good enough, perhaps the Civil Service people might not be so demanding.

Wheeling my bicycle into the station, I stopped a porter and asked him if it would be possible to leave it there for the day since I had to go to Belfast and I might not be home until late. The man greeted me with a big smile. "Surely", he said in a friendly voice, "we'll put it here in my room and it will be as safe as houses there until you come back. Is this the first time that you have ever been in Belfast?"

"How did you know that?" I asked, taken aback.

"It's not that hard to work it out by the way you have been going on", he said. "You had better watch yourself because you fellows from the country sometimes shy at the buses for a while till you get used to the city". He slapped his knee and laughed heartily at his own joke. "Do you know where you are going?" he asked when he had finished laughing.

"I think I do", I assured him. "I'm going to St. Mary's Training College".

"I used to court a girl that lived right beside it", he said and then proceeded to give me the same instructions that I had been given already. I thanked him and went to get my ticket as the train was due. I got an awful surprise when about a mile outside the town we were suddenly plunged into darkness. A man sitting across from me saw my astonishment. "It's the tunnel", he explained. "It's about a mile long. Did you not know about it?"

"I did not", I replied. "I never heard of it in my life".

The rest of the journey was uneventful and I arrived in Belfast with lots of time to spare. I found the Grosvenor Road and stood waiting at a bus stop. I got a surprise when the first bus came along. This bus has rubber wheels like the buses at home, but it had a contraption on the roof, which contacted a double set of overhead wires to give it power. I had seen my first trolley bus. I had hardly sat down when the conductor came along.

"Fares please", he said, holding out his hand.

"I want to go to the Falls Road", I said.

"Never been on a bus before?", he asked.

"Not a bus like this", I replied. "It's my first time in the city".

"That's tuppence", he said. "I'll give you a shout when it's time to get off".

The conductor warned me to get off just before the traffic lights and having done so I walked up to the junction. I spied a little café across the road and since I had more than an hour to spend I decided to get a snack before I went to the college, which I had been assured was only about five minutes away. I bought a newspaper and went into the café to spend a leisurely hour or so. At a quarter to two I came out and walked along the Falls Road until I came to St.Mary's.

A nun was standing just inside the main door with a clipboard in her hand. She came over to me. "I take it that you have come for an interview", she said. "What is your name?"

"I'm Arthur Daly Sister", I replied. It was the first time in my life that I had ever spoken to a nun.

She consulted her sheets and pointed down a long corridor to where chairs were placed outside a number of rooms. "Go down to where those green chairs are sitting outside room ten", she said. "Take a seat there and you will be called in before very long. The men are away for lunch at present but they are due back in a few minutes. Good luck and God bless".

"Thank you Sister", I said and took the seat as directed. A few minutes later a tall man came along the corridor and stopped beside me.

"You must be Mr. Daly", he said with a big friendly smile.

"Yes Sir", I answered.

"Come on in to the room and take a seat", he said, opening the door. "My colleague, Mr. Donnelly will be along in a minute or two. Did you have any trouble finding the place?"

"Not at all", I replied. "A couple of people had given me very good instructions and it was easy enough".

A stocky man of medium height with a waddling gait entered the room and greeted me with a grin. "I see you have made a start, Jack", he said to the first man, "this must be Mr. Daly".

"This is Mr. Donnelly, as you will have gathered", said the first man. "He is the Vice-Principal of Trench House, which is the men's Training College. This college is for women only. My name is Jack McCavert and I am in charge of speech and drama, mainly. Mr. Donnelly is our maths expert".

Mr. Donnelly looked at Jack and shook his head. "I don't know about the expert part", he said. "I can tell you, however, Mr. Daly, that you won't be learning any more Advanced Maths. We will be concentrating on ways of teaching the sort of maths that you learned in primary school most of the time. Even if you do a fourth year, it won't be much different".

Jack glanced down at his papers and then looked up at me, again with an enquiring smile. "I see that you come from the townland of Sessiagh, near Benburb", he said. "It may surprise you but I know that part of the country very well".

It surprised me so much that I gaped at him open mouthed and I could not think of anything to say. He went on to explain. "My wife was called Diamond, but the Hughes family of Lisban are her people on her mother's side. I suppose you know them".

"I do indeed", I agreed. "They are neighbours of ours and are all very friendly, especially with my father. I did not expect to meet someone today who was familiar with our out of the way place".

Jack rubbed his cheek thoughtfully. "There's no better way of getting to know a place than courting a girl who lives there, or who has relatives in it", he said. "I see that you have done exceptionally well in the exams, especially since it was your first attempt at them, wasn't it?"

"I was lucky enough Sir", I replied. This man put me completely at ease.

"Have you anything that you want to ask, Mr. Donnelly?" he said to his companion.

Mr. Donnelly looked up from where he had been writing on a sheet of paper and gazed at me in what I thought was a dreamy fashion. He sat like that for quite a few moments and then said, "no, that's all right, Jack", and went back to his writing. Jack consulted a sheet of paper and then said, "if you have not made any arrangements about digs, I have an address here that might suit you. It is in a street called St. Meryl Park and the lady is a Mrs.Geoghan. I think you should make arrangements today when you are here. Is that all right with you?"

I gasped in surprise. The interview was over. There had been no difficult or awkward questions. Indeed there had been no questions at all. There had been nothing except a very friendly conversation. "That would be fine, Sir," I answered, "but how do I find the place?"

"When you go out through the main gates", he said, "go across the road and you will find a bus stop not far away. Wait until a number twelve bus comes along and that will take you to the Glen Road. Ask the bus conductor to tell when you are near to St. Meryl Park. Cheerio now and we will be looking forward to seeing you in a couple of weeks time".

I was about to open the door to leave the room when Mr. McCavert added, "oh, by the way Arthur, your scholarship will amount to about two hundred and seventy pounds a year. Out of that you will have to pay your digs and buy any books you will need. There will be a wee bit over but not much. If you don't drink or smoke or gamble too much you will be able to survive".

"I don't do any of those Sir", I assured him.

"One last thing", he said. "The first payment usually does not come until a few weeks into the first term. You will have to try to survive until then".

I made my way out and across the road to the bus stop and it was only when I was waiting there that I realised that I had agreed to join the college without considering my other option. I got on a bus and after a short interval the conductor came for the fare. "I'm going to the Glen Road", I said, "but the name of the street that I want has gone out of my head".

I felt an awful fool as he looked down at me and shook his head. "What kind of man gets on a bus and doesn't know where he is going?" he asked, but he was obviously amused about my lapse of memory.

"I just can't remember the name of the place", I explained. "A man gave me the address a few minutes ago, but it has gone completely out of my head".

"We will soon be at the Glen Road", the conductor said in an understanding way. "I'll come back to you when we are going up the road and maybe you will remember by then". He went on about his business and I sat there trying to recall the name of the street. My mind was completely blank and I began to panic. I tried closing my eyes hoping that it might help, but nothing happened. I noticed the bus turning to the right at a junction and then I saw a notice with 'Glen Road' on it. I sat looking out of the window and reading the names of the streets but none of them rang a bell. Jack McCavert will think I am some fool if I have to go back to the college and explain this to him, I thought. Suddenly the name flashed back into my head just as the conductor was approaching.

"St. Meryl Park", I said, "I am fairly sure that was the name of the street".

"That would be right", agreed the conductor, "get off at the next stop and walk on up the road a wee bit and you will find it on the left. That will be threepence please".

I found the street without any bother. The house proved to be semi-detached like all the others in the street. I rang the doorbell. A small, sharp-featured, rather elderly woman with glasses, came to the door.

"Yes?" she said sharply.

"I was down at the Training College", I explained, "and Mr. McCavert gave me this address as a place where I might find lodgings".

"Oh, right," she said, "come on in".

We went into the living room, where her husband was sitting in a chair at the fire. I was instantly aware that the man was not well. He was smoking and every couple of minutes he was overcome with fits of coughing. Both husband and wife looked very serious, even dismal.

"This is Paddy, my husband", the woman said. "Our son has left home to take a job in Dublin and that means that we have a spare room. I thought that we might keep someone from the Training College, and that is why Mr. McCavert was able to give you my name. The rent will be two pounds, five shillings per week, which they tell me is normal for students from the College".

"That will be fine", I told her but really I was not too happy. There was not a very friendly atmosphere in the house and Paddy's continual coughing disturbed me. My mother had always told me about the scourge of TB and I was afraid of catching that dread disease. I may have been completely mistaken, but I was nearly certain that poor Paddy was suffering from it. At the same time, I was alone in a strange city, far from home and I had no means of finding alternative accommodation. Mrs Geoghan was studying me as I stood there wrestling with my thoughts.

"I will want the first week's money now, in advance", she said, "and there will be no waiting for money when you come to stay with us. I will always want to be paid a week in advance. Some of these students think people can stand out of their money for weeks on end. I'm having none of that".

At this stage I was starving. I had only eaten a scone since breakfast and I had been looking forward to having a reasonable meal before I got on the train. I searched in my pockets and managed to get the two pounds and five shillings. All I had left over was a threepenny bit and a couple of pennies. It would take all of that to get me back to the station. Reluctantly I handed over the money.

"That will do for now", said Mrs Geoghan, "but when you arrive for your first week I will want another week's rent. Do you want to see the room?"

She led me up the stairs, and into the front room of the house. It was quite big and had a large wardrobe, a dressing table and a small table with two chairs. There were two single beds, and Mrs Geoghan said, "you can pick whichever of these beds you prefer to have. I will probably have someone else as well but since you have come first, you can have first choice".

I chose a bed and she led me down the stairs and opened the front door. "You will be getting a key", she said, "but you won't need it until you come to stay. And by the way, I don't want you to be coming in at all hours of the morning. I want you to be in by half past nine in the evening unless there is something special on in the college. You will never bring any girls into this house at any time. Right, I'll see you in September".

She was about to shut the door when I asked, "excuse me, Mrs Geoghan, but how do I get back to the train station?"

She opened the door again and came out to the gate with me. She pointed up the way I had come and said, "take a bus up there on the Glen Road and it will leave you in Castle Street. Ask anyone there and they will show you how to get to the station. It's not far. Cheerio".

"Cheerio," I replied, "and thank you".

I arrived home about seven o'clock to find my mother and father sitting by the fire in earnest conversation. They had been rather worried about their only child's ability to look out for himself in the big city. They were also worried that I would make a mess of the interview and lose the opportunity of a reasonable job. There was an audible sigh of relief when I came into the kitchen.

"Well how did the interview go?" asked my mother in urgent, anxious tones.

"It went well enough", I replied. "Have you got anything to eat, I'm famished".

"Did you not get anything to eat and Belfast full of all sorts of eating houses?" asked Da.

"I got a bun and a cup of tea before the interview but I haven't had a bite since", I told him. My mother put my dinner on the table and I tore into it like a young wolf.

"Tell me this Boy", asked Da, "what were you doing that you could not go in somewhere, and get a bite to eat?"

"It was this way", I replied between bites, "Mr. McCavert told me to go to a place on the Glen Road and get myself fixed up with digs. The woman had to get the rent in advance and that left me with a few coppers to get the bus back to the city centre. I could not afford to get anything in the line of food".

"God dammit", growled Da, "there's not a damned bit of use in me wasting my breath talking. Didn't I always tell you never to go anywhere without some extra money in your pocket?"

I turned and stared into his face, feeling rather annoyed. "I had a couple of pounds extra surely Da", I said. "I never thought that I would be looking for digs today and I never thought that the woman would want a week's rent in advance".

"You should always be prepared for things like that", replied Da. "Was the interview hard?"

"Indeed it was not", I assured him. "Mr. McCavert was only interested in telling me that his wife was called Diamond and he knows this part of the country fairly well".

"Well dammit, that's a tarra to man altogether Sarah", said Da. "That must be the fellow that married a niece of the Hughes family across the fields there. I met him a lock of years ago one day and he is a real gentleman".

"There was another man with him called Donnelly", I added, "but he hardly said anything at all".

"Are the digs good?" asked Ma. "Do you need to bring bedclothes or anything?"

"That's all in", I assured her, pulling my chair up to the fire between them. "There's just one wee mouse in the meal as far as I can see".

The both looked at me with earnest faces. "What's the big problem?" demanded Da.

"Well, Mr. McCavert says that the scholarship will be about four pounds and ten shillings a week but it's paid in two lumps. The first one will come in the first term but he warned me that I will not get any money for six weeks or so and I will have to pay my own way until then".

"Well God dammit, Sarah, that might put out our light altogether", said Da with a great pretence of annoyance. "We've managed to keep you up till now Boy, and I have a sort of a notion that the ship is hardly going to sink in the next six weeks. If I was you, I wouldn't worry too much about it".

We discussed things for an hour or so and by that time I felt totally exhausted and told them that I was going to bed. Strangely, my first day in the big city had taken far more out of me than a whole week working in the fields might have done.

CHAPTER 27
LODGINGS LOTTERY

I discovered that I was not the only one who was leaving the townland of Sessiagh to go to Belfast at the end of that summer of 1954. Our next-door neighbours, Barney and Mrs Conlon, had sold their farm to Barney's nephew, Tom Conlon, and had decided to move to the city in their declining years. Barney called into our house on the day before he was ready to leave. "We're going away in the morning", he said. "I don't know if we're wise or not, for I'll miss the hunting and all the neighbours. It might be lonely living in the city where we don't know anybody. But it has got to the stage where I can't handle the farm anymore".

My mother and father were annoyed to be losing this couple who had been their closest neighbours and friends since they had been married twenty years beforehand. Da took Barney's hand and shook it warmly. "Be God, Barney", he said, "I would not fancy going to live in a place with all those houses round me. It's easy enough to take the man out of the country, but it's hard to take the country out of the man, as you will have heard people saying often enough. I hope you and Mary will be healthy and happy in the city. At least you will have plenty of help near at hand if you need it".

I noticed that Barney wiped a tear from his eye before he answered. "I've lived in the big cities of America and Australia and New Zealand in my time", he said slowly and thoughtfully. "I've worked with men of all colours and creeds but it has always been nice to come home. And I know that for dead sure this townland will always be home to me no matter how things go in Belfast".

He turned to me and took my hand. "I believe that you will be living in the same area as me Arthur", he said. "Any night that you have an hour or two to spare, call down to Riverdale Park and you will get a warm welcome. Don't forget, when you are running after all those nice girls in the city, that your old neighbours will welcome you to their new home. It would be lovely having someone from the old townland calling to see us".

"Thank you very much Barney", I said. "It will be nice to know that when I feel a bit lonely I'll have a place that will feel like a wee bit of home. I'll certainly be calling on you now and again".

I knocked on Geoghan's door about eight o'clock on the evening of the first Sunday in September. The course in the Training College was due to begin the following morning at ten o'clock. Mrs Geoghan opened the door and brought me in. "Your fellow student has already arrived", she said. "He's up in the room and since you know where it is you can go on up and get settled in. Breakfast will be at eight o'clock sharp, in the morning. As I was explaining to the other fellow you will have no call to use any of the house apart from the stairs and the bathroom. Meals, of course, will be in the living room".

I made my way up the stairs and knocked on the door of the room before entering. I got a pleasant surprise when I went in for sitting on one of the beds was my old friend from the College in Armagh, Chris Coulson. I was delighted to have someone whom I had known for a long time as a roommate.

"God, but I'm glad to see you", said Chris. "I didn't know who might be coming for that woman never told me your name. I have a feeling that these digs are going to be bloody awful. The first chance I get I'll find somewhere else where the people might be a bit more friendly. She is intent on keeping us penned up here like a couple of prisoners".

"I had a bad feeling about the place myself", I agreed, "but I didn't know the city and I had no chance of finding somewhere else. Maybe it will not be as bad as we think when things settle down".

"Don't cod yourself", replied Chris. "Living here would be like being in a prison. I bet you the men down in the Crumlin Road are a whole lot better off than we're going to be. Give me a week or so and I'll be saying goodbye. What kind of a woman would not offer us even a cup of tea this evening after our long journey to the city?"

Next morning we came down to breakfast to find that it was like being back in College in Armagh, except that the bread was toasted and the margarine was in a block. We had hardly finished the frugal meal when Mrs Geoghan said bluntly, "don't be hanging about down here. I have Paddy's breakfast to get ready". We went up to our room like two beaten dogs. The smell of frying bacon was wafting up the stairs to us. Chris stood in the middle of the room, rubbing his chin in obvious frustration, and looking at me.

"As sure as there's an eye in a goat", he said angrily, "if I don't get out of here damned soon, I'll strangle that hungry, ignorant, auld bitch".

I considered the situation for a moment. "I know how you feel, Chris", I said, "but that would not be an answer to anything. We should make up our minds to get out of here as soon as we can and as quietly as we can. We'll hear how the other students are fixed when we meet them up at Trench House".

On Thursday evening of that week, I went down to the city centre to buy some materials that were needed for the course in the College. Having finished my business, I got on to the Glen Road bus at Castle Street and sat down near the back of the bottom deck. It so happened that there were only about half a dozen people on the bus. The conductor, a smallish, rotund man with a very pleasant face came to collect the fare. "St. Meryl Park, please", I said.

"Are you in digs there?" he asked. "You're not a native of the city are you?"

"No", I replied, "I come from County Tyrone."

"I live in Andersonstown Park myself", he said. "We have a couple of students staying with us who have just started at the Training College. They seem to be very nice fellows but I have hardly had time to meet them for I have to work very long hours at this job".

He sat down sideways on the seat in front of me, holding the ticket machine on his lap. He was obviously tired but there was a look of friendship and fun on his face, and especially in his eyes, as he twisted round to look into my face.

"Where are you staying in St. Meryl Park?" he asked.

"I'm staying with a Mrs Geoghan at present", I told him. "I just moved in at the start of the week?"

I thought I saw a look of horror flit across his face. "Are the digs good?" he asked.

"Would you happen to have any extra room in your house?" I asked him without answering his question.

"Oh, so you are not too happy where you are", he said softly, studying my face.

"Well, I would like to move as soon as possible", I answered.

He sat whistling through his teeth for a minute or two and obviously thinking the whole situation over in his mind. "We have a son at secondary school", he said at last. "He needs a room of his own and then the two students have a room. The wife and myself have the big room and the only room that is left is a wee box room. It is full to the ceiling with all sorts of rubbish at the minute. Maybe it could be cleared out if the wife agreed. I'll talk to her tonight and if you call in the next couple of days she will be able to tell you what she decides. I wouldn't like to promise anything mind, but we can try".

Tea that evening, like all other evenings, consisted of bread and jam and the jam was rationed. Mrs Geoghan made us feel that we were taking the last bite out of her mouth. As we were finishing the meal, Mrs Geoghan came into the room and surveyed the table. "It's good to see that you fellows have great appetites", she said, referring to the fact that every bit of the four slices of bread had disappeared. I didn't know whether to laugh, or accost her with some caustic remark when Chris asked, "would you ever have tried feeding a canary, Mrs Geoghan? A canary would think it had a great appetite if it was in this house for a while I can assure you".

I thought the woman was going to faint. She straightened up and her face went a deathly white. Her lips moved up and down but for a minute or so no words came out. At last she got control of herself and asked angrily, "are you not satisfied with the food being served in this house Mr. Coulson?"

Chris looked up at her and smirked. Then he looked down at the table and shook his head. Finally he rose from the table and towered over her. "I can't make up my mind whether you are a greedy skinflint and buck stupid with it Mrs Geoghan", he said angrily, "or maybe you have never seen anything approaching decency in you life. You should be locked up somewhere for the protection of the rest of the human race".

I was sure the woman was going to have a heart attack or a seizure. She took a few small steps backward towards Paddy's chair and grasped hold of the back of it. She was breathing hard and her eyes were popping out of her head. "Get out", she squealed, "get out of this house this minute and never come back".

Chris looked very cool and totally under control. He looked back at the woman calmly and rubbed his chin slowly as though considering what he should do. It seemed a long time before he replied, but it was probably not more that half a minute at the most. "I will get out", he said slowly and deliberately, "and I will not come back, of that you can be sure. But my rent is paid until the end of this week and the end of this week is when I will be going. And I'll tell you something else. Tomorrow morning I will make my own breakfast and I'll be using some of that lovely butter that you keep for yourselves. And be sure to have the two pounds five ready to give back to me, that I gave you for next week".

Mrs Geoghan looked as though she had been shot. She struggled to speak but only gasps came from her mouth for a long time. Eventually she stuttered, "you'll be getting no money back from me. It's hard earned with your bad manners and impertinence. And I want you to get out now, immediately".

"I was talking to my uncle who is a well-known solicitor in Enniskillen", said Chris quietly, "and I happen to know that I can stay until my rent runs out. If you don't give back the money for next week, we'll put you out of house and home. It's up to you but the uncle assured me that he'd like to have a go at you".

The woman stood like a statue for a several moments while her husband went into a fit of terrible coughing. She turned to console him and when he recovered she went over to the sideboard and took Chris's money out of a biscuit box. "Here's your blasted money", she screamed, "and the quicker you get out of this house the better. I wish to God I'd never cast eyes on you in my life".

"The feeling's mutual, believe me", said Chris and turning, he stomped off up to our room.

During this long and unpleasant encounter I was sitting at the table trying to pretend that I did not exist. I got up and went to follow Chris up to the room. Mrs Geoghan put her hand on my arm to stop me and said, "I'm sorry you had to sit through all of that, Arthur". It was the first time that she had called me by my name and I simply shook my head and went up the stair. Chris had his case open on his bed and was packing it when I went into the room.

"Be God, you didn't mince your words there, Chris", I said. "It's quare and lucky that you have an uncle who is a solicitor and can tell you your rights".

Chris sat down on the bed and laughed quietly though the laugh seemed totally devoid of humour. "The only uncle I have is a farmer", he said with a knowing smile, "but it scared the devil out of that auld bitch downstairs. You know me. I'm not easily raised, but I don't like people to take me for a fool altogether. I'm moving in with four other boys who have a flat down at Cavendish Street. I'll be able to move on Saturday morning. Are you thinking of staying on here? Had you not got enough of this kind of grub when we were in Armagh?"

"I met a man this evening and I may have a place to go if I'm lucky Chris", I said. "In all the excitement at tea, she forgot to ask me for next week's money. I hope to God that I don't have to stay here next week".

CHAPTER 28
A STROKE OF GOOD FORTUNE

The next morning as we were walking to the College, at the top of Andersonstown Park we met in with two other students coming out of the gate of a house. One was a fellow from Larne called Francis O'Rourke and the other was Michael Gillespie from west Tyrone. As we went along Chris fell into conversation with Francis and I got talking to Michael. After a while I asked him casually, "are you in digs in that house we saw you coming out of?"

"That's right", he said. "We moved in last week on the advice of Mr. McCavert".

"What are the digs like?" I enquired. "Is the food good?"

"Mrs Andrews is an excellent cook", said Michael, "and we are treated like members of the family. For dead sure we won't starve as long as we're in that house. What are your own digs like?"

"Bloody awful", I said. "Really bloody awful. But tell me Michael, would your landlord happen to be a bus conductor?"

Michael gave a gasp of surprise. "How did you

know that?" he asked. "Jimmy definitely works on the buses and I think he is a conductor".

I did not pay much attention to what was going on in our lectures that day. I was in deep thought. I felt that I could not abide much more of the Geoghan household and I was desperate to find alternative accommodation. I decided on a plan of action, although I knew it had very little chance of being successful. I managed to slip away half an hour early and on my way home I knocked at the Andrews' house. After a short interval a middle-aged lady opened the door. She had a lovely warm round face, lit up by sparkling brown eyes. "Can I help you?" she asked in a friendly way and I noticed a trace of southern accent in her voice.

"I'm very sorry to disturb you", I said awkwardly, "but I think I met your husband on the bus last night. I was wondering if he had mentioned it to you".

She studied me for a few seconds and then said, "it must have been you that Jimmy was telling me about. He was telling me that he had met this young fellow from the country. He was asking me if I could take another person in to stay as he thought you were not too happy. Come on in here to the sitting room and we'll have a chat".

She led me into the sitting room and asked me to sit down in one of her big armchairs. She sat in the other one and studied me. "I really had not thought of taking anyone else", she said. "My son has one room and the two students have the other one. I don't have the room to take any more".

She must have seen my face drop, for she asked, "are you really desperate? Surely it can't be that bad?"

I was at a loss to know what to say, because I considered that the Geoghans were only up the street and, therefore, were her neighbours. At home we would consider people neighbours who lived miles away and these two families were only a couple of hundred yards apart. I looked into Mrs Andrew's eyes as she was looking into mine and I felt a great warmth. I knew I could really trust this lady.

"It's a very unpleasant situation at the minute Mrs Andrews", I said. "I'm going to have to get out very soon, someway or other. I'm sorry for calling on you like this and I understand your situation. Would you happen to know anyone around here who might like to have someone like me?"

Mrs Andrews sat there still looking at me with the slightest trace of a smile on her face. "Where exactly do you come from?" she asked.

"We live outside the village of Benburb in the County Tyrone", I told her. "This week has been the first time I have ever been in Belfast in my life".

"Are you feeling a bit lost?" she enquired.

"Well, it's not too bad because I already know some of the other students at the College", I said. "But it's hard to find a place to stay when I don't know the city".

"Jimmy was very taken with you", she said very

slowly. "He is trying to persuade me to make room for you. It would mean clearing out a wee box room. Come on upstairs and I'll show it to you and you can decide if you think you could manage to live in it".

My heart was now thumping. I could not really believe that I had a chance of getting into the house. At the same time, I was worried lest I should say anything to offend this lady. From the landing, she pointed out the various rooms in the house and then she opened the door of another room. It had a bed beside a hot-press, but it was piled high with various boxes right up to the ceiling. There was a small table in one corner but it too was loaded with boxes. Mrs Andrews was standing with her hands raised, as though in prayer. "I don't know what has come over me", she said. "Why under God am I showing someone this awful mess and me supposed to be real proud of my house? There must be something wrong with my head".

"Have you got a place to put some of your boxes Mrs Andrews?" I asked. "If some of them were removed this room would be great".

"Oh Lord bless us son", she said and went into fits of laughter, "they'll all have to go. Most of them should have gone to the dump years ago. The others can go up into the loft. When would you think of moving in, if I said it was possible?"

"My father always told me not to annoy the dog when he was not bothering me", I replied. "I don't often take Da's advice, so would it be possible to move in for Monday? That would be Sunday evening".

Mrs Andrews looked at me, clearly surprised. Then she burst into a fit of laughter once more. "You don't intend to give me much time to get the room ready for you", she said. "Would you not wait a week and let us get a chance to decorate it and make it fit for habitation?"

"Mrs Andrews", I said, "please do not worry yourself about the room. I'd be delighted with it if you are willing to let me have it. Please do not go to a lot of bother. Really it will be fine if that suits you".

The lady stood studying me for quite a while. She then shook her head as though mystified. "You know", she said, "I had really no intention of taking in another student. I told Jimmy that last night. But OK, we'll try and have some place ready for you for Sunday night. By the way I never asked you what your name was".

"I'm Arthur Daly", I said, "and you will never know how grateful I am to you for taking me in. I hope that I will be able to be some help rather than be a hindrance to you in the house. Thank you very much indeed".

"In this house", she said, "you will be expected to act like one of the family. We will all eat together, except when Jimmy is away on his long shifts at work. If you feel peckish between meals I hope you will go to the kitchen and fix something for yourself. And the boys have got into the habit of making a cup of tea for everybody fairly late at night. I hope you will muck in too".

"That sounds great Mrs Andrews", I said. "I can't thank you enough and I'll be looking forward to seeing you all on Sunday night. I had not intended to go home this weekend, but now I will. May I leave my case here over the next couple of days because I don't want to have to go back to the other house on Sunday evening if I can help it?"

"Oh, that will be OK", she said giving me a friendly push. "Next thing you'll be asking me to put you up for this night as well. Go on and good luck".

I went back to Geoghan's to find Chris pushing the last few items into his case. He snapped it shut and took it by the handle as it rested on the bed. "You can give that woman my best wishes", he said. "I hope you don't have too long to put up with her. Good luck and goodbye". He lifted his case, went down the stairs and slammed the front door behind him.

I packed my own case, which wasn't too difficult since I hadn't really unpacked it. I checked to make sure that I had left nothing behind and then I went down the stairs and left my case at the door. I went over to the living room door, knocked it and opened it slightly to put my head into the room. Paddy was sitting in his chair reading and Mrs Geoghan was knitting by the fire. She looked up clearly rather surprised.

"I'm heading off now", I said quietly. "I have decided to go home for the weekend and I haven't a lot of time before the train goes".

"I have just realised", said MrsGeoghan, "that you have not paid for next week's rent yet and you have to do that before you go".

"I won't be coming back here", I said, "so there is no rent to be paid. I just called in to say goodbye".

It seemed to me that the woman went slightly pale and she certainly dropped her knitting on to her lap as though it had suddenly become hot. Slowly she rose from her chair and looked first at Paddy and then at me. I closed the door behind me and that was the last I ever saw of them.

I moved into the Andrews house on Sunday evening, and when Mrs Andrews took me up the stairs I could hardly believe my eyes. The little room had been freshly papered and painted. The bed was neatly made and a small wardrobe was standing in one corner. On the side of the wardrobe, above a small desk, a reading lamp had been fitted. A very comfortable looking chair was sitting at the desk. I stood there open mouthed in amazement. "Mrs Andrews", I gasped, "there was no need for all of this. The room was grand the way it was but thank you very much. I'll pay you the rent now".

"You'll do no such thing", she said, "you can give me the two pounds at the end of the week, like everyone else. Now get settled in and come down for a cup of tea".

CHAPTER 29
THINGS BLOWING IN THE WIND

Michael and Frank were somewhat surprised to find that I had joined them but we soon became quite friendly and walked the mile and a half to and from the college together each day for the next few weeks. On wet days, one could get a trolley bus from the bottom of the Park as far as the terminus, which was at the entrance to Casement Park. It cost money and was not a very big help since it only took us a small part of the way. I thought about the situation and decided that, if I had a bicycle it would save money and time. It would also be very handy for going down to the Central Library if I wanted to do some study there.

On my next visit home I asked the guard on the train if it would be possible to take my bike with me when I was travelling to and from the city. He assured me that it would be no problem at all and since I was a paying passenger the bike could travel free. It meant that I had a cheap mode of travel down to the station on Friday evenings and back to the digs on Sunday. To my great surprise I set a new trend and within a month or so, a couple of dozen students appeared with bicycles and it became recognised as a normal thing. Mrs Andrews only charged two pounds for rent, which she insisted was the normal rate so I was saving five shillings a week as well.

The digs were really excellent. The food was first class and plentiful, and we were treated as members of the family in every respect. Everyone was perfectly happy until a disturbing event occurred one Sunday in early spring of the following year.

It was a beautiful morning when for the first time the sun, shining from a blue sky, gave the first hint of real warmth. Mrs Andrews had gone out early to ten o'clock Mass in St.Teresa's church and I was just about to follow her when Michael came down the stairs with some clothes over his arm. He looked somewhat concerned.

"I have a big date tonight", he said. "I have been trying to get this girl to come out with me for ages. I need to wash some socks and some underpants or I'll be smelling like a dunghill. Have you any idea where I could wash them?"

"Did you ask Mrs Andrews?" I enquired.

"No", he said, "I wanted to get them done while she is out and Jimmy is away at work. I think I'll wash them in the sink".

"Well, I suppose you know best", I replied doubtfully.

"But where the hell could I get them dried?" he asked.

"You could put up a line in the back yard", I replied in jovial manner, knowing he was useless with his hands. I went off to the chapel.

It so happened that Mrs Andrews and I met at the door of the church at the end of Mass and we sauntered back towards the house together, chatting and enjoying the beautiful morning. We were halfway along St. Meryl Park when Mrs Andrews gave an agonised cry and exclaimed, "Jesus, Mary and Saint Joseph, I'm ruined. I'll never live this down".

I took her by the arm for I thought she was feeling weak and I wanted to steady her. "What is wrong, Mrs Andrews", I asked, "are you feeling faint?"

"Oh the Lord save us and take care of us", she murmured, "how am I going to face people after this?" She was pointing towards the house in horror.

I looked in the direction indicated and could hardly believe what I was seeing. A sweeping brush was protruding from the front upstairs window held there by pieces of cord tied to the hinges of the window. And fixed to the brush shaft were socks, underpants and a shirt, all blowing gently in the breeze. Mrs Andrews had gone a sickly pale and she now leaned heavily on my arm. "My God", she whispered, "what are the neighbours going to think? I'm disgraced".

Mrs Andrews took off down the street at a trot and when she reached the house she rushed up the stairs and into the room occupied by Michael and Frank. Michael was lying on the bed, calmly reading a book, with both sections of the window wide open.

The head of the brush was resting against the central pane and blue cords tied to the tip of the handle held the entire brush in place. The clothes were still waving in the breeze.

"Under God, have you gone mad altogether?" Mrs Andrews demanded from Michael. "Have you set out to disgrace us in front of the whole neighbourhood?" She rushed over to the window and pulled the brush back into the room.

"What's wrong?" asked Michael rather angrily and apparently totally surprised. He rose from the bed. "Watch my clothes", he snapped. "I was only trying to get them dried. Why couldn't you have left them where they were?" Mrs Andrews stood in the middle of the room with the brush still in her hands and the cords still tied to the window. She was now obviously as horrified by Michael's attitude as by what he had done.

"Surely this is not the way you dry clothes at home?" she stammered at last. "Surely you would not disgrace your mother by putting clothes out through the front window of the house like that? I don't know how I'm going to face the neighbours. Oh God be merciful to me but what have I done to deserve this?"

"I have my rent paid and this is my room and I can do whatever I like in it", said Michael angrily. "Put those clothes back where you got them".

I had been standing at the door of the room when the acrimonious conversation took place. Mrs

Andrews gasped and looked as though she had been turned to stone. At that moment Frank came in through the front door and came up the stairs. He walked past me into the room.

"What has been going one here?" asked Frank. "Why are the clothes pinned to the brush and why is the brush tied to the window?"

"I was trying to get a few things dried for tonight", said Michael, "and to hear Mrs Andrews here you'd think that I'd set the house on fire".

"It was a darned funny place to dry clothes", said Frank.

"I don't see anything funny about it", said Mrs Andrews, "and I don't see anything funny about the nasty comments that Mr. Gillespie has made. I am now giving him five days notice to leave the house and I would prefer it to be sooner if he can find other accommodation. And by the way, Mr. Gillespie, you have not paid your rent. At this moment you owe me for the past two weeks, as you well know. I want you to leave this house as soon as possible".

At this stage I slipped quietly into my room and sat down at the desk with a book. I could not concentrate to read, however, and I tried to hear what was going on in the next room. Frank tried at first get Mrs Andrews to understand that Michael had meant no harm, and that such a thing would never happen again. Mrs Andrews told him that Michael had said things which she would not take from anyone in her own house and that she wanted him to get out as soon as possible and there was not going back on that. Frank told her that Michael was his best friend and he didn't want to be separated from him.

"Mr. O'Rourke", she said bluntly, "if you want to continue to enjoy Mr. Gillespie's company, you have a clear choice. You are free to leave with him". She stomped off down the stairs.

The two boys stayed in the room for about an hour but I could not hear what was being said. At a few minutes before noon I heard them going down the stairs and then the front door slammed. I sat in the room and tried to read, but I was upset and since it was a lovely day I decided I would go for a walk and get my head cleared. I was about to open the front door when Mrs Andrews came out of the kitchen.

"Just a minute, Arthur", she said. "I know you were not involved in the trouble this morning but I'm so upset that I don't feel like keeping anyone any longer. Would you like to move somewhere else too?"

I looked into her face and I could see that she was still very angry and very shocked. I walked along the hall until I was beside her. "Mrs Andrews", I said, "a few months ago you took me in when I really needed somewhere decent to stay. Since then you have treated me as you have treated your own son, Pat, and I have been really happy in this house. Please take a while to think it over and if you still want me to go, then I'll look for somewhere else. But really I don't want to leave if you will let me stay. You and

Jimmy have been like a mother and father to me and I can't thank you enough. Please give it a day or two before you make up your mind".

That year Pat was doing his senior exam and unknown to Mrs Andrews I had been giving him help with his Irish and English. He had suggested that he should ask his mother to pay me something for the help but I had made him promise not to mention anything at all about our arrangement to his mother. Later that Sunday evening he came to me with a piece of Irish, which was too difficult for him. While we were working on it, he asked me about the row, which had taken place earlier in the day and asked me if I felt that his mother had been unfair to the two boys. I had to admit that I thought she had been completely justified but that she was thinking of making me leave as well. He intimated to me that if I left, he was going to be in deep trouble with the Irish especially and pleaded with me to stay at all costs. I suggested that under these circumstances he might have a quiet word with his mother.

The result was that I was allowed to remain in the house for another year and a very happy year it proved to be. About a month before the summer holidays of that second year Mrs Andrews stopped me as I was about to go home one Friday evening. She told me that she had been to the doctor and her news was not very good. She was advised to do as little work as possible and she asked me to find somewhere else to stay. She said that there was no rush but that she wanted to give me a chance to find somewhere else to stay in the following September.

Not long after I had come to the house, I found out that Pat was going with a girl called Kathleen Rosbotham. One night I met them at a dance and spent quite a bit of time in their company. Pat had decided that he did not want to go with her any longer. I decided that I rather liked her and for a few months I went out, more or less steadily with her. Most of the time we went for long walks about once a week in the neighbourhood and now and again we went to the pictures.

My companions in the Training College noticed our relationship when we went to dances and they were intrigued with her surname. At first they changed it to Ramsbottom, and later to my utter disgust they said it sounded better as 'sheep's arse'. This situation was a source of great amusement to my friends and fifty years later they still have a laugh about it when we meet. Needless to say I did not see much humour in it!

CHAPTER 30
A MAN TO REMEMBER

I had heard rumours of students who were having a great time in a house in Denewood Park, which was only a couple of hundred yards from the Andrews' house. The place was owned by a noted character in the locality called Gerry Henvey. He had a greengrocery business and he toured the district selling his produce from a van. I already knew Gerry slightly because he had sometimes called with the Andrews and I had spoken to him on a few occasions. I spied him serving a customer a day or so after Mrs Andrews had spoken to me and I asked him if there would be any chance of staying with him. He told me to call up to the house that evening so that I could meet his wife, Agnes, and find out what she had to say.

I arrived at Gerry's that evening about eight o'clock to find him loading the van for the next day. "Give me a hand to finish loading this van", said Gerry, "and then we'll go into the house and face the wife. What part of the world do you come from anyway?"

"I come from Tyrone", I told him, as I carried boxes

of fruit and vegetables over to him. "We live out in the country near a wee village called Benburb".

"We have a grand sort of a fellow living with us at present", said Gerry. "He's from a place called Coalisland and he is called Jim Cavanagh".

"Oh, I know Jim fairly well", I said. "His brother, John is in our class up at the college and he and I are very good friends indeed".

We finished loading the van, and Gerry took me into the house. Jim Cavanagh was sitting in an armchair at the fire, talking to Gerry's wife, Agnes, who was ironing at the other side of the fire.

"This is young Daly", said Gerry addressing Agnes. "I was thinking that he could share the wee room up stairs with big John. He comes from the same part of the country as Jim here".

I had expected to spend five or ten minutes on this visit at the most, but I left Henvey's the next morning at half past two. Gerry had started a debate about politics and it became long and heated and the next-door neighbours banged the wall a few times to warn us that they were being kept awake by the shouting. It was a scenario to which I was to become very accustomed when I moved in at the start of the following September.

Big John, as Gerry had referred to him, was a retired man called John Connolly. He was big and strong and had spent his life labouring on all sorts of projects in various parts of the British Isles. He had originally come from a farming background high up in the Mourne Mountains. For the first few days as we shared the room, I felt that he was rather resentful of my presence but before very long we became firm friends. I think John resented all students because they were getting chances that he had been denied. After a couple of weeks, in the nightly arguments in the sitting room he would always take my part whether I was right or wrong and on a few occasions he challenged Gerry or Jim Cavanagh to fight. It never came to anything but it usually ended the debate for the night, much I am sure, to the satisfaction of the neighbours.

Agnes Henvey had come from near Banbridge and I got the impression that she never really liked city life and longed for her home in rural surroundings. She made no secret of the fact that she had a soft spot for the boys from the country and loved to sit and talk to us when there was a quiet time. She had a young son, Gerard, who was only a few months old when I took up residence and for the first time in my life I had the opportunity of studying the rearing of a baby. Agnes was an excellent cook and we were totally spoiled by the quantity and quality of her culinary output. Gerry used the sitting room as a store and we were free to go and take anything we wished at any time. It was in Henvey's that I learned to put segments of orange on toast as a late supper. I don't know where Gerry got his oranges but I have never tasted fruit of that quality since.

A few weeks after I came to stay, Gerry invited

two young nurses from the City Hospital to come and spend an evening with us. He warned Jim Cavanagh and myself that they were lovely girls, whom he could guarantee would be 'good courts' and he commanded us to make sure to be about during their stay. Both girls came from South Armagh and one of them was related to Agnes. They were lovely girls as Gerry had said, but neither Jim nor myself developed an overwhelming desire for their prolonged company, much to Gerry's disgust. To be honest I don't think either of them was in the least disappointed either.

As usual, Gerry got an argument going and the girls stayed until after the last bus had gone. He decided that he would leave them back to the hospital in his van and he also insisted that a fellow called Jim Ó Kane and I accompany them on the journey. At that time there had been an outbreak of IRA activity and we had not gone very far when we encountered a road -block manned by the 'B' specials.

I was in the back of the van and did not see the road-block, and I don't know what happened to Gerry. For some reason he did not stop but drove through the check point and shouted at all of us to lie flat on the floor of the van as he put his foot to the floor and sped away from it. I think I heard shouts ordering us to stop. We were all petrified, waiting for the van to be riddled with bullets. For some reason, no shots were fired and we managed to reach the hospital in safety. We were shocked and rather terrified, Gerry most of all. On the way home

Gerry chose a roundabout route so as not to have to encounter the same group of 'security forces'.

A few months later Gerry found himself in a bit of trouble with his neighbours. He had a habit of pulling damaged outer leaves from cabbages and other vegetables and throwing them on the path at the side of the house. Gradually a mound of rotting material built up and as the weather got warmer the odour was anything but pleasant. There was a little walkway near the house, which led to St. Meryl Park and I noticed that the odour was very noticeable even before one came to the path. After many angry complaints from neighbours, Gerry was finally visited by two men from the environmental health department and given a couple of days to get the mess cleared up.

He hired a man with a pick-up truck to do the work, but was unwilling to pay for any more than the removal of two loads and the result was that there was still a small amount of really nasty stuff left. Gerry explained to me that he intended to fill it into bags and go and dump it up in Colin Glen. He asked me if I would give him a hand with this unpleasant task. The van was completely full by the time we had finished filling bags and the spare wheel had to be forced in at the back door.

We arrived at Colin Glen, which is a really beautiful spot and we stopped beside a little bridge. Gerry opened the back of the van and took out the spare wheel and, for some reason, placed it on the roof. He pulled a bag from the van and carried it over to the wall of the bridge and dumped it over. I took a second bag and did likewise, except that I picked a spot about three yards away from that chosen by Gerry. I dumped the material over the wall and came back to the van for more. I thought I heard a shout from somewhere but paid little attention.

I put my next bag on the wall and emptied it as before. This time I definitely heard a shout, or rather a string of expletives. It was obvious that it was coming from directly beneath me. I looked over the wall to see a man and a girl trying to free themselves from the deluge of filthy vegetation, which had landed on top of them while they were courting. The man was threatening to cut our throats or worse if we would only wait until he had climbed the steep bank to the road. Gerry was looking over the wall, clearly somewhat amused by the situation.

"There's only a couple of bags left", hissed Gerry. "We'll dump them over and clear out before that boy can get up here to get at us".

We dumped the two bags as suggested and the poor man, who was trying to scramble up the bank, was completely enveloped once more in stinking filth. He slid backwards and ended up lying, on the broad of his back, on top of the rubbish already dumped. The girl too had got a second, or third, helping, but since she had moved to one side it was minor compared to the deluge suffered by her boyfriend. The man was yelling blue murder in very colourful language. Gerry ran to the van and jumped in behind the wheel.

"Come on", he yelled to me, "we'll get out of here now before that boy gets the peelers for us".

Gerry turned the van as quickly as he could and we sped off towards home. We arrived safely and once more he asked me to give him a hand to load the van for the next morning. We were working away at this task when a thought suddenly struck me. "Where did you put the spare wheel, Gerry?", I asked. Gerry's answer was colourful but unprintable. The wheel was nowhere to be seen.

We got into the van again and drove slowly back to the spot in the glen, but there was no sign of the wheel and fortunately no sign of the courting couple. The wheel must have slid off the roof at a corner and probably bounced over a hedge. It was never seen again.

A few months after I had settled into life with the Henveys, a new student came to join us. To my great surprise it was Michael Gillespie who had had a row with Francis O'Rourke and had left his former digs. By this time our English course was in full swing and Michael had come to the conclusion that he was the equal, if not superior, to some of the great poets and writers of the Twentieth Century. In spite of holding firmly to this opinion, he was not in the top five of six people in the class.

Shortly after he came to stay with us, he decided that he would write what he called a 'symphonic poem'. The poem attempted to describe the life of his neighbours in the mountains of west Tyrone, using the underlying symbolism of the journey of a salmon from the sea to the breeding grounds in the upper reaches of a river. Some time after he had begun this massive work, he came to a surprising decision. He decided that to concentrate completely, he would have to stay in bed and would not come downstairs even for food. There was no doubt, he said, that the other members of the household would bring him up enough food to sustain him in his massive task. He would not wash nor shave and neither would he allow any woman to enter his room and this included Mrs Henvey.

I don't know what explanation Michael gave to the college authorities for his long absence from all lectures but it did not cause any bother of which I was aware. His sojourn in isolation lasted for eight weeks and in the later stages, when I called with a morsel of food now and again, his appearance had changed remarkably. He had a fairly long dark beard and his face was pale and gaunt. He looked like someone who had been sleeping rough and who was in the final stages of some dread disease. We began to fear for his physical and mental survival.

I was out at a dance one night and came in to the house about half-past eleven to find Mrs Henvey alone in the living- room and ironing at the side of the fire. As was her usual custom she asked me would I mind staying for half an hour or so to keep her company, because she did not like being on her own late at night. I sat at the other side of the fire and chatted away to her as she worked.

This was the scene, when sometime after midnight, the handle of the door turned and the door itself opened very slowly. Mrs Henvey stood with the iron in her hand, petrified, her eyes glued to the slowly opening door. A few seconds later Michael's white, bearded face appeared, like some apparition from another world. "Jesus, Mary and Joseph take care of us", gasped Agnes, her eyes now fixed on the face in the doorway. "It's the ghost of our Jimmy", and she slumped over the ironing board, gasping for breath, the hot iron still clasped in her hand.

I jumped up and went to her aid. She tried to stand up again gasping for breath and scared out of her wits. "Jimmy, Jimmy, Jimmy", she gasped and fell limp into my arms. I eased her on to a chair, which Michael, who was now in the room, had brought over. "It's all right, Agnes", I whispered, "it's only Michael, who has got up from his bed at last. There's no need to worry".

It took Agnes a long time to recover from the shock of seeing the poet suddenly emerge from his self-imposed exile and for two or three days afterwards she looked at him with suspicion and, I think, a certain amount of fear. It was as though she were expecting him to come up with some scheme, which would scare the life and soul out of her once again. A couple of weeks later, she asked him politely to leave and soon after that Michael moved out to find new accommodation. It was to be the last time that I shared digs with him.

From my first days in Henveys I got to know Bernie Fusgoe. She lived in the next street and was married to a man who was of Italian extraction, or so I concluded from her surname. She looked very young for a woman who was the mother of a family and she dressed in such a way at to exhibit her female attractions for all to see. She was a regular customer of Gerry's and nearly every evening she would call round to replenish her supplies from the sitting room. She entered the room at Gerry's invitation and when he followed her there were all sorts of squeals and cries, the reason for which we could only surmise.

One night, Jim Cavanagh and I went to a dance and came home very late. As far as I can remember it was probably after two o'clock in the morning by the time we returned to Denewood Park. We discovered, to our horror, that both of us had forgotten our keys to the front door and much to our annoyance we had to ring and knock on the door until someone would hear us and let us into the house.

Eventually Gerry came downstairs and opened the door. He was dressed only in a vest, or simmit, as he called it and it barely reached his navel although he was a rather small man. When he saw who was at the door, a look of utter disappointment was obvious on his face.

"Och, to hell", he growled, "it's only you boys, sure

I thought it was Bernie". And with that, he turned abruptly and headed up the stairs. It was a sight not to be easily forgotten.

Jim came in to the sitting room and collapsed in and armchair in a fit of laughter. Now, nearly fifty years later, when I meet him he seldom fails to ask if I remember the night Gerry came downstairs ready to welcome the lovely Bernie.

I stayed in Henveys until after I had completed my fourth year finals, and I still remember the family, the various inhabitants and the house with affection and gratitude. I especially remember Agnes, who died not long after I left, still a young woman and one of the most gracious and big-hearted people whom I have had the privilege of meeting.

CHAPTER 31
THE RANCH

Although St. Joseph's Teacher Training College, Trench House, was somewhat ramshackle and unfinished, I found it to be a very friendly establishment. The fact that it was on the very edge of the city and surrounded by green fields made it feel like home. We were met and welcomed on our first morning by Fr. McEnaney, the Dean. "I hope you will all feel very much at home here", he said, wearing what seemed to be a permanent smile. "This old house was once the home of the Trench family, and we have taken it over and added to it in the previous ten years or more. We aim to keep the feeling of a family home about the place. The students of past years have helped to build the lecture rooms and other facilities, which you will find grouped round the quadrangle at the back. The place is not very swanky, but you will not be cold in the coming winter and I think I can assure you that you will be reasonably comfortable. The job of building has not been fully completed and some of you may be asked to help with the work in the next few months or years. I can personally give you a guarantee that your results will not suffer as a result of any time you might be asked to devote to the development of the college".

I happened to be sitting beside a fellow called Jimmy Donnelly, who came from County Down and played football for that county team. "That guy is far too sweet to be wholesome", he whispered, leaning across to me. "I wouldn't trust him as far as I could throw him".

I smiled and nodded, but the priest's attention had been attracted to us. "Is there something that you would like to ask?" he enquired, looking directly at me.

"We were just wondering when we might be getting the money for our keep, Father", I answered.

Fr. McEnaney turned to lift a folder from his desk and Jimmy took the opportunity to whisper, "good thinking, boy".

"Your allowance should be here in five or six weeks time", said the priest. "I will have charge of it and as soon as it comes I will let you know and you can come and collect it in my office, which is along the corridor outside this room. You will soon learn to refer to the money as your 'incidentals' so that is perhaps a new word, which will become an important part of your vocabulary. In the meantime if anyone is really stuck, he can come to me and I will try to lend him enough money to get him through until the grants arrive. Please don't ask me if you are able to manage on your own. I have you for music so we will now begin our first music session".

It did not surprise me that I found the music period a total waste of time. I was not musical and could not sing, and the whole thing was somewhat of a puzzle to me. I enjoyed listening to traditional Irish music and I could appreciate a good singer, but for some reason I could never reproduce the notes as other people did. Once more Jimmy took an opportunity to have a chat.

"I have been talking to a couple of lads who have been here for two or three years", he whispered. "They have been telling me that McEnaney is a bit like the head of the secret service. Indeed they say that he would have done well in the secret police when Hitler was about. He tries all the time to have a group of boys who will tell him what is going on in the digs, or when teams go away to play a game of football. He always has a sweet smile to your face, but he is liable to knife you in the back when you're off guard. Don't be surprised if he asks you to act as one of his spies".

"I have never been a spy in my life and I have no intention of starting now", I hissed. I felt rather annoyed that someone might even think that I might be party to such a scheme.

"Right", replied Jimmy, "but I think you will find out that he will manage to get a few fellows to do his dirty work".

I was to find that, to some extent, Jimmy's view

of the Dean's methods was accurate but on the other hand he was always helpful and had our best interests at heart.

The music lectures took place in the front room of the old house, which in former years had probably been the family sitting room. Fr. McEnaney stored his books in a small store at the back of it and this store was approached by means of a long dark corridor. He appointed a student called Brian McCall to go and fetch the books at the start of each lesson. He relied on Brian for many things and for that reason Brian was not too popular as he was suspected of being a spy.

We soon discovered that the little store was like an Aladdin's cave where all sorts of things had been discarded over the years. One such item was a skeleton about five feet tall. I was approached one day by one of my classmates called Sean McLaughlin, who was a scientist and an artist. "Would you like to give me a hand?" he asked. "I have an idea for playing a good trick on Brian when he goes to get McEnaney's books".

We went to the store and Sean got me to hold the skeleton while he painted some of the bones with florescent paint. He then painted a horrific face on a piece of stiff paper and fixed it to the skull and we suspended the skeleton in a corner opposite the door. Sean then removed the light bulb from its socket and replaced it with a special one, which did not show much light but made the paint glow in the darkness. By the time Sean had completed his work, once the light was switched on, the skeleton looked like someone who had just risen from the dead.

At the start of the next music lecture, Fr. McEnaney asked Brian to go and fetch his books as usual. Almost immediately, we heard a yell of horror and a few seconds later Brian came staggering through the door, his face a deathly white. "G- G- G-Ghost", he stammered, looking in horror at Fr. McEnaney, and fell on the floor in a faint.

A couple of people, who had experience in first aid, rushed to help and Brian slowly regained consciousness. "Ghost", he gasped, his eyes wild with fright. "Ghost in the store".

Having assured himself that Brian had not suffered any permanent damage, Fr. McEnaney went out and examined the store. He came back in a couple of minutes, obviously annoyed. "I suppose", he said, "that there is no use in my asking the smart fellow or fellows who set this up to come forward and admit it. It was a foolish and potentially very dangerous thing to do and if I find out who was behind it, I will take serious action. Poor Brian here might well have had a heart attack and if that had happened I wonder how those responsible would have felt".

Fr. McEnaney never found out who was responsible and in a short time the incident was forgotten, except for the fact that from that day, Brian totally refused to go and fetch the books.

As soon as the music class finished on the first

morning, a fairly tall, middle-aged gentleman came in and stood for a minute or two looking all round the room as though searching for something or someone. Having stood thus for half a minute or so, he gave a big sigh and said, "thirty-eight, that's eight or nine too many. We will have to get rid of a good few of you fine fellows before the end of the year. I wonder now which of you will be saying goodbye".

Once more he stood surveying us, perhaps in an attempt to gauge what effect his kindly introduction was having. "My name is J.J. Campbell", he announced slowly. "I am in charge of education and as such I am the most important person in this institution, so far as you people are concerned. Indeed, I might tell you, many people would claim that I am one of the most important people in this province of Ulster, if not on the entire island of Ireland. Soon you will be learning about intelligence quotients in your studies, but I can tell you now that my I.Q is so high that it goes off the scale altogether at the top end. I am a genius and you will soon realise that I use my extraordinary gifts in a most constructive way".

Mr Campbell then settled into our first education lecture, which, like every one of his lectures that would follow over the next few years, was as dead and boring as it could possibly be. He seemed to go out of his way to make his presence as uninspiring for us as he could. I have wondered ever since if he did this deliberately, in order to show us that it was exactly the wrong way to handle a class.

Education was a pretty boring subject at the best of times, but he killed it outright. We soon discovered that, behind this acerbic exterior, he was kind, gentle and helpful on a one-to-one basis, and was, as he kept insisting, a very intelligent man indeed. He spent endless hours showing us how to structure reading lessons, so as to make them lively and interesting for our future students. He insisted that the key to good teaching was to make it enjoyable and entertaining, which is the main reason why I have always wondered if he was playing a game with us in his own lectures. His threat to get rid of eight or nine of us proved groundless. One fellow left after three or four months but otherwise all of us completed the course.

Mr. Campbell was in no way typical of the rest of the staff. His colleagues treated us like mature adults, which I found surprising and very pleasant, having been treated like a child in Armagh. It took me some time to realise that no one was going harass me, whether I worked or not. I was responsible for my own actions. This approach astounded me, since I think that I was somewhat late in maturing, perhaps because of the fact that I was an only child.

The President of the College was a priest called Dr. Rogers. He had been born in India, where his father had held some important post with the British army, or administration. The 'Doc', as we called him, was fairly dark-skinned and looked somewhat foreign, although both his parents, as far as I know, were white people. At that time, he was probably in his late forties or early fifties. He wandered about the building and the grounds looking down at the ground most of the time, as though searching for something, which he had lost. He spoke in an unusual, clipped manner, and always managed to sound extremely funny, even when dealing with the most dull and uninteresting subjects. He had searching blue eyes, which gave the totally false impression that he was constantly on the look-out for some wrong-doing in everyone he met. He was a recognised historian; but his most notable attribute was his declared detestation of women.

On the first Wednesday afternoon of each month the Doc said a Mass for the students in St. Agnes's Church, which was only about three quarters of a mile from Trench House. He had a very special homily, which he delivered at the start of each year. Fifty years later I still remember the greater part of it clearly.

"This afternoon, my dear young friends, I want to direct my remarks, if I may say so, especially to those young fellows who have joined us from the backward, rural areas of this country. As they sit here, they are at a disadvantage since they have seen little except the hidden sides of cabbages or whin bushes. For those of you who do not know, whin bushes are known as gorse amongst civilized people, but if I were to talk about gorse, these young men would have not the slightest idea what I was talking about. Those of you who have been reared in towns might well ask me why our young friends are so familiar with the concealed areas behind whins, and various other plants. It is, if I may say so, because they spend many hours sitting on their hunkers behind such plants, contemplating nature and possibly meditating on the wonders of life. They find themselves thus occupied since our horrible modern toilets have not yet reached the places from which they come".

These revelations were met with howls of laughter, and he stopped to let them subside. He was clearly very pleased with the response to his opening remarks.

"You may laugh, gentlemen, but I have to assure you that these young friends of ours from forsaken rural parts, are in many ways the most fortunate members of the human race. They perform their bodily functions in a manner, which is truly natural, a manner designed by nature, and in so doing have time to contemplate the important aspects of life in a fashion, which has been denied to those of us who are unfortunate enough to have to sit upright on modern conveniences. Those of you who have been on holiday overseas will know that, that most civilized race, the French, realise the importance of these things. Their toilets are simply a hole in the ground, over which one crouches in a most uncomfortable, but perfectly healthy position".

Once more the whole congregation burst into laughter and those of us who were newcomers looked at each other in wonder, amazed by the content of this sermon. It was unlike anything we had ever heard before. But then we were soon to learn that the Doc was a very different person from anyone we had ever met before, or were likely to meet in the future.

"My next words, my dear young gentlemen from the margins of civilization", he continued, "are addressed directly to you. You may dismiss them at your peril, but if you do, some day you will look back on your life and you will wonder in sorrow and regret at how wise and prophetic Doctor Rogers was. I want to warn you about the awful and permanent danger of women. I make no exceptions; I want to warn you about women. They are a living, walking, constant threat to mankind. Attractive yes, but deadly".

The reaction to these words was a mixture of mirth and astonishment. I think I was typical of most of my peers. I was trying to work out if this man was taking a hand out of me. There was a sudden pregnant silence. Everyone wanted to hear more.

"The writer, or writers, of the first book of the Old Testament, if I may say so, were very wise indeed. He, or they, realised the threat that I am trying, probably in vain, to warn you about. They saw poor Adam completely overwhelmed, not by the lure of apples but by the desire to fondle the two semi-orbs placed on the most prominent part of the female form, designed specifically for the destruction of man. Even I, when I go to teach history in your sister college, find it difficult to keep my eyes averted from such female, delicate attractions. In modern times they are packaged in a more provocative manner than ever before in human history. Modern woman, in her deviousness has discovered that things slightly hidden are made even more alluring".

The laughter, which greeted this revelation, was long and uncontrolled. The picture painted by the Doctor's words, and the manner in which it was presented would have done credit to any music-hall comedian. He stood for a long time looking down at the floor, apparently unsurprised and unmoved by the reaction to his warning. He waited until order was restored and he continued:

"I have to tell you, my ignorant young friends that you may well be blinded by the bright lights of the big city, and the dangerous attractions, which those lights hold. The lights may be divided into two different colours but the fact that some are red is not the real danger. The real danger, which few people recognise, is that there are two kinds of women, the professional and the amateur. It may surprise you to hear me say that the professional is not, by any stretch of the imagination, nearly so dangerous as her amateur counterpart. Many foolish men simply pay a fee to them and go on their way. The services are temporary and if you are lucky so is their hold on you. I am not suggesting that you visit them; that would be totally wrong. But I want to contrast them with their amateur counterparts.

"Unlike the professionals, the amateurs are everywhere seeking to lure the male gender to destruction. They can appear so warm, so delightful, so keen to please, so attractive to the weakest parts of human nature. I want to warn you now that you may compete with the professionals, but you will never fathom the depths of the amateurs. I want to give you an example of what I am trying to say by relating for you a true story from history.

"About five thousand years ago, as some of you will know, a great civilization grew up in the valley of the Nile, in a land, which today we call Egypt. This civilization became so advanced and so skilled in building that some of their monuments remain to this day as wonders of the world.

"Amongst the many rulers of those ancient times there was a queen who had a reputation for exceptional beauty and outstanding intelligence. She was an object of desire to all the men around her. She also had the reputation of unbounded ambition and ruled her people with a rod of iron. Anyone who was thought to pose the slightest threat to her power and position was wiped out with cruel efficiency. The loss of a million lives mattered little to this thoughtful, beautiful and ambitious lady.

"This queen had twin sons and when they reached their teenage years a whisper went round the great palace and its court, that the boys were plotting against their mother. I have to tell you that all the evidence we have would suggest that this rumour was totally without foundation; totally false.

"At that time it was the custom for important

people in Egypt to have every part of their bodies tattooed. All manner of exotic animals and scenes were depicted in the brightest colours imaginable. As soon as the queen heard the whispers about her sons, she had the two young men very slowly skinned alive and the skin treated to make shades for the torches, which at that time were used to light the corridors and rooms of the palace.

"A perfect example, if I may say so, gentlemen, of the gentle sex".

We were to discover that each year the Doc gave the same lecture, perhaps very slightly modified, to the women in St. Mary's. The result was that the slightest mention of his name had the girls spitting fire. They detested him with much the same venom with which he professed to detest them.

Three years later, I was doing a new fourth year course, which was completely based in the women's college. It meant that four of us spent a whole glorious year surrounded by three hundred girls. We soon realised that nobody took much notice of us and during a short break each morning we had to put our heads down and shoulder our way through the crowd if we wanted to get a cup of coffee at a small counter. It may seem a very ungentlemanly thing to do, but if one wanted a cup of coffee, there was little option.

One morning I was making my way towards the counter in the usual manner, when my arm was grabbed as I was passing a pillar in the middle of the hall. The Doc was using the pillar as a place of shelter where he might be safe from the mad stampede. He had books under each arm and he looked totally lost and distressed.

"Mr. Daly", he gasped in obvious relief, "I am delighted to see you. You are the first of my species I have seen today. Please stay with me and keep me company until this scene of madness is no more".

At that moment the Doc looked very small and pitiful, even frightened. He was leaning against the pillar with his gown wrapped around him as though to protect himself from the milling crowd. It was only when the crowd had disappeared after a few minutes that he straightened up and assumed his usual posture and air of authority. "Mr. Daly", he said, "I am delighted that you were here to keep me company. This place has for me a distinct resemblance to the trenches of the First World War. All that is missing is the mud and the rats".

"Would you like to have a cup of coffee or tea, and a scone, Doctor?" I asked. "The ladies at the serving hatch are clearing up but there would still be some things left".

The Doctor looked startled, and stood for a moment looking down at the floor without saying a word. He then looked at me as though waking from a dream. "Mr. Daly", he said slowly, "if I may say so, you have taken me unawares. Students do not normally ask me to have a cup of tea. I do not normally have tea at this time of the day. I do feel a little thirsty at the moment, however, and I will accept your offer. Where can we sit?"

"There is a small table in the corner there, Doctor", I said, pointing to the table, "and there are a couple of chairs, which the girls use when they are organising things. Would you prefer tea or coffee?"

"I'll have a cup of coffee, if I may, and nothing else", he replied.

As soon as we sat down, the Doctor's eyes seemed to penetrate my very being as he looked at me across the little table. It was certainly not an uncomfortable feeling; it was just unusual and somehow friendly and caring.

"Mr Daly", he said slowly, "do you not feel very uncomfortable and lost in this establishment, surrounded by these hordes of predatory females?"

"I feel quite at ease, Doctor", I replied light-heartedly . "The four of us on the course settled in very quickly and no one takes the slightest bit of notice of us".

At that juncture a group of girls passed through the hall on their way to some activity. One of them was a small red-haired girl from near Banbridge called Mona Byrne and I had been going out with her for a few weeks. As she passed she raised her fists and scowled at me behind the Doc's back.

The Doctor, unaware of what was going on, was shaking his head and slowly sipping his coffee. "Mr. Daly", he asked, "am I right in thinking that you were a boarder at a secondary school?"

"Yes Doctor", I replied, mystified as to how he was able to know this. "I was a boarder at Armagh College".

"So you have been away from home for quite a few years", he said. "Did you not feel very separated from your parents and brothers and sisters?"

"I have no brothers or sisters, Doctor", I replied. "I am an only child but for a while in my first year I did feel a terrible home-sickness. It passed after a few weeks and from that time on it was not so bad".

"And how did you feel about being cut off from your mother?" he asked.

I thought this a very strange question, coming from this proclaimed hater of women. I wondered why he was so anxious to know how I felt about this subject. I took quite a few moments to think before answering. While I was still considering my reply, the group of girls passed once more, this time going in the opposite direction. They were carrying a red paper banner about four feet long and a foot deep, stretched out between them. On it, in heavy black letters, was the word 'traitor'. They went on their way obviously quite pleased with themselves.

"You know, Doctor", I answered slowly and thoughtfully, "as a child at home I spent very little of my time in my mother's company. I was usually out round our wee farm working, or running the fields scourging a hoop. But looking back, I now realise that any day when my mother was not at home was a bad and lonely day for me".

The Doctor sat bolt upright, looking intensely into my eyes. "Mr. Daly", he said in a surprised tone, "I am beginning to wonder if we are speaking the same language. I have heard of people being scourged and I could imagine some cruel person scourging an animal but why on earth would anyone scourge a hoop. What could a hoop have done on you that you might wish to scourge it?"

I laughed. "I used to run over the fields with a short stick in my hand with which I guided the rim from the old wheel of a bicycle", I explained. "Sometimes I would use the stick to hit the hoop rather than holding it steady. It was a form of play that most of my friends were fond of. I must have spent hundreds of hours running the fields with my hoop. It is called scourging a hoop in the part of the country where I live".

The Doctor looked down at the table and shook his head, as though thoroughly perplexed. At last he looked up at me once more. "Mr. Daly", he said, "I have noticed that you spend an inordinate amount of time trying to beat the devil out of a round piece of leather with that bat of yours, which I am led to believe is called a hurley stick".

I nearly fell off my seat in surprise. I had taken up hurling in my first year and we had formed a hurling team and taken part in the Antrim leagues. Never in my wildest dreams, however, would I have thought that the Doctor would have been aware of this, nor of the fact that we practised most evenings in the field at the back of the college. He smiled at my obvious surprise.

"Mr. Daly", he continued, "I would have to be very blind not to see you fellows acting so strangely as I look out of my office window. But I am interested in what you said about how you felt when your mother was not at home. In my own case, if I may say so, I was sent off to boarding school at six years old and that boarding school was hundreds of miles away from my home. If I may say so, I hardly had a chance to get to know my mother. The boarding school was a lonely and heartless place, where one had no caring friends amongst the staff".

He was now looking at me, but there was a far-away look in his eyes, as though he were dreaming. A moment later he rose and explained to me that he would have to hurry to get the bus up to Trench House for his next lecture. "Mr. Daly", he said, "it has been a real pleasure talking to you. I must get into the habit of having informal meetings with my students more often. I hope you learn as much from my history lectures as I have learned from you in this short space of time".

I assured him that there was an awful lot to learn from his lectures and that I enjoyed them, though I could not imagine what he might have learned from me. I sat at the table thinking for a long while after he had gone. It seemed to me that the man suffered from a deep frustration and sadness, which resulted from being separated from his mother as such an early age. I thought that it explained a great deal about his declared antipathy to women. I have felt very thankful ever since that sheer chance had given me the opportunity of having that short conversation with him. I have a strong feeling that the Doctor's problem with women was that, deep down, he was terrified by them and reacted accordingly.

CHAPTER 32
TROUBLE WITH A SPADE

I found myself assigned to a subject called rural science, which was in the care of Mr. Reilly who was generally known as 'Roots'. The subject was restricted to those who did not have a background in general science and we were known, and to some extent derided, as the 'clod-hoppers'. In good weather we spent our time in the garden or the greenhouse and in very bad weather we had normal indoor lectures on plant biology.

At one stage towards the end our first year Roots was showing us the traditional methods of preparing a garden by double digging or even treble digging. Many of the students were from town backgrounds and did not find digging easy. He was engaged on this process one day when an inspector arrived. The inspector was an Englishman who had written books about greenhouse techniques and was recognised as one of the leading experts in the British Isles. It was easy to see that Mr. Reilly was very ill at ease. A number of the students in turn exhibited their inability to handle a spade proficiently and Mr. Reilly did his best to show them how it should be done. In truth he was little better than they were in my opinion. After one such exhibition he handed me the spade and asked me to have a go.

I looked in disgust at the little English spade, which he had handed me and then I walked over to a wheelbarrow and exchanged it for a lovely new Irish spade. As soon as I lifted it I realised that it was beautifully balanced and it felt as light as a feather. It was a masterpiece of craftsmanship. I went back to the plot and began digging and nobody said anything for about five minutes. Even though I was doing something, which I had spent endless hours doing at home, I felt rather foolish with everyone's eyes on me.

"Stop", said Roots at last and reached out to take the spade out of my hands. He handed it to someone else and asked him to have a go.

"Could I interrupt, please Mr. Reilly?" asked the inspector, coming forward. "I want to ask this gentleman a few questions".

"That's fine", said Roots uneasily.

The inspector turned to me and asked, "why did you change spades when Mr. Reilly asked you to dig?"

I wondered if I had got myself into trouble and I did not want to insult the Englishman but I reckoned that I had no option but to be honest.

"I cannot see Sir", I said, "how anyone could really dig with that little tool. Whatever it was made for it was certainly not made for prolonged or heavy digging. Even Mr. Reilly was killing himself and if he had to dig a large area of ground he would be exhausted in no time at all".

The inspector walked over and lifted the little spade from the barrow where I had left it. He placed it beside the Irish spade, which I had picked. "Could you explain to me", he asked, "why you think one of these spades is better than the other?" The question was put in an inquiring and kindly tone, which told me that the man really wanted to know.

"The spade should be used as a lever", I answered, feeling very ill at ease, "and the man using it should allow the lever to do the work. The small spade is too straight, its handle is too short and its blade is the wrong shape. The big spade will do the work almost without any effort if it is handled correctly".

"Where did you learn to dig?" asked the inspector. "Have you been working on building sites in England?"

"Not at all", I answered, "but we have a couple of acres of strawberries at home and in my holidays I sometimes spend thirteen or fourteen hours a day digging in them and I have been doing that for years".

"Did you work out that explanation about the lever on your own while you were working?" he asked.

"No", I answered. "My father explained that to me years ago and showed me how to use the spade so that I could make it do most of the work. At least that is what I try to do".

"Very interesting", said the inspector, rubbing his chin and looking thoughtfully at the Irish spade. "Is your father good with the spade himself?"

"I would doubt very much Sir", I said, "if you would find a better man with a spade anywhere, or indeed with any farm tool that you might care to give him".

The inspector turned to Mr. Reilly. "I think, Mr. Reilly", he said, "that if you want to demonstrate the correct method of handling a spade you would do well always to employ this young gentleman. I have only once seen a spade handled with equal proficiency and that was by an Irish navvy on a building site some years ago. Even though I am English and his explanation is dismissive of the English spade, I have to admit that what he says makes a lot of sense".

The two men wandered off towards the college and we were left alone until the period ended. We were making our way out of the garden when Roots came striding down the path, red faced and clearly annoyed. He strode straight to me.

"Did you go out of your way to make a fool of me out there?" he asked angrily.

"I did not indeed Mr. Reilly", I answered. "I thought I did everything I was asked to do and I answered any questions that I was asked as best I could. I don't know what else I could have done".

"I suppose you think you know so much more than I do about this subject that you could give me lessons in every aspect of it", he snapped.

"I do not indeed", I answered. "I knew nothing at all about mixing composts nor about how to use a greenhouse. I have learned an awful lot so far and I know that there are oceans of things that I still don't know. It's just that I happened to have one of the best teachers in the world on how to use a spade".

"Well, since you regard yourself as such a marvellous man with a spade", he said, "you can take the next two periods and dig that patch of ground that has been marked out. I'll tell the Dean what I have assigned you to do".

I looked at the patch of ground that he had indicated and thought about what had happened. I felt that I was being accused of wrongdoing when I had not committed any crime. I was about to tell him to go and dig it himself when I realised that the next period was music and it was a lovely day to spend in the open air. I walked over, lifted the spade and began to dig.

There was an uneasy relationship between Mr. Reilly and myself in the next couple of years and I certainly felt ill at ease in his company. Things came to a head when I was finishing third year and had chosen a new fourth year course, which was to be based in the women's college. I had no longer any connection with Mr. Reilly nor with rural science.

The twelve people on our course were given the opportunity of going to Dublin to visit a school for deaf girls there and four lecturers were asked to transport us in their cars. It so happened that the four men on the course were assigned to Mr. Reilly's car.

We started off at half past nine or so and Mr. Reilly drove like a bat out of hell, explaining that he had business to transact on the way and he was short of time. The traffic was heavy in Newry and Dundalk, however, and it was nearly eleven o'clock when we arrived in Drogheda. He drove into a car park and stopped. He got out of the car and explained that he had people to see in the town but that he would not be very long. We were to stay in the car until he came back and then we would go for a meal.

More than an hour and a half went past before Mr.Reilly reappeared and we were starving. He rushed up to the car, jumped in and started the engine. He handed us a paper bag in which we discovered four buns and four small bottles of lemonade. "I got badly held up", he said. "There is no time to go for a meal because we have to be at the school for a quarter past two. That will have to do you until after the visit".

The visit to the school was a really wonderful experience. The girls were totally deaf but they were able to put on an exhibition of Irish dance and song and managed to communicate with us almost as though everything was normal. It was explained to us that music had to be somewhat louder than normal because they had learned to pick up the vibrations of sound from the walls, ceilings and floors. In conversation they had to lip-read. I found it a very humiliating and enlightening experience, to see how those girls and their teachers were able to cope with such profound disability. They were so full of the joy of life that I still marvel at their smiles and laughter to this day.

The one thing, which cast a shadow over the entire day was hunger. I was so famished that I had a light head and my three companions in the car said that they felt exactly the same. It did not help when we discovered that the eight girls, who had travelled in three cars, driven by other lecturers, had been treated to a sumptuous lunch and were completely at ease. One of our group, a fellow from Dungannon called Mickey McLaughlan, kept muttering that Reilly had taken a good lunch in Drogheda while we, like stupid fools, sat in the car. When the visit was over Mr. Reilly informed us that he was in a hurry and there would be no chance to have a meal before we got home.

A couple of days later I was working one evening in the library in Trench House and most unusually, it happened that I was completely alone. I had been there for about half an hour when Dr. Rogers came in and started searching for a book. "Mr. Daly", he said, "it is a great joy, if I may say so, to see that you are making good use of the library. Have you read many of these books, which decorate the walls?"

"I have scanned through some of them Doctor", I replied, "and I have read four or five, I suppose".

"Myself", he said, opening his arms to indicate the entire shelves, "I have either read or written every one of them". With this remark he picked a book and turned to go out. He was about to open the door when he turned and looked back at me. "Mr. Daly", he asked, "did you enjoy the day out, which your group had in Dublin?"

"It was a really enlightening experience to see how those girls and their teachers were able to overcome deafness", I replied. "It was something that I had not thought a lot about before and I learned a lot. It was an experience, which I would have hated to have missed. It would have been a really enjoyable day but for the hunger".

The doctor slowly let go of the handle of the door and came back and stood directly opposite me at the table. He left his book down on the table and held the back of a chair in both hands and leaned over it towards me. He gazed intently into my eyes.

"And why, if I may be so bold as to ask, Mr. Daly, did it happen that you were hungry?" he demanded.

"Well Doctor", I replied, "the four of us boys were with Mr. Reilly and he was in a hurry all day so that we did not have time to get anything to eat except a bun each and a wee bottle of lemonade at Drogheda".

The Doctor leant over the chair so that he was a little closer to me. "Surely", he said, "you left here just before nine o'clock in the morning and you did not have to be in Dublin until after two o'clock in the afternoon. Where did you spend all that time?"

"Mr. Reilly left us in a car park in Drogheda, Doctor", I explained. "He said he would be a very short time but he was away for well over an hour. He gave us each a bun and a wee bottle of lemonade and then he rushed directly to the school in Dublin. He had promised that we could have a meal but he said there was no time. When the visit was over he rushed home as he explained that he had an urgent appointment".

The Doctor straightened up without taking his eyes from my face. "Do you mean to tell me Mr. Daly", he asked in clipped tones, "that you four men did not have a morsel to eat all day except a bun? Have I been hearing correctly?"

"I'm afraid that is what happened Doctor, but in truth I don't think it was anybody's fault", I replied quietly, now aware that he was becoming very annoyed and angry. He stood for a long time staring at me and shaking his head. Finally he lifted his book and slammed it down on the back of the chair.

"Mr. Daly", he said, "I can only say that I am dismayed and disappointed and I am very angry. I want you to tell your three companions that I apologise to them from the bottom of my heart. That day was supposed to be an acknowledgement to all of you for choosing to do a new and difficult course next year. You were all meant to have a very special day out. By the way, were the women treated in the same manner?"

"Apparently they had a fabulous lunch Doctor", I answered. "And then they had another meal on the way home. They had a great day altogether. Mr. Reilly had us back in Belfast before seven o'clock but they did not get back until nearly eleven".

"This is most embarrassing", said the Doctor. "I have to tell you Mr. Daly, that Mr. Reilly was given sufficient funds to treat you men royally. The black hole of Calcutta is the only place fit for him and I can tell you he will wish he were there when I get an opportunity to speak to him. I feel let down and thoroughly ashamed".

"Och, it's not that important Doctor", I said. "I would not have missed seeing the work in that school for the world and in many ways it was a wonderful day. Please don't worry about it".

"Well, I hope that you enjoy the course next year", he replied, "and I certainly hope that nothing like this ever happens to you again".

He took his book and went out but it was easy to see that he was still very annoyed.

A few days later I was lifting my bicycle at the front of Trench House when Roots came striding out of the garden wearing a pair of wellingtons. He marched so purposefully towards me that I thought for a moment he was about to hit me. I began to mount my bicycle as though I had not seen him.

"Stop there for a minute", he shouted, "I want to talk to you".

I got off the bike and leaned against it looking at him. He was red faced and looked really annoyed.

"You can count your lucky stars that you have all your exams finished", he said, glaring at me. "If you were not in that situation I'd make you think twice before you open that big mouth of yours, you slabber".

I didn't say a word but went over and left my bike against the wall again. I turned calmly and faced him. "You seem to have a crow to pick with me", I said quietly. "That's fine with me. Come on now, this minute and we'll sort it out in Doctor Rogers's office. I saw him going in a few minutes ago. I'm sure he'd love to act as referee. I'm sure that he'd be delighted to hear that in addition to all your other derelictions of duty, you are now threatening his students".

I walked towards the main door but Mr. Reilly stood as though rooted to the ground. I was already going up the steps when he called, "Where are you going?"

"I'm going to the Doctor's office", I replied over my shoulder and climbed another step.

"There's no need for that", he called to me, "we'll forget about the whole thing".

"I'm afraid my memory doesn't work that way", I called back and walked into the building. I slipped into the library and found a place where I could see him but he couldn't see me. He stood at the front of the building for a couple of minutes as though unsure what to do and then he turned and went slowly towards the potting shed to change his footwear. I felt fairly sure that it would be a long time before he tried to play another dirty trick on any of his students.

It was a great but very pleasant surprise when I discovered that dancing classes were part of our curriculum at Trench House. The classes were held in the Kingsway ballroom, which was in King's Street in the city centre and they lasted for two hours every Thursday evening. For us first years a sheet was put up on the notice board, which paired us each with a girl from the women's Training College. It was an attempt to break the ice and to let us get to know some of the girls. I have no idea how Dr. Rogers felt about the arrangement but he must have agreed to it.

As soon as the sheet appeared on the board, I was approached by one of my classmates called Danny Slattery. "I see that you have been given my girl friend as your partner", he said. "We have been going together for a couple of years and I would like to change partners with you for the rest of the year".

Naturally I agreed immediately since I had never set eyes on either girl and secondly Danny was well over six feet in height and built like a tank. Danny was actually very gentle and friendly but I can't imagine anyone picking a fight with him if they could avoid it. It emerged that very few of us stayed for long with the girl who had been chosen for us and very soon the lesson became like an ordinary dance where everyone picked his or her own partner for each dance.

The teacher was a wonderful dancer called Victor Silvester who had won prestigious dancing competitions all over the world. He had his wife as assistant and, as far as I could judge, she was as good, if not better, than he was. I marvelled at the gracefulness with which they could sweep round the floor, their feet and bodies in perfect unison.

The dancing classes were a very pleasant interlude but I did not benefit from them as much as most of my companions. My feet completely refused to respond in the manner desired, or rather I suppose my mind did not inform them correctly as to what they were supposed to do. As I responded to the rhythm of the music as I felt it was natural to respond, Victor sadly shook his head and tried to show me what I was doing wrong. Mrs Silvester even took me apart for special sessions but all her efforts were to no avail. I came to the conclusion that for dead sure I would never be a dancer.

There was one very obvious disadvantage in not being proficient at the dancing. It was much more difficult to get to know a girl and the fact that her poor toes were suffering was not the best form of introduction. At the dances at home my friend Tommy Jordan was not much better that I was but he had developed an interesting way of explaining his problem to a girl with whom he was dancing for the first time.

"You seem to be a wee bit awkward at the dancing", he would say to her when they had completed a couple of rounds of the hall.

"What do you mean?" she would answer haughtily, "you have my poor toes all tramped black and blue".

"I can't understand this at all", was Tommy's stock reply. "I can dance the very best with any girl in this hall but you and you have the whole toes tramped out of my shoes".

CHAPTER 33
GAELIC CONNECTIONS

There was another ballroom near to The Kingsway, which was called The Orchid and it had a dance, which started just as our dancing class was ending. It was very popular and many of us made our way there each Thursday evening. It was at The Orchid that I met a girl from Gaoth Dobhair in Donegal and we started to go out together about once a week. We went for long walks or spent hours over a cup of tea or coffee in the Continental Café, which was in Castle Street. Not a word of English was ever spoken for Máire was a native Irish speaker and my command of the language improved immensely.

We had been going out for about six months when I became aware of her staring into my face in the café, one evening. "Why are you looking at me like that, Máire?" I asked, feeling a little puzzled and uneasy.

"This is the last time that I am going out with you", she answered quietly.

"Why is that?" I asked. "Have you met someone else?"

"No, it's not that", she replied. "But I have come

to the conclusion that you have not got the slightest interest in me really. I think that you are only interested in my Irish. You insist on speaking Irish all the time and I have the feeling that you only want to improve your command of the language. Can you truthfully tell me that I'm wrong? Otherwise, it's time we parted company".

I sat there for a minute or two, feeling embarrassed and very guilty. "I have enjoyed going out with you very much indeed, Maire", I said at last. "I would hate to think that we can't remain good friends".

The girl shook her head and laughed quietly. "I knew I was right", she said. "You have managed to improve your Irish over the past few months and that was what was attracting you. It was your aim all the time. I have a boyfriend back at home too and it's not fair to go out with someone else if I'm going to marry him. There's a girl I know from home and her Irish is as good as mine. Maybe you'd like to go out with her for a while, that is if you have time to go out with anyone with all this hurling that you are so fond of. I'll introduce you to her and see if she can do anything with you if you like".

"Oh, so you were two-timing the both of us", I said with a grin and a wink. "You're not as nice a girl as I thought you were. You're a right rogue".

Maire shook her head and rose from her seat. "I'm going off to meet a friend", she said and walked out of the café. I never saw her again although I went to The Orchid for years afterwards.

Across the street from the Orchid was the Barmen's Club. It was on the second floor of a big building but I am not sure why it had got its name. It was really a place where diehard republicans went for a night out or perhaps to plot a little treason. I loved it because of the high standard of ceili dancing and the preponderance of traditional music.

The third venue where I spent a lot of time was the Ard Scoil, which was just off Castle Street. There were lots of Irish classes held there as well as plays and dancing competitions. Soon after I discovered the place, someone in authority suggested that I take responsibility for the very young children who were considered impossible to control. I am not sure that anyone considered that they could be taught.

There must have been well over fifty of them in one class and their ages ranged from five to seven or eight. I am fairly sure that their parents were not too anxious about whether they learned any Irish or not but they were probably delighted to get them out of the house for a while and to have the services of a free child minder. I felt that the time I spent with the children was nearly chaotic but the people in charge assured me that I was doing a marvellous job. They seemed truly amazed that anyone could attain the level of control, which I had. They told me that it was almost miraculous and pleaded with me to continue in the post, which was, of course, voluntary.

I would probably have thought that they were

taking a hand out of me but for the fact that they insisted that I act as judge at the biggest Irish dancing contest of the year. I tried to argue that I knew nothing about judging Irish dancing but they insisted that anyone who could do such a marvellous job with the small children was well able to adjudicate at this important event. I have no doubt that had the dancers or their teachers known my background knowledge of dancing, there would have been a riot.

The competition lasted for over four hours and I marked the competitors according to how I felt about their performance. I had not the slightest clue about the finer intricacies of the steps. In the end everyone agreed that I had done a very satisfactory job and had acted very fairly. I look back on it as one of the times when I had foolishly got myself into an impossible position and through sheer luck managed to escape in one piece. The people in charge tried to book me for another event but I reckoned that great luck usually doesn't strike twice in the same place and I flatly refused.

It was at the Ard Scoil that I met Sean Kearney. Sean was a small man, probably in his early thirties, who seemed to be in charge of everything even though his command of the language was not great. He expended lots of energy in organising and seemed always to be on the move directing people. He muttered a few basic words or phrases now and then but generally communicated in English. A week after I had adjudicated the dancing competition, he stopped me as I was coming out of the room with the small children.

"I have to say that you are doing a great job here altogether", he said, shaking my hand. He had the coldest, motionless blue eyes I have ever seen in my life and I had the impression that he felt that I should do exactly as he wished no matter what that was. I felt really uncomfortable in his company. "Thanks very much", I muttered, attempting to go on my way. He took me by the arm and held me in a grip like a vice.

"I want to talk to you", he said and the tone of his voice suggested that I had no say in the matter. "I have been watching your work with the youngsters and I want you to take over a class of adults for me. There are twenty-two young girls in it about twenty years of age and they are dead keen. It would be for about two hours on a Wednesday evening starting at seven o'clock and it is held up in Cyprus Street. You can't say no".

The steel blue eyes had never moved while he was speaking and I read in them a message that defied me to refuse. I was annoyed that this man was demanding that I do a job and giving me no chance of refusing. At the same time the idea of teaching a class of around twenty young women was appealing. I looked at a picture on the wall behind him to his left, avoiding the constant glare in his eyes.

"I have a lot of things on my plate at the minute", I said quietly but firmly. "I don't think I should take on any more for the time being. Maybe next year I will consider it again if you are still interested".

Once again my arm was held in a vice-like grip. "Come with me now", he persisted in a slightly angry tone. "I want to show you the set-up that we have in Cyprus Street. It is only a couple of hundred yards away and is on your road home. You can hardly say that is too much to ask".

We walked down the hall together and I collected my bicycle in the porch at the front door. I wheeled the bike as we walked along the footpath for a few hundred yards and then turned left into a small side street. It was a lovely moonlit night but it was getting late and I was not at all happy in this man's company. He took out keys and opened the front door of a small house on the right.

"Leave your bicycle there beside the window", he commanded. "Follow me up the stairs and I'll show you our wee club".

Two rooms on the first floor of the little house had been recently renovated to some extent and now served as reasonable classrooms with fairly big blackboards on one wall. All around the room were pictures of republican heroes with a huge copy of the 1916 proclamation in pride of place on the back wall. The place had a homely feel and I could visualise twenty young women seated on the chairs, which had arm rests as supports for writing materials.

Sean stood on my left staring steadily into my face. "Well", he said after a few seconds, "what do you think of the work we have done here in the last few weeks? Surely this would be a grand place to help a group of lovely girls acquire a grasp of the language? If you agree to give it a try, I'll arrange for someone else to take over down at the Ard Scoil and that will save you a bit of time. What do you say?"

I stood for a while gazing at the pictures around the room as though I had a great interest in them. I was avoiding looking at Sean but I was aware of his constant gaze and I was feeling more and more ill at ease. "Surely it would be unfair to leave the wee ones in the lurch?" I said at last.

"We have a girl who can take over for a month or so", he replied curtly. "Will you give it a go next Wednesday?"

"You suggested a two hour session", I said slowly and thoughtfully, "that seems a bit long to me".

"There will be a break of twenty minutes or so in the middle", he said. "It's more like an hour and a half and by the time they get settled down it will be less than that".

"Right", I said at last, "I'll give it a try on Wednesday but if I'm not happy that will be the end of it and I'll not take any arguments".

"That is all I was asking for", he replied and led me down the stairs. I rode up the Falls Road in the moonlight that night, wondering what I had let myself in for. There was something about Sean Kearney that I found threatening and I was definitely very uncomfortable in his company. I felt that I had been railroaded into agreeing to take the class and I was sorry that I had agreed. By the time I reached the digs I had almost made up my mind not to turn up on Wednesday.

On Wednesday evening the rain was coming down in torrents and I sat on the edge of my bed for a long time debating whether or not I should go down town. Finally I decided that my word had been given and that it would be unfair to let the girls down. I took the trolley bus down to Castle Street. The door of the house in Cyprus Street was open and I made my way up the stairs to find Sean Kearney addressing the girls. They looked totally cowed and every girl in the room had an open exercise book with a pen poised above it as though about to write for all she was worth.

"I have been telling these girls that you have come all the way from the country to help them", said Sean. "I have warned them to be quiet and respectful and not to give any bother or they will have me to deal with. Now girls, I'll leave you with Mr. Ó Dálaigh." He walked out and pulled the door behind him.

I looked at the girls for a few moments and then I started to laugh softly. They looked at me as though I had gone mad. "Do you know why I'm laughing?" I asked. Nobody spoke and I reckoned that everyone was afraid to speak.

"I'm laughing because you all look as if I am some sort of ogre about to devour you", I explained. "And why have you all got exercise books and pens?"

"Mr. Kearney warned us to take down everything

you would say, or write on the board", ventured one girl.

"Well," I said, "you can put them all away because you are not going to do any writing. We are going to try to talk and play games". Forty minutes later the chairs had all been moved. The girls were in pairs and they were trying to converse with one another. There was quite a lot of productive noise and the fear seemed to have evaporated. Suddenly the door burst open and Sean Kearney came in with a book in his hand.

"Silence", he roared, "attention".

He opened the book and started to read. The story was set in the war of independence and it told about the bravery and suffering of a young man from county Limerick who was a dedicated enemy of everything and everyone British. Sean read for nearly half an hour, at times repeating especially emotive sentences and totally ignoring me. At last he snapped the book shut, warned the girls to be on their best behaviour and started to walk out.

"Excuse me Mr. Kearney", I said angrily, walking across the room to face him. "You asked me to come and take this class and you have the cheek to burst into the room like a savage and disrupt us. How do you explain your lack of manners and your boorish behaviour? You are a disgrace to yourself and to the country you claim to love".

He stood there stunned and silent but I could see seething anger in his cold eyes. I turned to the girls.

"I'm sorry girls", I said softly. "I can't work under these conditions. I thought we were getting on well and I've enjoyed the short time I've had with you. Cheerio and good luck".

I was walking past Sean Kearney to the door when one girl stood up and said, "I want to ask you wait a minute please, Mr. Ó Dalaigh? I have learned more in that class than I've learned in the past couple of months. Please don't leave us when we're just starting. We all enjoyed the class". A chorus of assenting chuckles greeted her remarks. I stood for a moment studying their eager faces and I felt guilty about walking out on them. At the same time I sensed Kearney's mounting anger beside me.

"I would love to stay and try to help you", I said at last, "but I can't work in these conditions. I'm sorry but there's nothing that I can do about it". Once again I turned to leave the room.

"Wait a minute there", said Kearney, his voice full of reluctance and suppressed anger. "Why do you find the history of your country so disgusting? Are you some sort of Brit?"

I looked into his face again and I found the anger he clearly felt almost frightening. I gazed directly into his eyes with what I hoped was determination and disgust.

"That rubbish has nothing to do with the history of my country", I snapped. "It's a load of hog-wash thought up to trap the young and the innocent into hatred and danger. I love the language and everything to do with it. Every person born or living on this island should be able to walk into any Irish class and feel happy and wanted there as far as I'm concerned. I'm certainly not going to be part of a scheme to trap these young people with lies and half-truths. If you want to do this kind of brain washing; do it yourself".

Once again I turned to go out.

"Will you change your mind if I knock the door nicely and apologise for interrupting your work?" he asked. His voice was now much calmer and almost pleading.

"I will not indeed", I answered over my shoulder. "I will take the language class right through and when I'm finished everyone will go home. If that doesn't suit you, find someone else who will act as your lap-dog".

"This place is about a lot more than the language", he growled. "It's about a whole way of life and a way of thinking for which many men and women have given their lives".

"You have answered your own questions and I've already explained why I object to your actions", I said curtly and put my hand on the handle of the door to open it. One of the girls stood up and said, "I think that in fair play we should have a vote on this".

A chorus of 'hear, hear' greeted her words and I thought Sean Kearney was going to choke with anger and frustration.

"We came here to learn our language", the girl continued, her voice steady. "I would like for Mr. Ó

Dálaigh to stay and I'm voting that we do things the way we want. I found those readings dead boring anyway. Anybody who agrees with me can put up her hand".

A forest of hands shot up eagerly. Only two girls at the back kept their hands down and I later learned that they were cousins of Sean's. I stood with my hand still on the handle of the door while Kearney stood as though rooted to the floor. He remained so for a long time and there was a tense silence in the room. Finally he turned and faced the class.

"If I agree to what you ask", he said curtly, "how many of you will agree to remain for twenty minutes or half an hour when the Irish class is over?"

The two girls at the back raised their hands but all the others looked up at him defiantly and folded their arms. He shuffled his feet on the floor, puzzled and annoyed.

"All right", he snapped at last, "you can have your flaming Irish class but I'm disgusted. I go to all the bother of providing these premises and this is the way I'm treated. He rushed past me through the door, which I had opened and he disappeared into a room downstairs. I stayed with the class for two very happy years and I hope the girls gained something worthwhile from their work. I met one girl many years later and she had gained her doctorate in Celtic Studies at the Queen's University of Belfast. Her hearty thanks for getting her started on the road were a very satisfying reward for my efforts.

Blackwatertown Boys' School circa 1948.

Front seated (left to right)

Eddie Donaghy, Francie Mallon, Al Gorman, Billy McCormick, Eamon Murphy, Patsy McCann, Seanie Collins, Malachy McCusker, Sean Gorman, Oliver Brannigan, Ignatius McCusker, Seamus Hegarty.

Second Row

Peter Collins, Sean Hughes, Seamus Mallon, Larry Dobbin, Thomas Jordan, Brendan McCusker, Jim McCormick, Henry Hughes, Mickey Madden, John Madden, Peter Maddigan, Tom Smith, John Connolly, Francie Nugent.

Third row

Barney Hughes, Sean Brannigan, Denis Moley, Joe Daly, Malachy Conlon, Jim Fox, Arthur McKeever, Charlie Hughes, Art Ó Dálaigh, Denis Flannigan.

Back row

Sean Kelly, Pat Mallon, Horace Murphy, John McKeever, Terry Smith, Francie Daly, Pat Gorman, Jim Donaghy, Packie Daly.

Mr. Billy Colgan. Principal of Blackwatertown Boys' School in the 1940s.

CHAPTER 34
INTRODUCTION TO PSYCHOLOGY

Towards the end of our first year at the Ranch Mr. Campbell announced that we were to have a visiting lecturer for a couple of weeks on Tuesday mornings. She was a psychologist and her name was Miss Primrose. She would talk to us about various aspects of trouble and problems occurring in families and how this might impinge on children when they came to school. In his usual sarcastic manner he suggested that we use every little brain cell that we had been given to try and work out even a little bit of what she might be talking about. He asked that we give her our full attention and treat her with respect and decorum.

"I've heard of this auld doll", whispered Sean Ó Connell, who was sitting beside me. "She is some sort of hypochondriac and surrounds herself with all sorts of medicines and takes swigs out of the various bottles while she is talking. She has three or four false teeth at the front of her mouth and she has a habit of lifting them out on the end of her tongue every few minutes. She's supposed to be a rare auld blade altogether".

"You make her sound like a very entertaining visitor", I answered, intrigued by the images Sean has conjured up in my mind.

"Wait till you see", said Sean. "When she moves she's like a Red Indian wigwam with half the tribe in it. She's a bit like Campbell himself and tells everyone that she's a genius".

"I can't wait", I answered, tongue in cheek.

In Gaelic football circles Sean was already recognised at that time as one of the best forwards in Ireland.

The morning of the first lecture came and in walked a young woman who looked like a model except that she was not much over five feet in height. I had seen pictures of the French beauty, Brigette Bardot, and I was convinced I was now looking at her identical twin except that this young lady had auburn hair in place of the blonde mass, which was one of the hallmarks of Bardot. She was dressed in a lovely light brown suit, the skirt of which only reached to about four inches above her knees. Her beautifully-sculpted legs stretched elegantly down to a pair of red, very high-heeled shoes. She had a white silk blouse, which was sufficiently opened at the front to expose what one could only describe as her very generous cleavage. Around her neck she wore a gold chain and from it hung a little gold cross, which dangled in her cleavage as she moved. Pat Casey was sitting behind me and he gave me a dig in the back. "How would you like a night out with that bit of stuff?" he chuckled.

The entire class was sitting mesmerised as the young lady introduced herself and then walked over to the lectern. I felt somewhat crestfallen at the thought that the wooden surround would conceal most of this heavenly vision as it did with all lecturers. There was a chorus of only slightly suppressed grunts and groans and intakes of breath as thirty-seven healthy young men of twenty gazed at their visitor.

My fears proved groundless. The girl laid her books on the lectern, lifted the high stool from its platform, placed it on the floor at our side of the lectern and climbed up to sit on it. She put one foot on one of the rails, which joined the front legs of the stool and then crossed her legs. She then leaned sideways and opened her books to start the lecture. She explained that she would talk for a few minutes on each of the sections to be covered and then she would pause to let us take notes or discuss any problems we might have.

She must have been very aware that every pair of eyes in the room were riveted on her and that her every movement was met with ecstatic groans of delight and anguish as fellows squirmed on their seats. She sat there, however, as though perfectly at ease and I began to wonder if she were carrying out some sort of experiment. She must surely have realised the effect she was having on this particular audience. She was a fine speaker but I doubt very much if any young man in the room remembered or even really heard much of what she said. She had just started her talk when there was a knock on the door and Mr. Breslin, our English lecturer, came in and explained that he might have left a book behind. There was no book and he left with a big smile on his face.

Every few minutes the girl had a habit of straightening up and crossing her legs in the opposite direction and this movement gave her audience the opportunity of a greater appreciation of delights, which were very inadequately hidden in the first place. Yelps or groans of tortured delight could be heard all around the room and there was a rustling of clothing as fellows twisted and turned on their seats.

I got another dig in the back from Casey soon after she began her talk. "What do you think of psychology now Boy?" he asked in a fierce whisper. We were sitting directly in front of her and every time she moved we were enveloped in a waft of exotic perfume. Casey prodded me as one of the waves hit us. "God be praised", he whispered, "but I think I must have landed in heaven and as far as I can make out, I didn't even have to die".

I glanced sideways and Sean Ó Connell looked as though he were in a lovely dream and as I let my eyes wander round the rest of the room everyone looked the same. Apart from her voice there was not a sound anywhere except for the expectant breathing of the entranced men. Casey thumped me in the back again and whispered, "calm down, you dog; you'll do yourself an injury".

I was convinced I was looking at Bardot's twin.

The lecture ended and the girl climbed down from her perch and lifted her books to leave. "You have been a very good audience indeed", she said with a lovely big smile. "I hope that I have been able to alert you to some of the more unusual aspects of human nature, which you are likely to encounter in your work. Are there any questions before I leave?"

There was a long silence as everyone gazed at her. She was about to turn to leave when Pat Casey spoke. "You have certainly alerted me to some aspects of human nature in which I am very interested and I can't thank you enough", he said. "By the way, would you be doing anything tonight?"

The girl stepped back in surprise, then burst out laughing, shook her head and flounced out of the room. For a long time everyone sat as though in a trance, looking at each other as though awakening slowly from a wonderful dream.

"That was some Indian tepee", I said to Sean. "If I thought that's what hypochondria does to people, I'd be dead keen to study it all the time".

"That was some exhibition", he said solemnly. "I never saw anything like that in my life. It's like something out of one of those films that they show down in the Mayfair cinema that we're not supposed to go and see. I can't wait until next week".

At that moment Joe Feeney, who had been sitting on the other side of the lectern came over to me. He put his two hands on the front of my desk and leaned down looking into my face. "Next week Art", he said, "I want to change seats with you. You and me have always been good friends and from where I'm sitting I could see damn all except her head and the toes of her shoes. You got a real eyeful today and that should be enough for you. You can't be too greedy. The Lord will reward you".

I looked up into his eager face and I tried to be very serious. "You know Joe", I said as earnestly as I could, "Fr. McEnaney asked us to take these seats so that the lecturers could get to know us by looking at that plan, which he has glued to the table of the lectern. You know that it would break my heart to do anything, which might annoy the Dean. Into the bargain I have become very fond of this wee seat of mine. You can have this seat, however, every day for the next week since you and I have been such good friends".

"God Art, thanks very much indeed", he said with a smile. "I'm going to fairly enjoy her lecture next week".

"Oh, I'm sorry Joe", I said, "I must not have made myself clear. You can have this seat every day for the next week but not for her next lecture. I'm dead interested in this psychology and I'd hate to miss even a very little bit of it. Sorry".

"Maybe you could ask her to sit on the other side of the lectern next week, Joe", said Pat Casey from behind me. "If she does then I'll be over there sharing your seat with you".

I was leaving the room to go to the next lecture

when I met Sean Breslin in the corridor. I could see laughter in his eyes. "Arthur", he said, trying hard to pretend to look serious, "I have a feeling that you have a desperate need to go to confession as soon as possible. I'll try and arrange for the Doc. to hear your confession before the next lecture".

"And why do you think I would need to go to confession Mr. Breslin?" I asked, trying hard not to laugh out loud.

"Well, you have just spent the past hour wallowing in eroticism and bad thoughts", he replied. "Even looking at risqué pictures is forbidden by holy mother church and I would be deeply concerned for your immortal soul".

"Thanks a million for your deep concern Mr. Breslin", I said, "but why do you think that I would have been wallowing in eroticism as you describe?"

"Oh, I've noticed that you are particularly sensitive to all sorts of erotic symbolism in poetry and drama", he said. "You're sensitive and perceptive generally, but you tend to excel in that field. And today I noticed that you managed to get yourself positioned so as to get full value of any eroticism that might be about".

"And what is it that makes you such an expert on wallowing as you describe Mr. Breslin?" I asked.

"Oh that's easy", he answered and burst out laughing. "I myself spent the previous half hour or so wallowing likewise in the staff room and I can wallow with the best of them, I can assure you.

However I'm married and allowed to enjoy that sort of thing". He walked on, shaking with laughter and he was gone before I had a chance to reply.

I was about to get on my bike when Joe Feeney came up to me. "I was serious in there about changing seats Art", he said. "Would you change your mind if I bribed you?"

"And what sort of bribe might you have in mind Joe?" I asked. "As I have tried to warn you I have developed an overwhelming affection for that seat lately".

"Our local football team is having a day out next Sunday", he said. "We are taking a bus and going down to Ballyhornan in County Down. I have an extra ticket and I'll give it to you if you change seats with me when that dame comes back next week. There will be a cup of coffee before we leave and when we arrive in Ballyhornan we'll have two or three hours to swim and fool about on a lovely beach. I know how keen you have become on swimming since the start of the year. This would be a great chance to swim in the sea instead of a pool. There will be a four-course dinner afterwards in an hotel and then there will be music and a bit of craic. I can assure you that it will be a very enjoyable day. Now what do you say to that offer?"

"Be God, here, Joe, that dame must have bewitched you altogether", I said trying to evaluate Joe's offer. "I'd be worried that studying all that forbidden territory might have a bad effect on you. You might have to go to confession and maybe you wouldn't get absolution".

"Damn you anyway Art", he growled. "I know that you don't give two damns about my soul's welfare but what do you say to my offer?"

I stood holding the bike and looking at him. I knew that Mrs Andrews would have the lunch ready and I did not want to be late.

"How long do you want to change desks for?" I asked.

"Holy God would you try to be reasonable?" he squealed. "Don't you know, as well as there's a head on your body, that I only want to change for that one lecture? What's your answer?"

"Right", I said. "If it gives you satisfaction Joe, we'll change places for the one lecture".

"Thanks a million", he said with a relieved tone in his voice, "be at St. Paul's chapel at twelve o'clock on Sunday".

Sunday was a beautiful spring day. The coffee and scones in St. Paul's hall were lovely as was the trip on the bus down to Ballyhornan. Everyone went out their way to be friendly and make their guest feel welcome. I had gone to the baths in Peter's Hill every week on a Thursday evening and thanks to the efforts of our coach, Johnny McGivern, I had learned to swim. I found it doubly pleasurable to swim in the sea and feel the buoyancy of the water. We had games of rounders on the beach and at six o'clock went for a wholesome dinner. Afterwards Irish dancers and musicians entertained us for a couple of hours so that we weren't back in the city until ten o'clock. It had been a really marvellous day.

On Tuesday just before our visitor was due to arrive Joe and I changed places and I could not help noticing how smug he looked as he took my place. As I took my new seat, Jim Harbinson, who was in the desk next to me, looked at me as though he were sure there was something seriously wrong with me. "What the hell has taken you over here?" he asked. "We can see damn all with that bloody lectern and you have left the best seat in the room. Is your head cut?"

"Och, you might be right about my head being cut Jim", I replied. "But sure I love to share things with my friends. It's just that I'm a real good Christian".

One could sense the air of expectation as the time approached for the psychologist to arrive. She arrived dead on time and when she walked in I nearly fell off my seat. She was still lovely but now she was dressed in a skirt, which reached her ankles and she had a military style tunic, which was buttoned right up to her neck. An audible gasp of disappointment went round the room. I looked across to where Joe was sitting and the look on his face could not have shown more disappointment had he got news that everyone belonging to him had been killed. I felt like laughing out loud.

A few minutes into the lecture a note was passed to me from Joe:

"You are one lucky frigger. If you fell into the river

you'd come up with your pockets full of fish. Damn you anyway but you must have second sight".

I heard a story about a psychologist a few years ago and I tried to tell it in verse. It has nothing to do with what happened in the above incident but I found it amusing.

THE PSYCHOLOGIST

It was a bleak December evening
with a dull sky, threatening snow,
And Gerry Mahon to a restaurant,
for a meal resolved to go.
The place was packed with people
being a noted spot to eat,
But the owner was a lifelong friend
and found him a spare seat.

Since the staff were very busy
Gerry had to wait a while,
He bought a drink and gazed around;
greeted people with a smile.
He spied a gorgeous female
at the bar all on her own,
He thought 'company'd be preferable
to eating all alone'.

He marched up to her bravely
and he tapped her on the arm.
"Excuse me", he said gently,
"I don't mean you any harm.
For my meal I'd like a partner
who'd partake in friendly chat,
If you'd care to share my table
I'd be very pleased with that".

The girl jumped up wildly
and threw her arms up in the air.
Her eyes then filled with anger
and she tossed her long dark hair.
"What? What?" she screamed out loudly,
"are you crazy in the head?
What makes you think that I would care
this night to share your bed?"

The diners from their dinners
at this scream at once did stop.
Throughout the crowded restaurant
you could hear a small pin drop.
Poor Gerry's face glowed crimson
as he slipped back to his place,
He was thinking there'd be people
who would savour his disgrace.

It was clear the girl's onslaught
had not been well deserved,
But as he reached his table
his meal was just being served.
He sat down to his dinner
and did his best to eat.
But shame overwhelmed his pleasure
and he squirmed on his seat.

From the tables all around him
he could hear some loud guffaws,
Was there something very funny

about the food inside those jaws?
There were ladies Gerry'd overlooked
at a party or a dance
Enjoying sweet and deep revenge
now they'd been given the chance.

The noise throughout the restaurant
had attained its normal pitch,
But Gerry felt as flustered
as if he'd been dragged naked through a ditch.
It was then the girl approached him
and bent down beside his head,
In soft sweet tones and gentle voice
these words to him she said.

"I am sorry, my dear friendly man,
if I have destroyed your meal.
In front of all these people,
I know how rotten you must feel.
I'm a student of psychology
at the university,
And embarrassment of people
is what I want to see".

"When folk are real embarrassed
I have to study what they do.
And that is why, unfairly,
I was so rude to you.
I really hope you understand
why I put you to this test,

But of all the folk encountered
your reactions have been the best".

"Your friends must all have wondered,
what got into your head,
To make you ask a stranger
to go home and share your bed.
So I must sincerely thank you
for helping with my task,
I would love to share your table
if now you'd kindly ask".

Gerry sat there in stunned silence;
the girl slowly turned away.
He resolved that she'd remember
this bleak December day.
He looked up and he watched her
as she walked back to the bar,
Then his angry shout poleaxed her
before she got that far.

"Why try now to seduce me
as I eat my dinner here?
That I'd think to take your offer
there was not the slightest fear.
How soft and sweet and gentle
your voice in whisper sounds,
But what made you think I'd pay you
a cool three hundred pounds?"

CHAPTER 35
LOOSE ON THE COMMUNITY

Twice each year Ranch students, like the girls in St. Mary's, had to go out to various schools around the city for teaching practice. The first session was a three-week period immediately before Christmas and the second was a similar period immediately following the Easter holidays. These sessions tended to be an unpleasant reminder of the life that lay before us at the chalk face and were in stark contrast to the rather cosseted life style of the Training College. In truth our life there was very easy going and an almost perfect example of what many people might consider as living in an ivory tower.

I got a shock when I entered the school for my very first teaching practice. It was, I think, called St. Gall's and was quite close to Clonard monastery. It was run by an Order of Brothers and on that first morning I went up the stairs to find the head Brother standing on the landing with a big strap in his hand. He was about to come and shake hands with me when a woman rushed past me at the top of the stairs. She was red faced and obviously very angry.

"Where is that wee fat shit that beat the arse of my son last Friday evening?" she roared. "Wait till I get my hands on his throat and I'll take the bloody head clean off him".

The Brother walked forward so that he blocked her passage on the top step. He held the strap in his right hand and pointed down the stairs with his left.

"Get to hell down those bloody stairs this minute, before I kick your big fat arse down them and out onto the street", he shouted. I could see the confidence and the anger draining from the woman's face as she looked up at him. She turned round meekly and did as she was ordered. He watched her until she was half way down. "And don't ever dare to come back here and try to insult one of my teachers", he yelled. "If you ever darken that door again, I'll kick your arse the whole way up the Falls Road before you have time to insult anybody".

The woman looked over her shoulder like a badly beaten dog and continued on her way. The Brother turned to me and held out his hand. "You must be one of our students", he said. "You arrived at just the right time to see how to handle troublesome people. That was a very good lesson. You never give them time to make trouble. You stamp it out before it has time to take root".

That first teaching practice proved to really enjoyable and the teacher with whom I was placed was both friendly and very helpful. Students generally dreaded lecturers from the Training College coming to visit them but I only had one visit towards the end of the period and that was by Jack McCavert. He took me outside at the end of the class.

"You are doing very well for your first attempt at teaching", he said, putting a friendly hand on my shoulder. "You still have an awful lot to learn of course but that will come with time. Aim for the very top". He gave me a friendly handshake and went on his way.

There was a lot of talk amongst the students about a school down in Eliza Street, which was beside the docks and very near to the Inglis bakery. The children were supposed to be impossible and everyone dreaded being sent there but enivitably on every teaching practice, someone was. I was sent there at the start of my second year and I approached the place in fear and trepidation.

The children proved to be very friendly but did not respond to discipline in the usual manner. They wanted to be close to people and I found that when teaching, one or two of them would take me by the hands and if I sat down they would climb all over me. The only trouble was that sometimes there would be squabble in a bid to get sitting on my knee or putting their arms round my shoulder. The teacher explained that they were very natural and were great children if one did not mind them being very close. "In my opinion the only way to handle them is to behave like a hen with a flock of chickens", he said. "Most students find that very difficult and to be truthful many find it impossible". After a couple of days I found the whole thing very pleasant and in spite of all the warnings I had heard I really enjoyed my time there. It was an experience I would hate to have missed.

"How will I manage if one of the lecturers comes to see me?" I asked the teacher on the first day. "Mr. Campbell is due to visit me and everyone dreads the very sight of him".

"First of all", he said, "you must realise that most of these children have been up at five o'clock or soon after and have been waiting for maybe an hour or more outside the bakery. They are given any bread or cakes that have been left over from the day before. That can mean a lot to some of their families. In some cases it can mean survival. As regards the classroom, well there are two ways to handle it. You can try and impose discipline as you would in most other schools and attempt to stand out at the front and teach. In my opinion you will have no chance if you do that. On the other hand you can sit amongst them and talk to them like a kindly father. I find that works well as you may have noticed. I won't tell you what to do; it's up to you".

Mr. Campbell didn't come but Mr. Breslin did and it was towards the end of the second week. By that time I had got used to sitting with children all round me and some clambering all over me. While some of the youngsters moved about, they did not make much noise and they seemed interested in what was being taught. I continued as normal while Mr. Breslin sat and took notes. At the end of the lesson he took me out into the hall.

"I am absolutely delighted to see how you adapted to this school and these children", he said. "I see that you have taken a lesson out of Mr. Tierney's book and joined them rather than try to dominate them. I think that is the only way to succeed but it is a difficult thing to do for a novice teacher. It takes courage and a lot of common sense. If you can succeed in this school, it is my opinion you can succeed anywhere and that is why I am so delighted".

"As you say, Mr Breslin", I answered, "it is only common sense, which is needed".

He looked at me and for once he was serious. "Arthur", he said solemnly, "common sense is a very rare commodity, I have found. I don't know who called it common but that is the one thing that it certainly is not. You think about that and I believe that you will discover that I am right".

For one of my early teaching practices I was sent to a school in Flax Street, which was in Ardoyne. Following Jimmy Andrews' instructions, I cycled down the Falls Road as far as the Springfield Road Junction, turned left up the Springfield and then turned right at Cupar Street and continued along Manor Street. It was only a short distance from there to the school and it was a very pleasant journey.

One morning in the first week I was cycling along Cupar Street and as usual there were lots of cars parked on each side of the road. A big red lorry was double-parked on my side of the street but I paid little attention to it and started to cycle past it. The driver suddenly flung the door open when I was about a yard short of it. I could not stop in time and I slammed into the open door with my face and chest. I seemed to be suspended in mid-air for a moment and then I dropped down and landed on my backside in the middle of the road. My bike continued on its way for a few yards and ended up lying between two cars. Physically I was not really hurt except that my nose was bleeding, but my dignity was shattered and I felt really foolish.

It was very embarrassing when people gathered round me from all directions asking if I was all right. I got up and tried to dust off my clothes and did my best to appear as if nothing had happened. The thing that worried me most was that the blood had stained the front of my shirt and I considered that I was not going to look very dignified in front of a class. The driver had jumped down from the lorry and was part of the crowd around me.

"Are you blind or do you never look where you are bloody well going?" he snarled. "Young people nowadays would need somebody looking after them all the bloody time. You're not hurt, are you?"

I was about to assure him that I was not really hurt when a woman intervened. "I was walking on that footpath on the other side of the street", she said, pointing across the street. "I saw what happened. You flung that door open without looking what you were doing and this poor fellow had no chance of avoiding it. If he wants to get the police for you, I'll tell them exactly what I saw".

"Thank you very much", I said to her. "I'm not hurt and there's no need to get the police. It was just a wee accident".

"I'm sorry", said the driver. "I should have looked before I opened the door". We shook hands.

I went over to collect my bike to discover that my books and my lunch had fallen from the carrier. The books were lying scattered on the road but had not taken any harm. A big brown dog was running down the street with my lunch in his mouth, however, and looking very pleased with his loot. It was not a great start to a school day.

In Flax Street I was placed with a teacher called Tom Honey. He allowed me to teach most of the day instead of the couple of lessons, which I was supposed to take. He sat at the back of the room and took notes on everything I did and at the end of each lesson he took a few minutes to discuss my performance.

"You will never gain confidence", he explained, "unless you have the chance of working a normal school day. You will find too, that you will get used to me criticising you and when those people from the Training College come to see you, you will take no notice of them at all".

*A big dog was looking very pleased with his booty
as he headed off with my lunch.*

At lunchtime Tom took his lunch at his desk and he invited me to join him and keep him in conversation. "Did you ever hear of the Legion of Mary?" he asked one day.

"Is that some sort of religious organisation?" I enquired. "I think I have heard of it but I know nothing about it".

"I am the President of the biggest presidium in Belfast", he said, "I would love if you would agree to join us. Will you come along to the next meeting and I'll introduce you?"

"What sort of work do you do?" I asked suspiciously. "I'm not that fond of praying".

"We don't pray that much at all", he replied. "We go out and visit lonely people or people who are in trouble and we might stay for an hour or two to keep them company or to clean the house for instance. It's mostly practical work. Come along and if you don't like it you can always leave".

It was hard to refuse this man who had been so helpful to me and I agreed to go along to the next meeting. Everyone was very friendly and welcoming and I was teamed with Gerry McCusker from Omagh, who like myself, was a student at Trench House. Gerry was one year ahead of me but we soon became very firm friends.

In the first couple of months our visits were very routine. It was simply a matter of going along and keeping some old person company for an hour or so and maybe washing the dishes or cleaning the floor. One of our regular visits was to an elderly man who lived in very poor conditions in a big house off the Antrim Road. We were warned that he had been a professor but had opted out of normal life and had become a recluse. He did not mind people calling but could be argumentative and difficult. He refused to wash himself or any part of the house and the only food he got was what people brought him from time to time.

The first time Gerry and I called we nearly turned back in the hall to run away. The stench was overpowering and I remember feeling physically sick for quite a few minutes. As we sat down to talk in the living room I slowly got used to the smell and by the time we were leaving it was hardly noticeable. On each ensuing visit, however, we had to get through the odour barrier.

The man was clothed in rags and he had a grey beard, which reached down to his waist. His hair was long and tumbling and all we could see were two bright eyes, which glistened between the thick folds of hair on his head and those of his beard. He very quickly discovered that we were students and took a great delight in trying to catch us out. This was not too difficult for it soon became obvious that he had a wealth of knowledge, the breadth and depth of which was astounding. He had been a classical scholar and he assured us that he was better acquainted with the agora in Athens and the forum in Rome than he was with the centre of Belfast.

I think it was on our third visit that Gerry decided to see if he could persuade him to have a priest call. "Excuse me for asking Professor", he said, "but I was wondering if you would like someone to call and take you to Mass on Sunday".

The old man jumped as though a bee had stung him on the bottom and the bright eyes glared into Gerry's face.

"And why, my dear young fellow, would you think that I might wish to go to a church?" he asked. I could detect an unusual eagerness in his voice and I suspected that Gerry was going exactly where the professor wished him to go. Gerry sat thinking for a moment before he answered.

"I was thinking that maybe you would like to have

a conversation with someone who takes the place of God", he replied, but there was a hint of uncertainty in his voice.

"With God did you say?" said the Professor slowly. "And what makes you think that there is such a person?"

"Och, now, Professor", said Gerry, "sure everyone, who has any sense, knows there is a God".

The old man sat bolt upright, still looking hard at Gerry. He pointed his gloved finger to his chest as he answered, "well I can assure you for certain that I don't know if there is a God and in fact I doubt it very much. Now give me a reasonable answer please. What makes you think there is a God?"

"You and I are very complex beings", answered Gerry. "Somebody with intelligence must have made us".

"And why do you think that?" asked the old man once more.

"Let us look at it this way", said Gerry. "I want you to imagine that you are walking through a huge wood. Everything around you is natural but suddenly you see something bright shining in the undergrowth. You pick it up and discover it is a watch. Surely you would say, 'someone must have made that and the person who made it must have had great intelligence'. But we are far more complex than any watch so someone must have made us and we call him God".

"And who made your God?" asked the old man and there was a air of confidence in his voice like that of a chess player announcing 'check mate'.

"Nobody made him", said Gerry. "He was always there".

"So you give me the example of a watch, to prove that someone must have made a man but then you tell me that nobody made the person who made the man. Surely you can see that there is a dreadful gap in your logic. You have answered me with a *non sequitur*. Would your silent friend not agree with me?" he asked, looking at me.

"I'm afraid no one can prove that there is a God", I answered. "I think it is futile even to try".

"Oh, he exists all right", said the old man, "but only in the minds or in the imaginations of people who claim to believe in him, and I am not one of them".

We left that night and Gerry was very unhappy. At the next meeting of the Legion we were informed that the professor had been found dead the day after we had visited him. I had become rather fond of the old man and I felt a deep sadness to hear of his sudden and lonely death.

A few weeks later we were asked to visit a family where a man had been beating his wife. He was an alcoholic and had been drinking any money that came into the house with the result that the two young children were short of food and clothing. His wife was distraught and had approached the Legion to see if they might be able to help.

"What the blazes do they expect us to do?" Gerry

asked me as we were on the way to get the bus home after the meeting. "I don't like the sound of this at all and I have a good notion to forget the whole thing. My father warned me never to get mixed up in other peoples' business".

"My father always said that only a fool would get in between a husband and his wife", I said thoughtfully. "He assured me that it would end up with both of them attacking the outsider, but och, sure we can go along and have a chat with them anyway, and see what the story is Gerry. If they feel that we're interfering we can always leave".

"Right", replied Gerry, "but I'm telling you I don't like the thought of the whole thing. I have a bad feeling about it".

The family lived near Cromac Street. We went down to the city centre on the bus together and found the house without any bother and knocked at the door. It was about half past eight on a cold winter's night. A small woman came to the door, her clothes somewhat dishevelled and her face red as though she had been crying. We explained we were from the Legion and had been asked to call.

"Thank God", she whispered. "Come on in. He's been on the drink all day".

We followed her into a small room, which at home we would have called a kitchen but she called it a sitting room. There was a big black range with some pots cooking on it and the only furniture in the room was a white deal table and four chairs. Sitting at the other side of the table from us was a huge man, with bleary eyes and tattoos all over his muscled arms. He looked across the table at us as if he were having trouble seeing us.

"Who the effen hell are you and what do you want?" he mumbled angrily.

"We are from the Legion and we were asked to call because we heard that your children were short of food", replied Gerry warily.

"You what?" the man yelled, rising on his elbows and glaring across the table at us.

"We called to see if you would like help with the children's food", I said softly, moving back towards the door at the same time.

"Wait till I get an effen knife out of this effen drawer", he roared "and I'll show you effers what help is".

A moment later we were out on the street and running for our lives, totally unaware of which direction we were taking. He was after us with a huge knife in his hand. For a big man, who was drunk, I was amazed at how quickly he could run. We both played in the hurling team and were regarded as being fast, but he was slowly gaining on us. Fortunately, when we had run about two hundred yards a trolley bus happened to be passing and we managed to jump aboard it even though it was going at full speed. We ended up holding on to each other and lying on the floor at the bottom of the steps, which led to the top deck.

"What do you two fools think you are up to?" yelled the conductor, rushing down between the seats of the bus. I recognised something familiar about the voice and I looked up to see Jimmy Andrews bending over us.

"Arthur!" he said in obvious disbelief. "Are you trying to kill yourself? It's not like you to be so damned foolish and stupid as to jump on a bus like that".

I stood up and pointed out of the back window. "We're running away from that wild man, yonder, Jimmy", I said. "He was threatening to cut our throats and I think he meant it".

Jimmy looked to where I was indicating and drew in his breath. "How did you get mixed up with that man?" he asked. "He's one of the most dangerous men in the city and a few years ago he was the Irish light-heavyweight boxing champion. Since he took to the drink he's lethal. But how the blazes did you get mixed up with him?"

"His wife came to the Legion for help", said Gerry. "They sent us down to see if we could do anything".

Jimmy stood there looking at us in amazement. He did not speak for a long time. At last he told us to take a seat and he would take us to the terminus as we were on the wrong bus and we would have to go to the end of the line and then come right back to the city centre in order to change over to the right one. "You're lucky to be alive," he said. "Anyone who sent two young fellows like you who do not know the city, to see a man like that, should be strung up. I don't care what organization they belong to, they should be strung up".

"I agree with you completely", said Gerry with a scowl. "They'll not be sending me anywhere else for I'll never go back near them in my life again". Gerry kept his word; he never appeared at another meeting.

A couple of months after our adventure Tom Honey decided that the Legion should try to meet people on the streets and it was agreed that the best way to do this was to have a bookstall at Bridge Street corner, which was quite close to the Albert Clock. Permission for this was sought from the police and after a couple of weeks it was granted. A small wooden bookcase on wheels was procured and members took their turns to stand beside it in pairs on a Saturday morning. Each pair did a two-hour stint but it was soon noted that very few people stopped or even passed the time of day with us.

I took over from Tom Honey one Saturday at eleven o'clock and my companion was a new recruit called Frank McKenna. I don't know what Frank did but he was a lot older than me and when I took over he had not arrived. About five minutes later he rode up on his bicycle, however, parked it against a little wall behind us and took his place beside me. He was wearing a heavy overcoat and had a hat, even though it was a warm day.

"I'm not one damned bit keen on this carry-on at

all", he said. "I come from the far end of Fermanagh and I know damn all about Belfast and its people. Have you been at this carry on long?"

"I have only been on a couple of times Frank", I answered. "It only started about a month ago".

"It's a bloody waste of time", he growled. "I wouldn't think much of clearing off now and never taking anything to do with the Legion in my life again. I don't know how I got mixed up with them in the first place. What do you say to people if they stop with you?"

"Och, I would just pass the time of day with them Frank, and maybe discuss some of our wee booklets with them. I keep hoping that they won't ask me too many awkward questions about the books for I haven't read any of them".

We stood there talking for about three-quarters of an hour and we were feeling rather bored when, to our surprise a group of five or six men stopped in a van and set up a similar type of bookstall about ten yards away. One of them was a tall young man dressed in clerical attire. He had a powerful voice and he used it to address the area in general, warning people of the terrible danger they were in if they did not do what God wanted them the do. He had a bitter spite at the Catholic Church and the Pope in particular. It was not long until a crowd gathered but they did not seem to notice us at all. The tall young clergyman had their full attention.

A few minutes later a police constable came along

and stood for a while watching what was happening and then he came over to us.

"Who is in charge here?" he asked.

"I suppose I am Constable", I answered.

"Well, I think you should pack up your gear, Sir, and clear off", he said. "There is a bit of a crowd gathering and it could lead to trouble".

"I'm afraid I have no authority to do that", I said. "We have to stay here for another hour and then we will hand over to the next pair".

"I'm telling you to pack up and clear out", he said angrily. "Can you not understand that?"

"Well Constable", I said, "there is just one problem. We have written permission from the Police Commission to be here and I have no authority to do as you say. I am only a foot soldier in the organization and I don't make decisions. You might like to have a word with this other group, however. I'd be surprised if they have any permission at all".

"So you won't move?" he growled as he moved away.

"You've got it at last", I said. "You are very bright".

I watched him as he walked off towards the Albert clock and then I turned to speak to Frank. His bicycle was gone and when I looked along the street he was disappearing round a corner about two hundred yards away and I never saw him again. I was on my own.

A few minutes later the constable came back but

now he had a sergeant with him. The young preacher had got into full flow by this time and the crowd was increasing by the minute. The sergeant came and looked at our bookcase. He studied it for a moment and then he looked up at me.

"I'm told that you have been advised to move and that you have refused to do so", he said. "Do you not think that was good advice?"

"It may be good advice", I agreed, "but I have not got the authority to move as I have explained to your constable. As I told him we have permission to be here but I don't think these other people have. I can't see why you can't move them if you are so worried".

"I think you are just being crooked and obstructive", he said. "It's not a very wise policy to adopt in this city".

"I can't see how I am being awkward or crooked when we have permission to be here from your head office", I said. "I'll bet you any money you care to mention that this other crowd have not got any permission at all. There was no bother until they arrived".

The sergeant walked over to the preacher. I did not hear what he said to him but I did hear the reply as did everyone within a hundred yards: 'I can assure you, Mister Policeman, that we are not for moving'.

The two policemen wandered off and some minutes later they arrived back with a senior officer. I am not sure exactly what his rank was but he carried a carved baton under one arm. Once again we went through the same ritual and by the time that conversation had ended, the next two men arrived to take over our stall.

There was a heated debate at the next Legion meeting about what we should do. The presidium was evenly divided about whether we should stay and demand our rights or whether it was wiser to leave and avoid trouble. They decided to stay on but a week later that decision was reversed. Crowds had got quite big and at times ugly and most people felt that no purpose could be served by demanding our rights. In my heart I knew that it was the right decision but I argued vehemently against it and when the decision went against me I left the Legion. In truth the incident gave me the excuse I had been seeking for some time.

I discovered later that the young preacher was called the Reverend Ian Paisley and that a fortnight after we left the corner, he left too.

CHAPTER 36
HOME TERRITORY

In third year, which hopefully ended with graduation as a primary school teacher, there was only one teaching practice but it lasted for the entire term following the Christmas holidays. In our case Easter was very late that year and the term was fifteen weeks long. It was, therefore, a fortnight to three weeks longer than average and I was not aware of anyone who was looking forward to it.

For this special practice we had a choice. We could allow the college authorities to allocate us a school in the city or we could apply to spend the practice in our own parish. The college authorities would arrange everything once we had made a decision and I don't think anyone was ever refused permission to spend the practice in his chosen school. I chose to go home to Blackwatertown where I had been for some years as a pupil.

The principal at the time was Frank McAvinchey whom I had known as a pupil although he had never taught me. Bill Colgan, who had been the principal while I had been at school had retired and Mr.

McAvinchey, who had been the assistant, had taken over. Having spent some years at Benburb school, I had gone straight into Mr. Colgan's room on going to Blackwatertown, and in recent years some of the men who had been at school at the time have told me that they envied my good fortune in never having been Frank's pupil.

Great changes had taken place in my home townland since I had gone to board in Armagh eight years before. Probably the biggest change was that electricity had been installed in the mid-fifties and so as I prepared my work I now had a strong, if somewhat harsh light. My mother had bought a television set before any of the neighbours had considered doing so. My father had objected and told her she was mad but soon became a complete addict.

The gravelled lane into our house had been concreted. I had come home after a fortnight's absence to find the job completed and expressed my surprise to my father.

"Thing's are moving on", he said. "We can't stand about waiting until people in Belfast tell us whether or not we should do a job. Nobody round here considered you an expert in that sort of work anyway".

Tractors had appeared at the end of the forties and in the early fifties and horses quickly faded from the scene. Our neighbour, Tom Jordan really made the biggest step upwards of all. He bought a lovely new Hillman Minx car. It was the first private car in the townland as far as I can remember and it was somewhat of a wonder to everyone. It was the beginning of a trend.

I can remember an occasion some years previously when Tom had similarly astounded the neighbours. It was just after the ending of the Second World War I think, when he bought a brand new Raleigh bicycle. It had gears, a case round the chain and a dynamo. People came from far and near to see it and it was a source of wonder for quite a while. People marvelled that any man could afford to spend £14.10s on a bicycle. It was more than the price of a good beef calf!

In our case, apart from the electricity and the television we had not really moved with the times.

In those days, in most Catholic schools, boys and girls had separate establishments. In Blackwatertown the boys' school was housed in an old creamery and the girls were across the road and I think the clergy felt that this was at a safe distance. Frank's wife Mary, was principal of the girls' school.. The creamery was too small to hold all the boys. The two senior classes, made up of boys more than twelve years old, were taught by Charles Dillon in a room at the back of the stage in a parochial hall, which was on the girls' side of the road. It was in a very poor state of repair and Doctor Rogers might well have described it as 'the black hole of Calcutta'. The creamery was certainly not fancy nor modern. The plaster was crumbling from the walls but each room had a big fire, which made the place homely and pleasant.

A few weeks before the term started I had one of the strokes of good fortune, which have occurred from time to time during my lifetime. For some reason I decided to write to Mr. McAvinchey and explain that for a whole term I would be giving him lots of bother and thanking him for agreeing to have me in the school. It was a very unusual thing to do as students took it for granted that arrangements made by the college authorities were sufficient notice and all they had to do was appear at the start of term. I got a surprise when I discovered Frank's attitude to this in the first couple of days.

"I must say I am glad to have you in the school for one very good reason", he said. "You had the courtesy to write and ask my permission and the sense to realise that you are somewhat of a burden on me and not a gift sent by God. I have heard of lots of your fellow students who never bother to inform the principal of the school to which they are going, that he is going to have an intruder. And some of them have the arrogance to think that they might even be an asset during their stay. If you had not written such a courteous letter I might well have refused to have you at all. As it is I will do my very best to help you and to see that you do as well as is humanly possible".

"Thank you very much, Mr. McAvinchey", I replied, completely surprised by his attitude and thankful that I had had the good fortune to write to him. It was a timely warning that I would have to be careful to take any advice he might give me and to follow his commands without question.

For the first six weeks Frank decreed that I should spend the time in the junior room with Pat Donnelly whom I had known well at the Training College. Pat lived on the edge of the village and was only in his second year of teaching. This meant that he was still on probation and it was unclear if it was legal for a student to spend part of his teaching practice with him. Frank assured me that he would be listening to all that was happening through the thin wall between the rooms and that he would explain this to any lecturers who would come to visit me. Pat had three classes in his room, primaries three, four and five. It required great effort, therefore, to get through the basic subjects with everyone and try to fulfil the timetable.

It was in Pat's room that I met one of the most interesting children I have ever met in my life. I will give him the name Peter. He was very retarded and although he was older than the other children he could neither write nor recognise his name. Pat tried his best to spend as much time with him as possible but to no avail. The boy spent his day in a desk at the back of the room with a big sheet of paper and a crayon and he simply scored the sheet in all directions. Most of the time he simply sat and listened but I doubt if he understood much.

At eleven o'clock on the first morning I got a great surprise. Pat called the boy up to the front of the room and nodded to him. He took off all his clothes until he was standing with only his trousers left. Pat then took him out and left him sitting on the toilet. The toilets were to the back of the school and reaching them entailed a forty-yard walk from the classroom. The set-up could only be described as primitive. A plank of wood with round holes in it at two-foot intervals was fixed above a water trough. Usually, the trough could be cleared by pulling a lever at one end to allow a flush of water to escape from a big iron tank located on top of a small tower.

At one stage before the end of teaching practice, the whole system clogged up and this created a real problem for everyone. Soon after it happened a young curate, who was on loan to the parish at the time, called one day at lunchtime.

"We have an awful problem at the present minute Father", explained Frank. "The toilets are all blocked up for the past couple of days and are almost impossible to use. I can tell you it is very unpleasant out there. You would need to get someone to come and sort it all out".

"Why are you telling me about it?" asked the priest.

"Now Father", said Frank in an exasperated tone, "you know as well as I do that the clergy are in charge and it is their responsibility to get things fixed when they go wrong".

"Did you try clearing it yourself?" asked the curate.

"I did have a go at it at the start but I couldn't get it going", said Frank. I could see that he was becoming annoyed and angry. The priest rose to leave. "Och, I wouldn't worry too much about it", he said over his shoulder. "For hundreds of years people went behind bushes and they never came to any harm. Send them out round the hedges and they will be fine". He closed the door behind him and was gone, which was probably just as well for he never heard the names Frank called him.

"You see", Pat explained when the boy was ready to go out to the toilet, "this lad has no control over his bodily motions and if I misjudge the time to prepare him and take him out I have to bring him home to get his clothes changed. If that happens there is a row down at the house and I am called every bad name under the sun. Wait till you see what happens when he comes in".

Five minutes later the boy arrived back, holding up his trousers and greeted us with a big smile. "Good Lad", said Pat, "now can you put on your shirt?"

"Can", said Peter and lifted his jacket.

"That's not your shirt, that's your jacket", Pat pointed out quietly. "Do you remember I showed you the shirt before the holidays?"

Pat lifted the shirt and handed it to him. To my utter surprise he tried to put it on upside down. It was the same with every garment. If he did not try to put it on upside down, he tried it inside out. I don't think there was one instance when he got it right.

"You see what I mean", said Pat. "I have to be careful to get him to go out in time and no matter what I do I can't teach him to put on his clothes. He's not going to learn anything while he's here. I think he's unteachable".

"I'll try and see if I can help while I'm here", I said. "I don't expect to get anywhere but I'll try. I don't have much time though, since Frank insists that I take four lessons every day".

"I'll have a bit more time with him while you're teaching". said Pat. "I doubt if there is any hope though".

In the fourth week Pat failed to turn up and word reached us that he had a bad flu and would not be in for the entire week. "You will take Pat's place this week", Frank informed me. "It will be a great chance for you to have the room to yourself with the children. Remember I'll be monitoring everything from next door".

That morning at eleven o'clock I called Peter up from the back and helped him to remove his clothes except for his trousers. He stood and looked up at me.

"Don't you know where to go now?" I asked.

"Do", he replied in his usual guttural manner.

"Right", I said. "Good man, now on you go".

The boy left the room and I continued teaching the rest of the class. Two or three minutes passed and suddenly the door burst open and Frank appeared in the doorway. He was red in the face and doing a sort of war dance. "Come here and see what you have done now", he ordered, indicating with his finger exactly what he expected me to do. I was completely mystified as to what could have happened. I knew I had not done exactly as Pat had been doing but I was sure that I had gone as far as necessary. As I reached the doorway, Frank grabbed me by the arm with one hand and pointed along the little corridor with the other.

"What do you think of your handiwork, smart fellow?" he asked.

The boy was standing outside Frank's room holding up his trousers and looking completely mystified as to why there was a fuss. On the little mat outside Frank's door were the entire contents of his bowels, sitting in a neat pile.

"What do you think of that?" snapped Frank.

I looked at Peter standing there still holding up his trousers. I looked at the little mat outside Frank's door. I could see Frank out of the corner of my eye still doing a little dance of anger in the corridor. I found it very difficult not to burst out laughing.

"Right, young fellow", said Frank angrily, "You caused that so you get rid of it and when you are off at the weekend you can get me a new mat. I'm not having that one back". Still in very bad temper he danced back into his room and slammed the door. I took the mat outside to the toilet and got rid of the mess and then put the mat in the bin. It must have taken the next ten minutes to get the boy dressed. I learned one very important lesson that day. Never again would I think that I knew better than an expert.

The religious inspection was due to take place in the middle of that week and Frank was very worried lest the school get a bad name. It was the custom that teachers whose school had been inspected would pass on questions to those still on the list. So intense was the pressure to do well that teachers would teach religion for the entire day. It was a situation, which surprised me and made no sense but I was not in a position to do anything about it.

"When Fr. Finn arrives", said Frank, "I will take over in your room and you can take my boys until he is ready to inspect them. I don't know how he will accept the fact that Pat is sick".

Fr. Finn was a native of the parish but had never served in it. In fact he had been a past pupil of the school when Frank was the assistant teacher but this did not lessen Frank's worry. He was not expected until about ten o'clock but he arrived while Frank and I were standing in the corridor chatting at a few minutes after nine.

"Good morning men", he said with a big smile. "I am running a bit ahead of time as I have to be in Dundalk in the afternoon".

"That's fine Father", said Frank but it was obvious that he was taken aback.

"I'll have a look at Pat's room if that is O.K", said the priest. "I know that not all the boys are in yet but maybe we can make a start nevertheless".

"Right", said Frank. "Arthur here will look after my room and I will go into Pat's room with you. Arthur had been taking Pat's classes this week as Pat had the flu".

The priest looked at me and asked, "Where do you come from Arthur?"

"Oh, I'm from the parish Father", I said. "I live just outside Benburb and I am on long teaching practice here. Mr. McAvinchey has been looking after me very well".

Frank turned to go towards Pat's room but Fr. Finn took him by the arm and stopped him. "No need to change about like that", he said, "I'll get a chance to get to know this fellow parishioner of mine. There is no need to worry. I know Pat Donnelly's work and it is excellent".

I could see that Frank was badly taken aback. He stood for a moment as though he was not sure what to do. Finally he asked the priest, "are you dead sure about this?"

"Oh, for heaven's sake relax", said Fr. Finn. "It's not the last judgement and we'll be fine. Come on", he said, taking me by the arm, "and we'll make a start".

Fr. Finn allowed me to teach for about fifteen minutes while he went round and talked in whispers to the boys. When he was sure that he had spoken to everyone he came up to me. "Could you give them some work to do and we'll have a chat?" he said.

When the boys had settled to work he sat on the edge of the teacher's desk and said, "I'm glad to get a chance to talk to a young teacher from my own parish. Everyone takes this inspection far too seriously. What would I know about advising teachers how to do their job? I have bother enough looking after myself".

"Oh, I'm sure you could give advice very well Father", I replied, "I got the impression that everyone looks on this inspection as if it's the most important thing in the world".

"It's daft", he said laughing quietly and looking up at the ceiling. "All this passing of notes round the schools makes a nonsense of the whole thing. But how have you been enjoying the chance to come back to your own parish?"

"It's been great and I've learned a lot", I said. "It's been very hard work though, because Frank expects very high standards".

"Right", said Fr. Finn. "That is an interesting lad you have in the corner down there. He more or less effed me off". The priest looked into my face and burst out laughing.

"I find him very interesting too", I agreed. "He's finds it almost impossible to learn anything and he uses the language of the home. Some people might think that they are being insulted but that is not the case at all".

"I agree completely", said Fr. Finn. "Tell me does Frank still use a sort of dummy confession box to show the children how to go to confession?"

"He might Father", I said in surprise. "I have never seen such a thing but I have only been back here for a few weeks and Frank never taught me when I was a pupil".

Fr. Finn paused and pursed his lips. "When I was a pupil", he said, "Frank used to use some such device. I remember going home past the Bell's house and some of the Bell boys were in Frank's room at the time. Bob had installed himself in an old shed with a wee square window in the side. He used a sheet of corrugated iron as a slide to open and close the window if you know what I mean. He pulled the tin back and forwards as the priest would do with the slide in the confession box".

"Who the hell's next there?" he roared and James came up to the window.

"How long is it since your last confession?" Bob asked when James had settled himself outside.

"It's a right while Father", James answered.

"What the hell have you been at since that?" asked Bob.

"I called my mother an auld hoor", admitted James.

"Go to hell you bastard, you", roared Bob and pulled the window closed.

"I have often wondered", laughed Fr. Finn, "what Frank would have thought of his handiwork if he seen and heard that exhibition. I had better go in and see how he is getting on. It's been great meeting you and I hope we soon get a chance of talking again".

Frank spent the first twenty minutes of lunchtime that day telling me how well things had gone in the religious inspection. Finally he drew breath, looked at me, and asked, "why did Fr. Finn spend so long with you by the way?"

"He was telling me jokes and stories", I answered.

"He was what?" asked Frank, and I could see that he could not believe what he was hearing.

"Och, he was telling me about funny things that he has seen and heard", I answered. "He seems to have a good sense of humour and to like to have a good laugh".

"Laugh be damned", growled Frank, "the inspection is nothing to be laughing about".

CHAPTER 37
WORK DAY AND NIGHT

At lunchtime each day and again at the end of every school day, Frank took out a notebook and went through each lesson I had taught. He must have given his class silent work to do and listened to every word that came through the partition to him. He pointed out where he thought I could have done a lot better and praised me for the things he considered I had done well. It was like having the entire set of lecturers from the Training College with me all the time. He demanded that I have a least three hand-made visual aids by the end of each week. It meant that by the time I had my lessons prepared I was often up until three o'clock in the morning working on the visual material.

"Well, that's a holy tarra, altogether", said my father. "Damn the likes of that bother ever I seen in my life to teach a lock of wee children. I thought teachers had no work to do at all. Be God Boy, you'd be nearly better to be breaking stones with me up in the quarry. Damn me but you are suffering under Pontius Pilate. If it goes on like this you'll not be going to bed at all. Damn me here, I say, those girls round the Donnelly Hill and the Brantry will be wondering what the hell has happened to you".

Soon after Pat came back an inspector came to see him teaching and to verify the end of his probation. It was a lady called Miss Boland, and the news was that she was almost impossible to please. I was teaching when she arrived and she asked me to continue for another half hour or so while she sat and took notes.

"You are doing very well at the teaching", she said. "But you would have to take half a day and clean under your nails. There must be half a stone of dirt in there".

"Just before you came in Miss Boland", I explained, "I was setting up a wormery with the children. I had to use layers of various types of soil and I did not have a chance to wash my hands afterwards".

"I'm afraid I don't buy that at all", she responded curtly. "There is no excuse under the sun for a teacher to have dirty nails. I hope I never see them like that again".

"I'll see to it", I said. "I'll leave the room now and let you carry on with Pat's inspection".

"Not at all", she said. "There's no need for that. You can sit down here at the back beside me. Maybe you will learn something for Pat is a very fine teacher".

Miss Boland marched to the back of the room and sat down at a small desk with Peter in the corner on her right. I did as instructed and took the seat on her left. Peter watched us as we took our seats and then became very industrious with his crayon. It looked as though he was completely devoted to some very important work.

Miss Boland opened her notebook and began to write. After half a minute or so out of the corner of my eye I could see Peter get up and move over beside her. It seemed as though he were trying to read what she had written, over her shoulder. He had his tongue out on one side of his mouth and saliva was slowly dripping from it. Miss Boland glanced up and Peter bolted back to his seat and set to work once more with his crayon. She continued to take notes.

About a minute later I saw him rise again and go back to exactly the same position by her side. The tongue was still dripping and it appeared as if he had a great interest in what she was writing. Once again she glanced up and once again he darted back and resumed work. This time, however, she rose quietly and slipped over beside him and stood looking over his shoulder. The crayon was going so fast that its noise was clearly audible above Pat Donnelly's voice. Miss Boland bent down beside Peter.

"What are you doing, son?" I heard her ask softly.

"Drawing", was the reply.

"And what is it you are drawing, son?"

"House".

"Is that a house son?"

"Fuck you, can't you see it's a house and a tractor beside it?"

Miss Boland stood up and burst into peals of

laughter. She came over to me and whispered, "it sounds as if I am very stupid indeed. That is perhaps the best telling off that I have had in all my life and in the vernacular too. Will you please take over from Pat now?"

She walked up to the front of the room and indicated to Pat that she wished to speak to him outside. She was still laughing as she disappeared out of the door.

Only two lecturers called to visit me during the weeks that I was with Pat. One was Sean Breslin and the other Fr. McEnaney. It was most unusual for the Dean to go out on teaching practice. Both of them simply sat and took notes as usual and at the end of the session told me that I was getting on fine and to keep it up. It was then time to move into Frank's room for the final nine weeks.

Frank allowed me to teach all day on the first Monday and likewise for the rest of the time. He sometimes took over for a few minutes at the end of a lesson and showed me how he would have handled some aspect with which he was not pleased. It was intensive and tiring and for a few days I could scarcely see the handlebars of the bike as I rode home. My mother was rather annoyed because I was so tired that I had no appetite for dinner for the first week or more. One lovely evening I took a chair and a wee table out to the street to prepare my work for the next day. I could hear my mother talking to Da as he took his dinner.

"God, Mick", she said in a concerned tone, "this fellow of ours will never stick the pace he is trying to keep up at the present time. He's so tired when he comes home that he is not fit to eat a bite. And then he takes a ten-minute nap and he's away working for hours getting things ready for the next day. He's up until three or four in the morning. It's not worth it at all. Could you not talk some sense into him?"

"What the hell do I know about teaching?" asked Da. "Sure it's only for a lock of weeks and then he'll be going back to the college. He's young and fit and he must know what he's doing".

"I thought he had it made when he got to that college", said Ma. "But there's nothing worth this. Maybe it would have been far better if he'd joined the Civil Service".

"Och, now Sarah", replied Da, "wouldn't you have been dead happy if he was away in London or some other big city in England? For dead sure it would be me that wouldn't be getting any sleep if that had happened".

At that point Ma closed the door and I didn't hear the rest of the conversation.

On the Friday of the first week after the changeover Frank sat looking at me intensely as we were finishing our lunch at his desk. I felt rather uncomfortable and I thought that he had seen something very wrong in my work and was about to tell me about it.

"Tell me Arthur", he said at last, "have you ever thought of going for the O.M"

It was my turn to look at him intensely. "The what?" I asked.

"The O.M." he repeated.

"What is it?" I asked.

"God bless me but some of you fellows never cease to surprise me", he said. "It's the award of Outstanding Merit and it had not been gained in any training college in this country for something like eighteen years".

"How did you hear about it?" I asked.

"Well now", he said with a sarcastic smile, "if you can't be bothered to look after your own business, someone has to do it for you. I did a bit of research before you arrived and I asked the lecturers who called to see you. I found out that the O.M is the highest award that any student on teaching practice can achieve. I had to go out of my way to get the information and that is how I know about it. I realise that some people round here might not believe it but sometimes you have to go out of your way to discover important facts".

"I think I have been in the top half of our class", I said. "I would love to be given the opportunity of doing a fourth year course in English and drama. That has been my objective for more than two years. I would be really happy if I succeed in that".

Frank sat and drummed his fingers on the desk and studied them as he did so. He did not speak for a long time. At last he looked up and I could see a trace of annoyance in his eyes. "Have you no ambition at all?" he asked. "Why don't you have a go at it anyway?"

"I don't think I would have any more chance than the man in the moon", I replied. "You have said that it has not been awarded for about eighteen years. Why should I be the one to break the mould?"

"Because I'm dead sure that you have a good chance of getting it", he replied firmly. "I have all your lecturers and Miss Boland thinking along the same lines. They have not decided one way or the other at the present time but we have a few weeks to go. I know you can get there if you put in the effort and don't make any dreadful blunders. If you get it everything in teaching will be wide open to you".

I gulped and took time to take a few deep breaths. "God, Frank", I said, "this is a very ambitious step to take. I would never have thought of going out on a limb like this at all. Besides, I don't honestly think I could work much harder. I have really been burning the candle at both ends for the past few weeks".

Frank slapped the palm of his hand down on the desk. "That's not a problem", he said. "Your work has been grand and if you can keep it up until the end of this term I have no doubt that you will be home and dry. You must be prepared for lecturers and inspectors at all times, however, and some of them may stay for nearly a full day. I want you to go full out for this for it would be a great accolade for this wee country school to have a past pupil and a student who has been awarded this honour. Why do you think I have been going to so much trouble to guide you?"

"I just thought you were going out of your way to help me", I answered. "I appreciate it very much. I know that many principals round the country don't bother that much. I'd already realised that I could never thank you enough".

"Right", said Frank. "We are taking the high road. Don't you dare to let me down".

During the first three weeks in Frank's room one lecturer called each week. Mr. Breslin called twice and I took the chance to inform him that I was very keen to do a fourth year in his subject.

"I can't see that you would have any problems as far as I am concerned", he said. "Mr. Campbell has been talking to me about you, however, and you should not make up your mind until next term when he will be talking to you. Keep up the good work and if you decide to go for English, I would certainly be happy. Good luck".

On Monday morning at the start of my fifth week I was leaving my bicycle against the wall when a car pulled up beside me. It was just after nine o'clock and class did not start until a quarter past. "I am glad to see that you are in good time", said a voice from the car. I looked round to discover that Mr. Campbell was speaking to me through the open window and that Mr. Donnelly was in the passenger seat beside him.

"That you very much", I said. "I hope you enjoy your visit to my part of the country".

They got out and came into the school with me and I introduced them to Frank. They stayed all that day until nearly three o'clock. The three men sat at the back and I was aware of them conversing in whispers as I worked with the boys. Frank took over as the two men were leaving and they indicated that they wished to speak to me outside.

"You did reasonably well", said Mr. Campbell looking very serious. "I think that with a bit of luck and a bit of hard work you will make a competent enough teacher some day if we are all spared that long. Mr. Donnelly here feels the same. I will be back to see you sometime. Cheerio for now".

I felt very crestfallen. I thought I had worked very hard all day and there had been no obvious problems. I went back into the room and told Frank what Mr. Campbell had said.

"His auld arse and pancakes", said Frank. "You worked there all day like a man who had been teaching for years and in spite of the fact that you had myself and two strangers sitting at the back of the room you acted as if you were completely at ease. I defy any of those toffee-nosed friggers to cope the way you did. As far as I am concerned that was some performance. Just make sure that tomorrow and every other day is the same".

I was in the middle of a religion class the next morning when the door knocked and Mr. Campbell appeared once more. This time, however, he had Miss Boland with him. They sat down beside Frank and at the end of the lesson Mr. Campbell called me down to him.

"Show me your notes for today's lessons, please", he said.

I gave him the notes and he indicated that he wished me to continue teaching as usual. Frank winked at me as I handed in the notes. The two men and Miss Boland sat there chatting for the next two lessons and then the two visitors rose to leave. As usual they indicated that they wished to speak to me alone.

"Have you made any progress with my friend next door?" asked Miss Boland.

"I'm afraid I haven't really", I confessed. "I have tried a few things that I read about but I would have to admit that they were not very successful".

"What did you try, may I ask?" she enquired.

"Well, Miss Boland", I said, "I found an idea where one gets some sandpaper and cuts out letters from it. I stuck these on cardboard flash cards so that the rough side was upward. I did out Peter's full name in this way. I then held his index finger and guided it over the letters as we spelled out his name. It's supposed to make an impact on the child's brain".

"And did it?" she asked with an air of hope in her voice.

"I'm afraid not", I admitted.

"What did he say when you presented him with your handiwork?" she asked.

"Do you really want to know, Miss Boland?" I asked.

"I certainly do", she replied firmly. "Let's have it".

"Well", I explained softly, "he lifted the cards and examined them from all angles. Then he looked me hard in the face and said, 'Jaysus, did you make them yourself?' I told him that I had made them the night before and he looked at them in wonder and said, "well, fuck me but that's a tarra".

Miss Boland burst out laughing and pushed Mr. Campbell on the shoulder. "I just knew that I would get a good laugh before I left here", she said. "I realised that Mr. Daly here has a sense of humour and that is very necessary in this profession. Some people who think they can teach, just don't have it", she said pointedly as they went out to the car.

As I came back into the room, Frank came towards me with his two hands held out before him as if in prayer. "Didn't I bloody warn you to be on your guard", he said. "Those two thought that by coming back today they would catch you out. Campbell nearly fell off his seat when he realised that your notes were up to the usual standard after yesterday. That's a big feather in your cap, boy. By the way, what the hell was Boland laughing about?"

I told him what had happened and he looked stunned. "You didn't tell her that story in those words", he said. "Surely you put a gloss on it".

"I didn't see that I had much choice, Frank", I said and I told him about the previous incident.

"By God, Boy", he said, "you took an awful chance there. I would never have imagined in a million years that she would abide language like that".

In the middle of the tenth week I was about to go through the school gate when a car drew up beside me. A very tall, middle-aged man got out and said, "Excuse me please. I'm looking for the primary school in this village. Can you help me?" He had a very polished English accent and one might say that he barked his words rather than spoke them.

"This is a primary school", I answered. "This is the Catholic school but there is another small Protestant school a few hundred yards away down a small road on the right".

"No", he said, "I think I must be in the right place. I'm looking for a student teacher called Daly".

"I'm afraid that's me", I replied. "I was just about to enter the school to start the day. Would you like to come on in?"

"My name is Mr. Wilkinson", the man answered. "I am in charge of physical education in Northern Ireland at present. I know from the time table, which I have been given that you are not due to take a class today but it would be helpful if you would take one for me first thing this morning. Do you think you could manage that?"

"I'm sure that will be fine Sir", I replied. "There is the principal, Mr. McAvinchey coming across the road. School is not due to start for another twenty minutes or so".

Frank agreed that I could take the first period for physical education but made it clear that he was only doing so as a great compliment to his visitor. He explained that it would be some time before all the pupils would arrive and that I had to take P.E. in the parochial hall across the road. He sent a boy over to Mrs McAvinchey asking her to send a cup of coffee across for the inspector. I used the time while they were taking the coffee to get ready for this unscheduled class. I was about to take the boys across the road to the hall when Mr. Wilkinson stopped me.

"Could I see your notes please?" he asked.

He took the notes and flicked through them for a minute or two. He picked one lesson, which I had taken about a fortnight previously.

"Do you remember this lesson?" he asked, handing me the open book.

"I remember it reasonably well I think", I replied, glancing through the notes. "It's a couple of weeks since I took that lesson".

"I want you to take that lesson for me this morning", he said. "I have not got much time so we'd better get started".

I was thinking hard as we made our way to the hall. Some of the specialists in P.E. had told me that Mr. Wilkinson had spent most of his life in the British Army in postings overseas. He had retired with the rank of Major. If he liked you, they said, he could be fairly understanding. If he didn't like you he was impossible. It was most unusual for the physical education inspector to bother with students who were not picking that subject for their fourth year. I had enjoyed taking the subject because the children were enthusiastic and cooperative but I had never even considered being inspected in it and I felt very nervous. Everything went fairly well, however, as far as I could judge and I was reasonably happy.

"What did you think of that performance?" Mr. Wilkinson asked when we were back in school. The question took me completely by surprise. I had expected him to tell me what he thought and I found it hard to know what to say.

"These children are great", I replied. "I do believe that if I asked them to climb up the walls they would try their best. They are very easy to work with and I think they enjoyed the period".

"Yes", he said firmly, "the children were great but I was not asking about them. I was asking about you and I think you were quite aware of that fact".

"To be honest", I said, "I made a few mistakes but I hope they were not too serious. I don't think I could have done very much better".

"You seem to be extremely fond of noise", he said.

"I'm not really", I said, wondering what he was talking about. "I love silence rather than noise".

"If you are so fond of silence", he said, "why did you gallop round the hall making so much noise in those outdoor shoes. It sounded like a herd of wild horses in that hall".

I felt completely at a loss what to say. The subject was not part of the curriculum for that day and I had left my gym shoes at home. In spite of all Frank's warnings I had been caught out but I doubted if even he could have foreseen this.

"I was sure I would not be taking P.E. today Sir", I explained but it sounded a poor excuse. "I took my gym shoes home and that is why I made so much noise. I'm sorry".

"No need to be sorry at all," he said with a friendly smile. "Actually the lesson was excellent, the equivalent of anything that my first year specialists have produced. I must have a word with your principal and then I shall have to scamper. It has been nice to meet you".

"Thank you very much, Mr. Wilkinson", I said. "It has been nice meeting you too and I'm sorry about the noise".

Frank left me in charge and went out with the inspector. To my great surprise he was away for nearly twenty minutes. He came back rubbing his hands and with a serious look on his face.

"You did it this morning, you boy you", he said.

"Oh God, I'm sorry Frank", I said earnestly. "I never thought of taking the flaming gym shoes and that was the one thing that he picked on. I'm sorry for letting you down but how the blazes was I expected to be prepared for that?"

Frank held out his hand. "Put it there, you boy you", he said. "That is supposed to be the most difficult man in the country to please and he thinks you are the bee's knees. I'm proud of you".

He called a boy up to the front. "Go over to Mrs McAvinchey, son", he said, "and tell her to send over two cups of her very best coffee". When the boy went out he said, "sit down here with me at the desk. We both need to relax after that. I thought we were scuppered this time. Who could have foreseen him coming today when you were not supposed to have his subject? I could not believe it when he told me how delighted he was".

At lunchtime on the Wednesday in Holy Week Frank gave me a big relieved smile as we were finishing our meal. "We can relax now", he said. "No one is going to come away out here with only a day and a half left. You can take it easy from now on and you have earned the rest. Just keep the notes up until the last minute as they will be looking at them when you go back to the college".

He had barely got the words out of his mouth when the door was knocked and Miss Boland and Mr. Campbell came in, accompanied by a third person. He was a stocky man with a goatee beard and I had never seen him before. "This is the Chief Inspector", said Miss Boland. "We would like Mr. Daly to take a class for him before the end of term".

Frank went noticeably pale. He rose to welcome the visitors and I could see that he was shaken. "Mr. Daly has already taken his classes for today", he said. "It's a pity you did not come a bit earlier".

"I know that it is very late", replied Miss Boland, "but we could not make it any sooner", She turned to me and asked, "would you have a lesson that you could take for the Chief Inspector immediately after lunchtime, please?"

"Which subject would you like me to teach?" I asked.

She turned to the Chief Inspector and said, "it should be your choice, Wilbur. What lesson would you like to see?"

"What is on offer?" he asked looking at me.

"I can take an English lesson, or a maths lesson or I could take one on nature study", I answered, trying to make the last sound like an afterthought.

"I think we'll have the nature study", he said. "That sounds interesting".

The boys came in and Frank arranged four seats for the onlookers at the back of the room. I had borrowed a book from Pat Donnelly, which he had recommended highly. I had prepared a lesson from it on the life of the badger. I thought it was a brilliant lesson but I had never used it even though I had prepared visual aids for it.

As the lesson started the visitors whispered softly to each other for a few minutes. Soon, however, I noticed that their eyes were fixed on me and there was no sound. The boys too were obviously enjoying the lesson. I felt that I had my audience in the palm of my hand and I began to really put on a demonstration. I had even copied a set of worksheets from Pat's book and I ended the class by distributing them. I could see that Frank was sitting mesmerised.

As the class began work on the sheets, the visitors rose and came up to me at the desk. "I think you know that was a very good lesson", said Miss Boland. "Mr. McAvinchey has tutored you well. He has even made you keep the best wine until the last. I know that the Chief Inspector will be pleased".

"I am very impressed indeed", added the Chief Inspector. "Can you show me your lesson notes for the entire teaching practice?"

I handed him the notes and he sat down at the teacher's desk and scanned through them. He stopped suddenly in the middle and pointed to one lesson. "I see that you have prepared a visual aid for this lesson", he said. "Can you show that to me now?"

Frank had carefully catalogued all the aids in a box and I was able to get the required one within a minute or two. "That's fine", he said. "We had better be going if we want to get back to Belfast on time. It has been a real pleasure visiting your school Mr. McAvinchey. I have to thank you very much on behalf of the Department for all the bother you have gone to with our student".

Frank was nearest the door and he opened it for them as they turned to leave. Miss Boland lingered and then turned and whispered to me.

"You have got your O.M", she said. "Congratulations. Just keep it under your hat until it is made official".

"Thank you very much indeed Miss Boland", I gasped. "I can hardly believe it and I will certainly do my best not let you down".

Frank left the visitors out to their car and it was probably ten minutes before he came back into the room. He smacked the front of his legs with the palms of his hands and asked, "where under the good God did you get that lesson, boy? It was bloody brilliant".

"I'm afraid it was a bit of plagiarism Frank", I said. "I copied it out of a book that Pat lent me when I was next door".

"But how the bloody hell did you have it ready and the two brilliant visual aids to go with it?" he asked.

"A year or so ago I was on teaching practice in Belfast with a man called Tom Honey, Frank", I explained. "Tom told me that it was a good idea to have a lesson always up your sleeve in case of emergencies. I thought it was very good advice and since then I have always followed that practice. I was hoping they would pick the nature study because I knew it was the best lesson I had".

"Damn you, sure you put it into their mouths", said Frank. "The way you suggested it they could hardly have asked for anything else. I thought I was cute but by God I could take lessons from you".

"Did you hear any news when you were outside with them?" I asked.

"What kind of news?" asked Frank. "What the hell are you talking about?"

"You mean to tell me that they didn't tell you anything?" I asked again.

"You have been straight with me all through your

time here", snapped Frank. "Don't start playing fancy games with me now".

"Miss Boland told me that I had got the O.M.", I said. "But she put me under a strict promise not to mention it to anyone. For God's sake don't open your mouth about it. I gave her my word of honour".

To my astonishment and to the astonishment of the class, Frank jumped into the air, clapped his hands above his head and gave a ringing cheer. I have never in my life seen as much satisfaction and joy in anyone's eyes.

"Jesus, that is great", he gasped. "That is really bloody great. I knew you could do it, you wee frigger. I'll tell Mrs McAvinchey, but that's as far as it will go until it's official".

"I was sure some of them would have informed you when you were outside with them", I said. "They must know that it was you who was responsible far more than me".

"They told me that you could have the next two days off but that was all", replied Frank. "You have the whole world at your feet now, Boy. Make sure that you make the most of it. I could not be more delighted if you were my own son. And by the way I think that woman Boland has a notion of you. You'd better watch yourself".

I felt somewhat sad at leaving the school and especially the children but at the same time I breathed a huge sigh of relief.

CHAPTER 38
FINAL STAGES

Towards the end of the Easter holidays I took a severe cold and on the final Sunday evening my mother tried to persuade me that I should stay at home until the worst of it had passed instead of returning to Belfast on time.

"You have been looking very pale for the past couple of days", she said, "and I don't like the sound of that cold at all. Stay in bed for a day or two and you will be a hundred per cent better. I don't like the thought of you going back to the city where we can't get in touch with you if you were to get any worse".

"Och, Ma, I only have a wee touch of the cold", I assured her. "I will be better in a couple of days and I want to hear all the news after the long teaching practice. I'll be fine, don't worry".

As I rode towards Dungannon on a lovely spring evening, however, I wondered if I might have been wiser to have followed her advice. Although I had given myself extra time for the journey and was going slowly, an uncomfortable cold sweat enveloped me and my legs felt so weak that I could hardly turn the pedals. In the train I started to shiver even though it was very warm in the compartment and some people were opening the windows for comfort. The short journey from the station to the digs felt as though it would never end.

As I came into the living room, I was dizzy and I felt like fainting.

"What's wrong with you, Arthur?" asked Agnes Henvey in a very worried voice. "You look like death warmed up. Go on up to bed and I'll bring you up a cup of tea".

"Thanks, Agnes", I replied. "I'll go up and get into bed but I don't feel like tea tonight. I'll try to get to sleep and hope that this cold will have lifted in the morning. Thanks very much anyway".

That night I slept only fitfully and when I did lose consciousness I had all sorts of weird dreams or nightmares. The next morning every part of my body was sore and I had a splitting headache. I came down to breakfast in my dressing gown but I did not feel like eating. Agnes took one look at me and I could see she was worried.

"You have a really bad flu and if we're not careful you'll give it to everyone in the house", she said. "Get up to bed this minute and I'll get in touch with Doctor Maguire straight away. You're not fit to go to him so he will have to come to you. Go up now and no arguments".

I did as she ordered immediately simply because I

was not fit to do otherwise. The doctor came before lunchtime and he agreed that I had a really bad flu.

"I'll give you these tablets", he said, "they are fairly new and very powerful and they should have you fixed in a couple of days. Take three a day and make sure that you drink plenty of water. You have brought that bad infection with you from the wilds of Tyrone. I suppose you are determined to share it with everyone here in the city".

The tablets were large and white and I later discovered that they were penicillin, which I had never heard of before. I managed to take three on that afternoon, even though I should probably only have taken two. The next day I felt even worse and in a vain attempt to get better I had taken my three tablets by six o'clock. I must have dozed off to sleep, and I don't remember anything else of that evening.

I woke up to find Gerry Henvey sitting at the side of my bed with a book in his hand but looking over the top of his glasses at me.

"Oh, so you are back with us", he said, in an obviously relieved tone. "You gave us some fright these last couple of days".

"What happened Gerry?" I asked. "Why are you sitting beside my bed like that?"

"Well, one of us has been sitting here most of the time these last three days", he replied. "What day do you think it is, by the way?"

"Well, I came back on Sunday", I said, "and I didn't go to the college on Monday. That was when the doctor came and I was still in bed on Tuesday. It must be Wednesday".

"Wednesday, my arse", replied Gerry. "It's Saturday afternoon and you have been out of the world completely for more than three days. You were raving and shouting and claiming that all sorts of animals and strange creatures were attacking you. Anybody would have thought that you were suffering from drink and had a dose of the DTs. Agnes had to change the bed two or three times a day because you were sweating so much that you were in pools of water. By God we have had some week trying to keep you in the bed in the first place".

I found it hard to believe or comprehend what he was saying. I remembered Tuesday evening but nothing else after that.

"What the blazes happened to me Gerry?" I asked.

"Do you remember those big white tablets you were so fond of?" he asked.

"I wasn't that fond of them", I assured him, "but the doctor was dead keen on them, however, and he said that they would cure me in no time at all".

"The doctor had to come back on Wednesday morning", said Gerry. "As soon as he looked at you he said that you must be allergic to penicillin and the tablets were having a very bad effect on you. He says that if you ever need medication in your life again you are to tell the doctors that you have an allergy to penicillin. By heavens there was one time a day or so ago and I thought we were going to lose you. You were going on like a lunatic and I thought we were going to have to get you locked up".

I lay back and tried to sort out my thoughts. I felt really guilty because the Henveys had been put to so much trouble and it was all my fault for not taking my mother's advice. Agnes and Gerry had a small child and it was the last thing in the world that they needed.

"God Gerry", I whispered, "I don't know how to thank you and Agnes for all the bother you have taken with me. I hope wee Gerard doesn't catch this dose. I should never have come back. It was dead stupid of me. How am I ever going to repay you?"

"Don't worry about that", replied Gerry. "As long as you are all right we are happy enough. I have a feeling that you will be back to normal in a day or so. I think you have turned the corner".

"Did anybody get in touch with Ma or Da?" I asked.

"At one stage we were on the point of trying to contact them but we were not sure how to manage that", replied Gerry. "Nobody was too sure of the address. We decided to leave it until there was a change in your condition for we did not want to worry them. Since you seem to be a bit better, maybe that was the best decision".

I heaved a big sigh of relief. "I think it was", I agreed, "but I will have something to listen to when I go home for not writing to them. My mother must be astray in the head".

I was not due to go home that weekend but my mother would have expected a letter, especially since I was not well before leaving home. Now there was no hope of one reaching her before Tuesday and I considered getting up and heading home immediately. I got out of bed to go to the toilet but I felt so weak that I decided that it would be foolish and probably impossible to undertake such a journey. I got back into bed and wrote a short note explaining that I had been in bed with flu for a couple of days but that I would be home the next weekend. I asked Gerry to get someone to post it that evening so that it would reach home as soon as possible. On Sunday I got up in the afternoon and sat by the fire for a couple of hours and on Monday I felt a great deal better. I decided to go back to the college on Tuesday.

Fr. McEnaney met me as I was about to enter the front door of Trench House.

"Hello Stranger", he greeted me, "so you have decided to honour us all with your presence. I suppose you thought that you had worked so hard on teaching practice that you could take an extra ten days or so of holidays".

"I was back in the digs all last week Father", I explained. "I had the mother and father of a flu and I was not fit to come back any sooner".

"A likely story indeed", he said scornfully. "You fellows from Tyrone think that you can pull the wool over the eyes of us simple city folk all the time".

I was taken completely aback by his attitude and I felt annoyed and angry.

"I'll have a medical certificate for you in the morning", I snapped. "I'll make it my business to see Doctor Maguire this evening and there will be no doubt about who is telling the truth. Even this morning my legs are as weak as water if you really want to know".

He took a step back and looked at me closely. "You do look a bit pale", he said and there was obvious concern in his voice now. "There is no real need for a certificate".

"I'll make sure that you get one anyway", I said. "I'll make sure that the doctor gives you a full explanation of what happened last week".

"You seem to be on your high horse", he said. "I was really only joking but maybe in the circumstances it was not a very good joke. I saw you coming up the path and I wanted to congratulate you on the great results last term. It's a great achievement and we are all very proud of you".

"Thanks Father", I said and went on my way.

There was a break at the end of the first two lectures and seven or eight of my classmates gathered around me. "The news broke last Tuesday", said Joe Feeney, "that someone had managed to get an O.M. It was Thursday evening before we heard who it was. How the hell did you manage it?"

There was a chorus of inquisitive mutterings as people stood shaking their heads. I was feeling tired and weak again by this time. The faces around me seemed to be floating in a mist.

"I had very little alternative", I muttered. "The principal in the school made me work like a slave all the time. I have not recovered fully from the flu and I'll have to go and sit down somewhere, by the way". I was astounded to discover, however, that almost everyone had been aware of the award of Outstanding Merit and had many had been hoping to achieve it.

The term soon settled down as normal and I was relieved when the wonder of what had happened died away. We were all looking forward to graduation in a few weeks time. Everyone had been very successful on teaching practice and this meant that it would be most unlikely that anyone would fail the final exams.

Towards the end of the second week I was walking up the little path, which led from the main road up to the college. I was wheeling my bike as the path was very narrow. About half way along I met Doctor Rogers, who was glaring down at the ground at his feet in his usual fashion. As we came abreast of each other he looked up suddenly.

"I am delighted to see you, Mr. Daly", he said. "I was looking for you last week but you were nowhere to be found".

"I had a very bad bout of flu Doctor", I explained. "I was in bed in the digs for over a week".

"Mr. Daly", he said, "if I may say so, you have

taken us all by surprise. You were cruising along at your ease in my opinion and it looked as though you would never do anything exceptional. But to my surprise, if I may say so, you suddenly blossomed forth like the buds in the springtime. An ordinary flower suddenly burst forth as the brightest bloom in the garden. You achieved something, which I was sure none of my students ever would. I have to congratulate you and assure you that I will take very great pleasure in writing 'Outstanding Merit' on your teaching certificate".

"Thank you very much indeed, Doctor Rogers", I said. "Now that we have met like this I would like to take this chance of telling you that I have enjoyed your history lectures and your sense of humour very much indeed".

"Nice of you to say so", he said, and continued on his way.

Three weeks later Mr. Campbell asked me to stay behind at the end of an education lecture.

"You had the unbounded pleasure of having me visit you quite a few times out in Blackwatertown", he said. "I hope you appreciate the extraordinary privilege, which that was. No one else was honoured in such a fashion".

As usual I found it hard to know what to say to this man. I was fairly sure that he was trying hard to be funny but his usual sarcastic manner made his attempt sound totally out of kilter. Suddenly I believed I knew why he found it so hard to communicate. I came to the sudden conclusion that he had no sense of humour and he was trying hard to compensate for this. I was fairly sure that things, which amused others simply puzzled him making his attempts to be funny seem somewhat ridiculous.

"Everyone was very understanding when I was there". I muttered. "All the lecturers and inspectors were very friendly and helpful".

"Have you given any consideration to which fourth year you will chose to do next year?" he asked.

"I have indeed", I replied. "I love Mr. Breslin's subject and I have been looking forward to being allowed to do a fourth year in English and drama. That has been my goal for well over two years now".

"I understand that", he replied, looking very thoughtful. "However, I am going to ask you to think about changing your mind. I am in the process of setting up a completely new fourth year at the present time and next year will be a sort of pilot run. I would be very satisfied if you would agree to take part. This is the first time that I have asked any student for a special favour. I am asking you".

I was astounded by Mr. Campbell's pleading attitude and by his request.

"What kind of fourth year is it?" I asked.

"The new secondary schools have a problem", he explained. "They have a fairly big section of their intake each year who have not learned to read or use number to any acceptable standard. The new course will train people to give these children special help. New special classes will be set up in a couple of year's time".

"That sounds to me like a very difficult job", I said, and I immediately pictured poor Peter in Blackwatertown. "It seems to me that the English and drama would be much more rewarding and much more fun. Do you not think, Mr. Campbell that the children are already very old to learn the basics when they reach secondary level?"

Mr. Campbell sat down on the top of one of the desks and looked up at me.

"Arthur", he said, "there is a lot in what you have just said but on the other hand English and drama teachers are two a penny. It is a part of teaching where advancement is likely to be slow. These new special classes will offer an allowance equal to any other post of responsibility and it will take effect as soon as you are appointed once you have gained your diploma at the end of a year. Other teachers will have to cope with these children in their subjects with no reward. In addition you would be entitled to hold any other post in the school at the same time. I am not saying that it will be easy but financially it will be worth while thinking about".

I stood there stunned. I would never in my wildest dreams have imagined that this man would call me by my first name. Knowing him as I did it astounded me. He was asking me to give up the one thing, which I yearned to achieve. And he was offering me a full year in education, which I detested. I was about to tell him that I would never consider such a thing when for some reason, which I can't explain, I changed my mind.

"Mr. Campbell", I said, "you have taken me completely by surprise. I had never even thought that far in advance. I loved working with the children in Blackwatertown and I would be inclined to go into primary teaching if the chance were offered. I will have to take time to think about this".

"Of course", he agreed, rising from the desk and moving slowly towards the door. "I just want you to think of the advantages of this new course. Ask people who are working in schools and they will tell you that English and drama in the classroom is a very different thing from what you experience here in Trench House. It seems to me that Sean Breslin has all you fellows enveloped in the mists of the Celtic Twilight. Don't let that blind you to the fact that things are very different out in the schools. In your situation you could easily be holding the equivalent of two posts of responsibility within a couple of years".

Next day I was passing through the hall when I met Mr. Breslin. "Excuse me, Mr. Breslin", I said, "I was wondering if you would have a few minutes sometime, to have a word with me".

"I have been expecting this", he answered. "Let us slip into the library and we can have a chat now".

I told him what Mr. Campbell had suggested.

"Well, I sort of warned you of this some weeks ago", he said. "As soon as you began to draw attention to yourself on teaching practice Mr. Campbell was determined to have you on his course. What do you think of the idea?"

"I can see the advantages", I answered. "On the other hand I love the English and I would love to have a chance to do a fourth year in it".

"I can't tell you what to do", he answered slowly. "I think, however, that what Mr. Campbell has told you makes good sense. I think that if I were you I would take the new course. At the same time you will be more than welcome in my group if you so choose. Take some more time to think the whole thing through".

A few days later Mr. Campbell again asked me to have a word with him at the end of his lecture.

"Well", he asked, "what has my star student decided? Have you decided to come with me on my new course? It should suit you because it is to be held down in St. Mary's and you can look forward to being surrounded by all those wonderful women".

"I have thought very carefully about it over the past few days, Mr. Campbell", I answered. "I find it very hard indeed to turn my back on Mr. Breslin's course but I have decided to take your offer. I must say, however, that I am not looking forward to it with the same enthusiasm. In fact I feel a wee bit like a man who has agreed to walk up the steps to the gallows".

"I am quite sure that you will never regret your decision", he replied, in a satisfied tone. "Anyone who takes my considered advice is not likely ever to regret it".

His parting remark made me even less confident about my decision.

The graduation ceremony was marked by a dress dance and dinner, held in St. Mary's. Once again a notice informed us that a partner had been picked for us. I felt a little self-conscious about this since I had never met the girl before. I need not have worried, however. She was very friendly and we both enjoyed the evening.

I had never heard of a dress dance in my life but some of my friends informed me that I would have to go down to a shop called Parsons & Parsons in the city centre to hire a dress suit. They assured me that I would be measured and that the suit would not be very expensive but that I would have to make sure to return it on time. At home a couple of weeks before the graduation I mentioned this to my mother.

"Do you mean to tell me that you would think of hiring a suit for the most important event in your life?" she asked tartly.

"That's what everyone does, Ma", I said, feeling very surprised at her attitude. "We only need the suit for the one evening and it is a very handy way to get it".

"Well, indeed you'll do no such thing", she said.

"You'll go down to the shop and buy a suit. Make sure that they measure you correctly and that they give you the best material available. And when you're at it get the shirt and all the trimmings as well. I'll pay for it no matter what it costs. You will have it for dress dances for years to come".

I was completely taken aback by this her dictatorial manner and I looked across at Da, who was sitting reading the paper with a big smile on his face. I knew that he had been paying more attention to our conversation than to the news of the day.

"What do you think about this, Da?" I asked.

"What are you talking about?" he asked, lowering the paper as though reluctant to do so and pretending that his concentration on the paper had been rudely interrupted.

"Ma wants me to buy a suit for the graduation dance", I replied. "I think it's a waste of money when I can hire one".

"What kind of dance is it?" he asked. "I thought you bought a new rigout a couple of weeks ago".

"I did surely", I answered. "This is a dress dance, however, and I'm told that I have to have a dress suit. But I was going to hire one like all the rest of the lads".

"What the hell are you asking me for?" he asked, but I could see that he found it hard not to laugh out loud. "Sure what the hell would I know about one of those big affairs? I'm damned lucky to have a suit to cover my back on a Sunday. I never saw one of those fancy suits in my life and I never met anybody who was daft enough to get into one of them".

"That makes two of us", I said. "The only thing is that I have to wear one for this dance. Do you not think I should hire it for the night?"

"Your mother was in the clothes trade in Glasgow, years before you were born", he said. "What the blazes are you asking me for when you have an expert sitting beside you?"

"That's right, Mick", Ma said, clearly delighted with my father's assertion of her competence. "I'll give him thirty pounds when he's going back on Sunday and on Monday afternoon he can go down and order the best suit they have. There'll be no son of ours going to a big do like that in somebody else's clothes. You never know who might have had them on last or what disease they might have had. I remember that great flu in 1918 and the way it spread through Glasgow. Coffins were piled up at the corners and in places they were seven feet high. He be getting into no second hand clothes".

Da straightened himself up in his chair and smirked. "I don't think, Boy, that there's much you or me could say about that. I doubt that you're going to have to buy a suit whether you want to or not. What the hell would I know about these fancy things ?"

I bought the suit at twenty-two pounds, which was a great deal of money at the time. My mother's prophesy about it coming in handy proved very accurate. Not only was I able to wear it on two consecutive years at graduation but I have worn it at numerous dress dances during the ensuing fifty years and, greatly to my wife's amusement, it is still to the fore.

CHAPTER 28
NEW HORIZONS

In the middle of the final term in our fourth year, advertisements began appearing in the press for teaching positions. One of them was for a specialist teacher in basic subjects who would take a special class in St. Thomas's Secondary School on the Whiterock Road in Belfast. The school was within an area, which I knew well, and I applied for the job. The interview lasted all of five minutes one evening, and I was appointed to the post.

I was especially looking forward to working in the school because the principal was a man called Michael McLaverty and I was very keen to meet him. I had known of him as a writer for years and I was excited at having the chance to get to know a famous author. I think that I was expecting to meet a truly exceptional man in every way but I was disappointed. Michael was friendly and approachable but very ordinary. In my opinion he was not a really capable principal and I don't think he was very happy in the post. He left most of the running of the school to the Vice Principal, Mr. McKeown.

I had been picked as one of a team of four people on duty in the first week of September. At lunchtime on the Tuesday I wandered towards the school yard and as I was about to enter it, I noticed a man working at the door. He had a big box of tools sitting beside him and he had just finished fixing a huge pane of glass into the door. Always being fascinated by skilled workmen, I stopped to talk to him.

"Was there an accident?" I asked. "That is a very big pane of glass that you have had to replace".

"Some blind, stupid effer walked right through the door", he informed me. He then went on to explain in very colourful language, how most of the people whom he had the misfortune to meet should not be allowed out on their own because they never looked where they were going. I chatted with him for a few minutes and then went sauntering along the side of the yard. I had gone perhaps fifteen or twenty yards when I heard a crash and an explosion of expletives behind me. I turned round to see the workman on his knees on the ground leaning over his workbox and surrounded by broken glass. He had finished the job, lifted his box and walked straight through the pane of glass, which he had just fitted. I walked back and reached him as he was surveying his handiwork. He glared at me.

"Don't you dare say one effen word", he growled. "What the hell took you back here anyway?"

"I just wanted to see if you were all right", I said.

"Did you get cut with any of these sharp pieces of glass".

"I never got a scratch", he replied, shaking his body to make sure that there were no shards of glass sticking in his clothes. "It was that bloody big heavy box that did the damage".

"Like you said", I remarked, "there are some right blind, stupid effers round here". I walked on about my business before he had time to think up a suitable reply.

My room was right beside the principal's office and Mr. McLaverty had a habit of calling in to ask one of the boys to do a message for him. Harry was one the most entertaining children I have ever met but I knew that he could not be trusted to do any sort of job reliably. It was not that poor Harry would not do his best but he was sure to get things wrong. He was always the most anxious to be picked but usually I managed to direct Mr. McLaverty's attention to someone else.

On day Mr. McLaverty came in and asked for a messenger. Harry almost knocked him down by running to him with his arm raised and a cheerful look of determination on his face.

"Oh, you are very keen to help me son", said Michael with a huge smile. "Now what would your name be?"

"I am Harry McKenna Sir", replied the boy jumping around him in joy at being noticed.

"Well Harry", said Michael, "I want you to take

this bucket down to the coal store and when you are down there bring up the milk. You will find the milk in a crate just outside the door of the store. Now, do you think you could do that?"

"I could surely sir", Harry assured him in glee.

Michael handed him the bucket and Harry disappeared down the stairs.

"I noticed that you keep Harry sitting in that little recess at the back of the room", said Michael, turning to me. "Have you got a reason for that?"

"I have a very good reason for it, Mr. McLaverty", I replied. "Every time I look at Harry I feel like bursting out laughing. Harry has caught on to this and he manages to twist his face so that I will certainly burst into laughter. Most of the time I manage not to look at him directly unless I am speaking to him".

"Is he a troublesome boy?" asked Michael.

"Not in the least", I replied. "He a very lovable and affectionate child but I don't want the class to think that I am paying him special attention".

"Right", said Michael thoughtfully and went back to his office.

Five minutes or so later, Michael flung the door open and stood in the corridor in a pose of complete bewilderment.

"Mr. Daly", he said, "Come out here till you see this". He stood there scratching his head.

I went to the door to find Harry standing looking at Michael with a bemused look on his face. He then turned to me and as usual stuck his two front teeth out so that he looked like a rabbit. On the floor at his feet was the big steel bucket. It was now filled with milk and a thousand bits of slack were floating on top of the milk. I burst into a fit of laughter and Mr. McLaverty looked at me in disgust.

"Mr. Daly", he said, "surely you don't think this is funny? All that milk is ruined. Do you not think that this boy should be able to do what his is asked to do? He actually went to the trouble of pouring thirty bottles of milk into a dirty bucket?"

"I'm sorry, Mr. McLaverty", I said, "but do you not think it is funny yourself when you look at it? If you really think about it Harry has done exactly what you asked him to do".

Michael stood there for a few moments scratching his head and surveying the scene around him. He looked into Harry's now earnest face and he too burst into laughter.

"I suppose one has to see the funny side of it", he agreed. "Is it not sad, however, that the boy can't do a reasonable job when he is asked to do so?"

"I suppose it is", I replied. "He can do a job if it is really straightforward and in this instance, as I said, if you think about it he did exactly what you asked him to do. I have no doubt that Harry will make his way in the world later on because he is a very lovable young fellow. Maybe some day when you have an easy job, you will ask him again".

"Right", said Michael. "Come with me now Harry and I'll give you your bar of chocolate. And then you can go downstairs and pour all that milk out at a drain. I hope that from now on you will know not to put milk into a coal bucket".

Harry assured Michael that he certainly would not do such a foolish thing again but I was not so sure that he would manage to keep that promise. Harry managed to keep me entertained for the year, which I spent in the school and I look back on him with great affection.

Michael McLaverty seemed to be obsessed with the idea that children who were behind in attainment should be helped to spend as much time as possible in the open air. If the weather was at all favourable he always opened my door after lunch time and pointed to the Black Mountain.

"Come on Mr. Daly, and take those children up that lovely mountain", he commanded. "This is no kind of day for them to be corralled here in school. I don't want to see you all until it is time to go home".

The result was that we spent quite a high percentage of our time wandering about on the lower slopes of the mountain. At that time there were hardly any houses between the school and the slopes and there was a narrow path from the Upper Springfield Road, which led to open ground. Sometimes I felt quite frustrated because I had lessons planned for an afternoon and I could not get them fitted in. It was also pretty difficult to find constructive ideas with which to fill the time.

One day as we were leaving the little path a goat

with two kids was grazing quite close to us. As soon as we approached they took off up the slopes but one of the kids had an injured leg and quite soon it fell behind. One of my more mischievous boys, Jack McStravick, began to chase the kid and in spite of my shouts, he continued after her until they disappeared round a crag. I asked one of the more responsible pupils to keep the class where we were and I went to find my missing pupil.

My heart missed a beat when I managed to climb round the big rock. The boy had followed the kid along a very narrow ledge and he was now stranded on the very edge of it. Below him was a sheer cliff some forty or fifty feet in height. The boy was standing with his back against the rock and I could see that he was utterly terrified. There was no sign of the kid, which must have managed to escape.

It was not difficult to climb up to the start of the ledge but almost as soon as I began to edge my way along it became so narrow that there was scarcely room for my feet. The rock at my back felt as though it was pushing me outward. I don't have a great head for heights and I began to feel a cold sweat enveloping me.

"Stay where you are Jack", I urged the boy in as quiet and calm a voice as I could muster. "Hold on to the rock and you'll be safe. I'll be with you in a minute".

I don't know what Jack thought but I certainly was not as sure of what I was saying as I tried to make out. Inch by inch I made my way painfully slowly towards Jack. I was about four feet away from him when I heard a shout from behind me.

"Hold on tight there Mr. Daly. If you fall you'll be killed stone dead".

I looked round in horror to find most of the class had now climbed round the rocky outcrop and were standing watching us.

"Stay where you are, boys", I managed to shout. "Don't dare come any further. I'll be back with you in no time".

I was now so frightened that I found it difficult to move my feet at all. I knew that if Jack were to fall I would not have any excuse for my actions. 'What sort of silly idiot would have brought a class of youngsters into dangerous territory like this?' I could imagine people asking when the news got out. It seemed like an age but at last my outstretched fingers were able to touch Jack's.

"Come very slowly toward me Jack", I urged. "Look at me and do not look down. Keep your eyes on me and move when I move".

It must have taken many minutes to make our way back to the start of the ledge but at last we made it. I gathered the class around me and we sat down and gazed out across the city spread beneath us. I tried to act as though nothing had happened but in reality I was trembling with terror at the thought of what might have happened.

Soon after I began working in St.Thomas's I

reluctantly had to change digs. Gerry Henvey decided to take in a crowd of new lodgers and at one stage there were thirteen or fourteen of us in the house. The food was still great and the craic was even better. There was only one bathroom in the house, however, and it was almost impossible to get out on time in the mornings and the one thing on which Michael McLaverty was very strict, was punctuality in the mornings. We had to sign in each morning and anyone who was in before ten past nine signed in black, those arriving between ten past nine and a quarter past signed in green and after that one had to sign in red. Michael relied on the honesty of his staff to use the correct colour but it soon became clear that he had no need of a red pen even though there were always latecomers.

I found that if I wanted to be in school on time I had to get up at half past six and that did not suit me at all. One of the teachers mentioned that he knew a lady who lived on the Grosvenor Road and volunteered to introduce me to her. He had heard her say that she was lonely in the house on her own and was thinking of taking a lodger.

Mrs Coulter was absolutely typical of the Belfast women I had seen in pictures. She was probably in her middle sixties when I got to know her and she was somewhat overweight to put it mildly. When going out she always wore a shawl except on very warm days in the middle of summer. She was very kindly and welcoming and treated me like a son. Her house was near to the school and this meant that I could walk when it wasn't raining. It was also near to the railway station, which was a bonus as well.

As soon as she discovered my interest in Irish, Mrs Coulter informed me that she was a life long republican and that she had been a courier during the Troubles in the Twenties. She assured me that she had a revolver secreted above the front door and she offered to let me examine it. I thanked her kindly for the offer but declined the invitation, stating that I knew nothing about guns and cared even less.

Not long after I moved in she told me that she had a son but that she did not allow him to come near the house.

"Why do you not wish to see your son?" I asked. "Surely if you go to the chapel and try to follow the commands of your religion, you should make peace with him no matter what he has done".

She rose from her seat and danced in anger before me, pointing her finger right into my face.

"And do you know what he did?" she asked. "He went and married a black Protestant from Ardoyne. If he was here this minute I'd cut him in stripes with a hatchet I have above the door beside the gun".

"Och now Mrs Coulter", I said, "surely he could have done thousands of worse things than that? Maybe if you'd got to know the girl you'd have found that she was quite nice".

I thought Mrs Coulter was going to have a fit. She did a sort of war dance in the middle of the floor.

"Nice? Did you say nice?" she gasped, glaring at me. "For six months after they set up house together I wandered the streets round Ardoyne with the hatchet under my coat. If I had managed to meet them I have chopped them in pieces. Maybe it's as well I didn't for if I had you wouldn't be talking to me now. I'd be sitting looking out of the Crumlin Road jail or else they'd have hanged me".

In the late spring I noticed Mrs Coulter looking at me very thoughtfully one day at dinner.

"You seem to be caught up in lots of things to do with Irish", she said eventually. "Would you happen to know where I might get a really good record of the Irish National Anthem?"

The question took me completely by surprise and I had to think for a while before answering. "As far as I know", I said, "the Radio Eireann Orchestra did an excellent one a couple of years ago and I think they have it on sale at the moment".

"How would I find out what price it is and how to go about getting it?" she asked. "I want to play it on that gramophone that you must have seen in the parlour".

The parlour was a very small room at the front of the house and only on one occasion when important visitors arrived had I ever seen it used. I knew that it was Mrs Coulter's pride and joy and was a sort of showpiece of her status. One of the many pieces of furniture, which crowded the little room, was a tall mahogany gramophone, which had to be wound up by means of a handle on the side, in order to get it to play.

"You know, Mrs Coulter", I said, "you will have to make sure to explain that you want the music on the old seventy-eight type of record. Some new records will not play on your machine".

"I'll not be explaining anything", she said with a knowing smile. "I want you to write to them and explain everything and I want you to get me the record as soon as possible".

About a fortnight later the record eventually arrived and Mrs Coulter made me sit on an armchair in the parlour to hear the first performance of the anthem. It was the first time in the months that I had been there that I was allowed to enter the parlour. She agreed that the record was excellent, just what she wanted, and she was delighted.

The following Sunday morning was beautifully warm and sunny. Mrs Coulter opened the parlour window, which greatly surprised me and at first I wondered was this something, which she did in summer. She also made sure that the front door was wide open too.

At half past ten, people began to pass the house on their way to a service in the Drew Memorial Church, which was fifty yards or so up the road. Their appearance was the cue for which Mrs Coulter had been waiting. She had the gramophone fully wound, the volume at maximum and the record in place. With a look of satisfaction, which it would be impossible to describe, she lowered the needle on to the record. As the music blared out, the startled looks on the faces of the passers by obviously fulfilled her wildest dreams. "Listen to that you Orange bastards", she murmured as she rubbed her hands and stood at attention to the music.

"For God's sake Mrs Coulter", I pleaded, "have a bit of sense and turn that volume down. If those were not quiet, decent people you would have a stone through your window or worse. How would you like people to go out of their way to annoy you going up to Clonard?"

"Let them listen to the anthem of their country", she sang as she waltzed around the room. "It'll give them something to think about for the rest of the day when they won't do any work".

I could see that there was no use trying to argue and I went up to my room and tried to read. The anthem ended and silence once again took over. Apparently Mrs Coulter tried the same experiment the next Sunday when I was away at home, but when nobody objected or paid much heed she let the matter rest there.

Almost immediately I got a real insight into how some of the people in the surrounding streets lived. Mrs Coulter was an agent for a money lender, and every Friday women came to the house to pay in deposits on money, which they had borrowed, or to beg for a new loan, or for an extension to an old one. She asked me on a few occasions to check her books for her and in doing so I was totally astounded by the amount of interest, which the lender was charging.

"Surely you don't mean to tell me, Mrs Coulter", I said, "that these people get a loan of ten pounds and they have to pay all the money back in eight weeks and they are charged four pounds interest. If they go over the eight weeks they have to pay six pounds. Have I made a mistake somewhere?"

"That would be right", she agreed. "Most of them get a loan of ten pounds and pay back at least fourteen. The man whom I work for tells me that he has to charge forty per cent interest because his money is not safe".

"But that is not forty per cent interest", I retorted. "It would only be forty percent interest if they were given a whole year to pay back the money. He is charging at least two hundred and fifty per cent and that is sheer robbery. People complain if a bank charges any more than ten per cent".

"Look", she said, "I get a few pounds out of it, the lender gets a bit out of it and the people are satisfied. Don't you go opening your mouth to anyone. Nobody is supposed to know it is going on".

We never discussed the business again but while I was there I often noticed people coming to the house in obvious distress. I discovered that they were terrified of being visited by the lender's enforcers. It was a way of life that made me feel sick.

Almost as soon as I began teaching, I wrote to parents on a number of occasions inviting them to come into the school to discuss the progress of their sons. Just over half of them came and I took the opportunity to have a fairly long conversation with them. One of the things, which emerged time after time, was that very few of the parents had ever been in the city centre or indeed outside of their immediate area. This completely amazed me and I mentioned it to some of the senior teachers. They were not surprised at all and accepted this as a local traditional way of life. As far as I could gather life was lived within the boundaries of a person's own parish.

Toward the end of the summer term a period of warm sunny weather set in and in the evenings, after school, I used to take the train and go down to Helen's Bay for a swim. On one such trip the thought struck me that it might be a good idea to take the class down to the beach while the good weather lasted. I mentioned my idea to Mr. McLaverty the following morning and he said he would think it over. Just before lunch he came into my room.

"Boys", he said, "Mr. Daly has mentioned to me that he is thinking of taking you all down to a beach on Belfast Lough for an afternoon. How many of you would like to go?"

Every hand in the room shot up and the eagerness on the children's faces was a joy to behold.

"Well," continued Michael, "you will have to get your parents to agree to let you go. They can either write me a note or they can call and see me here at the school. Do you understand that?"

The boys all assured him that they understood perfectly but I was not so sure.

"What Mr. McLaverty means", I explained, "is that if your parents do not give permission you will not be allowed to go. We would be in very serious bother if we took you out and your parents had not known about it and agreed. So if you want to go you must make sure that Mammy or Daddy give Mr. McLaverty permission to let you go. Harry, what do you have to do?"

Harry was up on his toes immediately with his hand stretched into the air as far as it would go.

"Please Sir, I have to tell Mammy and Daddy when I go home and get them to come and talk to Mr.McLaverty".

"That's exactly right", said Michael. "Now, I hope all the rest of you understand as well as Harry does. If your parents agree, Mr. Daly will take you down to the beach next Tuesday. That means that your parents have three days to get in touch with me".

Mr. McLaverty then turned to me. "I think this is a great idea", he said, "but it is a very big responsibility taking the whole class out on your own. Would you want me to arrange for another teacher to go along and help?"

"I don't want to disrupt the school at all, if I can help it", I answered. "Word has got out about what I'm thinking of doing and some of the staff think that I'm completely off in the head. I'll keep my fingers crossed and hopefully everything will be fine but thank you very much anyway".

"You will have to be very careful", said Michael, with a frown. "You have to get them down town and then to the train. Remember that none of these youngsters have ever been on a journey like this before. It's a big undertaking. By the way have you thought of what games or entertainment you will need on the beach?"

"If the weather remains like it is this week", I said, "I can't see that there will be any trouble. The landlady has a gas picnic stove and I'll get the loan of her pan and I'll fry a stone or so of sausages for them".

Tuesday was as fine a summer day as anyone could wish for. Michael came into our room at eleven o'clock.

"You know", he said, "we have been trying to get the parents to get in touch with us all year without result. And now every one of them has been in touch by yesterday. Most of them went to the trouble of actually calling at the school. I think that the reason for that, in the majority of cases, was that they did not think that they would be able to write a simple note. At any rate you can go off immediately after lunch".

The boys behaved impeccably on the journey and it was obvious that they were enthralled by the short time spent on the train. They played all sorts of games on the beach until they were tired and then we had our meal. Four pan loaves, twenty pounds of sausages and bottles of lemonade clearly seemed to them like manna from heaven. After the meal they sat around me and asked about all the various places, which they could see across the water. To my utter amazement, however, they spent most of the time just gazing at the water and the sky and murmuring about how beautiful it all was. Late in the evening I suggested we would have to start off for home.

The suggestion made them gather closer around me.

"Och, Sir", they pleaded, as though with one voice, "this is a lovely place. Do we really have to go back to Belfast where we never see the sea or the sky like this?"

"Now Boys", I chided, "you know that you have to go home. Your parents will be worried about you already. I have already kept you out far longer than I should".

"But", they murmured, "we might never get a day like this in our lives again. Just look at this lovely beach and the sea and all the lovely things around us. It would be great to stay here forever".

"Come on now", I ordered, "you know that we have to get back home. I am sure you will have many wonderful days later on. We'll go up the mountain every day if this weather continues and the city looks lovely from there".

They were not to be consoled, however, and on the train into Belfast they complained bitterly about having to go back to the dull, colourless city. I could not understand why these boys who had never been away from their parents before, did not yearn to get back home. In many ways I was delighted that I had brought them. I learned a great deal about them and saw them in a different light. They were almost like babies in this foreign environment. On the other hand I felt somewhat sorry. I felt that they had got a glimpse of something that could not be theirs. At the end of the day I felt a deep sadness and it stayed with me for some time afterwards.

CHAPTER 40
AN UNEXPECTED OFFER

I was at home for a weekend in May and when I was coming out of early Mass Fr. Moore took me to one side.

"I believe you are working in Belfast", he said. "How do you like living in the city? I was talking to your father some weeks ago and he assured me that you have been doing your best to court all the young women you happen to meet".

"Life's not bad at all, Father", I replied. "but you should know better than anyone not to listen to my father. City life is not like living in the country but in the good weather I take the chance of going to a beach two or three times a week. I also have my friends in the hurling team and that is very enjoyable".

"How would you like to have a job at home?" he asked.

I gasped. I had not even considered such a prospect because all the teachers in the parish were still quite young and I did not think that any new posts were needed.

"I would love to come home Father", I said eagerly.

"I don't see any chance of that at present, however".

"Pat Donnelly has made up his mind to leave teaching and go to the priesthood", he replied. "He has been preparing for this for some time and he will be going to a seminary in September. If you want the job, I can tell you now, it's yours".

"Thank you very much indeed Father", I said. "I will certainly take the post but I'm overwhelmed. I hadn't thought that a chance like this would come up for years to come".

"Right", he continued. "That's settled then. You can start immediately after the summer holidays. I want you to keep this quiet for a while as Pat has not told anyone what he is doing at this stage. The news will have to break soon, however. You can tell your parents but no one else".

"I will have to give in my notice in Belfast, Father", I pointed out. "It is only fair to give them as much notice as possible because leaving was the last thing on my mind and they have the staffing settled for next year".

"That's not a problem", he said. "Belfast is a long way from here and the news is not likely to come back this far. The job is yours but you will have to go and see the Parish Priest, Fr. Soraghan, as a matter of courtesy. As you know he has not been well and cannot leave the house really but technically he has the final say. It is only a matter of form. Make an appointment with him as soon as you can and get it over with. I hope you enjoy your new post".

"Thanks again Father", I said. "I know I will certainly love working here at home".

I rang Fr. Soraghan and made an appointment to see him the following Saturday. I then went home and told my parents the good news as we were sitting down to dinner.

"God be praised, but this is great news altogether", purred my mother. "Didn't I tell you, Mick that I was praying for something to come up and do you see the way God has worked things out for me?"

"For heaven's sake Sarah", replied Da with a laugh, "sure you're always praying for all sorts of things from one week's end to the next. If the man above listened to you half the time, he'd have no time to listen to anybody else".

"I tell you that it's my prayers that got him this job", Ma stated firmly. "Only I keep praying this house and everyone in it would go to the bad".

Da turned to me. "You'll have plenty of money about you now boy", he said. "You'll have the big teacher's salary and no need to spend money on lodgings. You'll be a real gentleman altogether".

"How much do you think the big teacher's salary is?" I asked.

Da spluttered into his dinner. "I don't know and I don't want to know", he replied firmly. "What a man earns is his own business and nobody else's".

"Well Da, no matter what you say I'm going to tell you. I get the princely sum of thirty nine pounds a month".

Da stopped eating and looked at me. I could see disbelief and surprise in his eyes. He looked down at his plate again and continued with his dinner without saying a word. Finally he looked up at me again.

"Thirty nine pounds a month?" he repeated in a questioning manner. "That's less than a tenner a week. Sure I'm getting that for breaking stones in the quarry and I have no schooling at all. Well, that's a tarra to man altogether. The only thing is that your pay will rise and mine won't. Anyway it's great that you're coming home".

First thing on Monday morning I told Mr. McLaverty what had happened. I could see that he was annoyed and disappointed.

"You promised when you were given the job here", he snapped, "that you wouldn't run away at the first opportunity and now that is exactly what you have done. Into the bargain you come along to me this morning and only give me a couple of week's notice before the holidays. I could hold you for three months after the summer holidays and how would that suit you?"

"If you want to do that, Mr. McLaverty", I said quietly, "you would be perfectly within your rights and I will abide by your decision. I'll have to tell Fr. Moore to hire a sub for that time. I did give a promise not to run away at the first opportunity and I really meant that. I could never have imagined that a job like this would come up in my own parish, however. I'm really sorry the way things have happened so suddenly".

Mr. McLaverty turned away from me and stood with his hands behind his back, looking out of the window. I could see that he was squeezing one hand with the other in an agitated way. He stood in this fashion for two or three minutes. Finally he turned round and looked me full in the face.

"Have you taken into consideration," he asked, "that next year your probation will be finished and you will be eligible for the allowance for the special class? That is seventy pounds a year at the present time and will make a big difference to your salary".

"I hadn't really thought about it Mr. McLaverty", I admitted, "but even with that increase I would still decide to go home".

He stood there looking at me and rubbing his chin with his hand. I could see that he was thinking and trying to work things out in his mind. Finally he slapped the desk with his hand.

"What would you say if I offered you a post of responsibility on top of the class allowance?" he asked. "Think about that and you'll find that I'm offering your at least a hundred and fifty pounds a year extra. That would more than compensate for having to pay for your digs and for any travel costs, which you might have during the year. There are senior teachers working here in the school and they have not got extra allowances to match what I'm offering you. And then you could spend all the time you like with that lovely young Brophy girl".

I gazed at him open mouthed for a minute,

completely taken aback by his final remark.

"How did you find out that I know Dolly, Mr. McLaverty?" I asked.

He laughed. "She comes from a lovely family", he replied, "and for many years I have been very friendly with her father. Indeed I am very friendly with all the family".

"I have only gone out with her a few times", I assured him. "It's nothing serious".

"I think that there are two opinions about that", he said. "I wouldn't like to see that wee girl hurt. But anyway what do you think of my offer?"

I felt embarrassed by Mr. McLaverty's generosity and by the fact that I was going to turn it down. I found it difficult to think of a form of words, which would not sound like an arrogant insult. It was my turn to stand looking out of the window. It must have been two or three minutes before I attempted to respond.

"Mr. McLaverty", I said, "that is a very generous offer and indeed all through this year you have always been very helpful and supportive. I honestly feel very bad about promising not to run away as you have put it, but I had no idea that something like this would crop up. I have given my word to Fr. Moore, however, and I'd find it hard to go back on that. Into the bargain, I also informed my parents of what had happened last weekend. They were delighted to hear that I was coming home again and since I'm an only child I think it would break their hearts if I changed my mind. In spite of all your kindness and generosity I'm afraid I'll have take Fr. Moore's offer".

To my great surprise Michael smiled and held out his hand. "Well, nobody can say I didn't try", he said, shaking my hand. "I can see that you have made up your mind very firmly and in that case all I can do is wish you the best of luck. You can tell the priest that you will be starting in September because there would be little purpose in my holding you here for a few weeks. I'm sorry to lose you and I hope that everything turns out well for you".

"Thank you very much indeed, Mr. McLaverty", I replied. "In many ways I'm sorry to leave because I have been very happy here. I think, however, that the man who wrote that wonderful story, 'The Wild Duck's Nest', will understand why I want to get back to the wilds of Tyrone".

"Oh, so you have been reading some of my writing?" he said.

"I have read quite a lot of it", I assured him. "I must say that I have enjoyed it immensely but that little story of the duck's nest on Rathlin island was a real masterpiece in my opinion".

"Thanks a lot for your appreciation", he said. "Once again, I want to wish you all the best in the next few years. And I can assure you that no matter how many of those years there are, in the end they will seem very short indeed".

My interview the following weekend with Fr. Soraghan was, by any standards, somewhat unique.

The old priest was reclining in an armchair in his sitting room but he welcomed me with the warm, childlike smile, which I had known so well as a boy.

"Take a seat there Arthur", he said, holding out his hand. "I hope you're not in a hurry because I have not seen you for ages and we have lots to talk about. I feel very lonely here in this room at times and it is very seldom that people call in to see me. It's no fun, I can tell you, being confined to a chair".

Looking at him there I felt a pang of sadness to think of one of Ireland's great athletes being so limited in his movements. He had never been very big but in his present condition he looked like a young child. In my mind I visualised him jumping over gates, or leaping across streams, as he went round the countryside visiting his parishioners as a young parish priest.

"I'm sorry to hear that you can't get out Father", I said. "I'm sure the camogie girls must miss you terribly every time they play".

"Did somebody tell me that you have taken up the hurling?" he asked.

"A long time ago I found a fairly good hurley stick at my granny's", I agreed. "Tommy Jordan also got a hurley somewhere and we used to practice in the fields around home. When I went to Belfast a group of us formed a team and we have been playing in the Antrim leagues and in college matches".

"So when you come home", he said with a big

satisfied smile, "you will be able to train the camogie girls for me".

"Lord, I don't know about that Father", I said. "I know a wee bit about hurling but I know nothing about camogie".

The old priest laughed and sat up in his seat. "If you can play one, you can play the other", he assured me. "As you know I come from Louth, which is not a hurling county and I have trained teams to win Ulster championships and All Irelands".

All during our conversation, Margaret his housekeeper, had been dusting round the room. I was aware that she was much more intent on listening to our conversation than she was in the work. By this time she was on her third tour round the room and it must have been difficult for her to find anything more to do. She stopped just short of the door and looked agitatedly into the old priest's face.

"Och now Father", she demanded earnestly, "are you going to yarn and blether there all day? I think it's time you gave the man the job and be done with it".

I have wondered ever since if I am the only person ever to have been appointed to a post by the priest's housekeeper.

CHAPTER 41
GREENHORN AT WORK

I soon discovered after moving home in that summer of 1959 that working in school was only one of the jobs that I was expected to do. In fact in the eyes of the priests of the parish it often seemed as hardly the most important. They gave the impression that helping to raise funds to build and equip the new secondary schools was a teacher's major function. Young teachers were expected to take part in every event held in the parish and in most cases to organise such events. The more important and eye-catching jobs were in the hands of senior staff while new recruits were expected to fulfil more menial duties. Jobs, which needed delicate handling and were likely to land one in trouble, were the natural province of the newcomer. Unless one wanted to be regarded as useless or incompetent, or some sort of ridiculous rebel, one had little option but to do exactly what one was told without question or complaint.

At that time, for about eight months of the year, there was a whist drive every Sunday night in the Parochial Hall on our side of the parish. It was preceded by tombola, which would later be better known as bingo. Both activities had to be very carefully run and supervised lest some of the experts in cheating should unfairly win the 'big' prizes on offer. Fr. Moore made it clear that jackpots should be kept for the longest possible time and it was a minor catastrophe that the parish should have to part with them at all. It was suggested, though never explicitly stated that should an organiser be responsible for the loss of a jackpot, he would be expected to pay the money out of his own pocket. In my own case it meant the if such a calamity should occur, it would mean the loss of half a year's salary at the very least.

Just before lunchtime on my second day in the school, Fr. Moore burst into my room in his usual hurried fashion. I think he loved to give the impression that he was constantly involved in very important business and thus had never a second to spare. I had been sitting with one of the children helping with his work and I rose at once and went to greet our visitor.

"I see that you have settled in already", he said, and smiled pleasantly. "I hope that you will enjoy your work here in our school and I am looking forward to us having a very profitable and friendly partnership for all concerned. You will be aware that the big whist drive will be starting before the end of the month. I want you to be in charge of the tombola and of course you will be helping at the whist as well. We have a new curate in the parish as you probably know and you will be working with him. I will look after things over in Moy and I will leave this side of the parish to the two of you".

"You know Father", I said, "this secondary school problem is putting an awful burden on you priests and on the people of the parish. I wonder if it is all necessary".

"What?" he exploded, jumping as though stung by a bee. "We have to raise the money. We have no alternative".

"But Father", I continued, "I have been looking at the four and two committee system and it seems to be working well in the one or two places where it has been tried. I can't see why we could not have given it a chance and then opted out if it was not to our liking".

"Oh the bishops know best", he replied, in a tone that told me he was not at all pleased with my remark. "We do what we are told and get on with it".

I thought of the constant nights of work before me and my heart fell like a stone. This would mean that I would not be able to get to a dance on a Sunday night and the best dances were always held on a Sunday. I was in a quandary. I could not very well refuse this man who had been so helpful to me over a long period but I thought that it would be worthwhile suggesting an alternative solution to his problems.

"You know Father", I said softly and hopefully, "I know nothing at all about whist or tombola and I would not be much use at running things. Maybe some of the other teachers could take charge for a few months. Cards are a complete puzzle to me and I have no interest in them at all. Others are likely to know what they are doing whereas I really would not have a clue".

"There's no need for you to worry", the priest said confidently, putting a friendly hand on my shoulder. "We have a fine group of men on the committee and they will keep both you and Fr. Bradley right. There's a meeting in the hall on Friday night and you will meet everybody then. It starts at eight o'clock so make sure not to be late. That's what I called in to tell you about. I have to be off now as I have business in Drogheda".

Fr. Moore swept out of the room as though he did not have a second to spare. I felt slightly annoyed that I had not been asked if it suited me to go to the meeting or if I would be willing to assist at the function. I had been told what to do and the idea that I might object had never surfaced. A few minutes later lunchtime began and as usual I took my sandwiches into Mr. McAvinchey's room where we dined together at his desk. Each day Mrs McAvinchey sent over a big pot of tea from her school across the road and thanks to Frank's generosity we shared the hot tea. I was somewhat surprised when Frank chatted about all sorts of things but did not mention Fr. Moore's visit. Eventually I brought the subject up myself.

"Fr. Moore did not give me much option but to take charge at the whist and tombola", I said. "I would have thought that somebody like yourself with plenty of experience might have been the ideal choice for a job like that".

Frank spluttered into his tea and stopped with a sandwich half way to his mouth and glared at me. I could see the red slowly spreading from his neck up to his face and I knew that he was annoyed and angry.

"Fr. Moore?" he growled at last. "And when and where did you see Fr. Moore, young fellow?"

I had learned on teaching practice that Frank only addressed me as 'young fellow' when he was annoyed with me and the more annoyed he was, the more distinctly and slowly he pronounced the words. Now he pronounced them very slowly and distinctly indeed. I wondered what I had done to really irritate him. Maybe it had been bad policy to let him know that I had tried to get him a job, or rather to palm it off on him.

"He called in to my room a few minutes ago", I answered as calmly as I could. "He was in a hurry but he told me that I had to work in the hall in Sunday night and go to a meeting on Friday night. I thought you would have known about it".

Frank jumped up suddenly, knocking his chair over on to the floor. He stood holding the edge of his desk with both hands, clearly ignoring the fact that he had not finished his lunch. He was now very red in the face indeed and he was glaring down at me as though I were his worst enemy in the world.

"Do you mean to tell me?" he spat through his teeth, "that that bloody man had the cheek and the bad manners to walk past my door and go into your room without telling me?"

I breathed a huge sigh of relief. I knew now that I was not the object of Frank's irritation. I found it hard not to laugh at his attitude about what seemed to me a very minor matter indeed.

"I did not realise that he had not called with you", I explained. "That's why I was surprised that you didn't mention him when I came in for lunch".

Frank stepped back from the desk, kicking the chair out of his way in the process and he stamped his feet angrily on the floor while holding his hands over his ears.

"I'm supposed to be the bloody principal here", he hissed, glaring down at me once more with venom in his eyes. "That bloody man thinks that he can treat me like a tramp on the street. Wouldn't you think that he'd have learned a wee bit of manners at his age and with all the training he had received?"

"He said he was in a hurry", I explained. "Maybe that is why he came on into my room without calling with you".

"Dammit", yelled Frank, once again doing an angry shuffle, "are you as bad as he is? Don't you know damned well that nobody and I mean nobody, is ever allowed to enter this building without getting my permission to do so? That, young fellow, goes for any of your friends or relations who might want to see you. It also applies to any parents of the children. No one goes in there to see you unless I give them permission. Have you got that into your head?"

I assured him that I had got the general idea and I was about to relax on my seat once again when I noticed that he was still glaring at me in annoyance. He pointed a finger down at my nose.

"As long as ever you are working in this school", he hissed, "never you dare to act the smart fellow and land me with a job, young fellow. I was working here when you were still in the pram and I have done my stint. Don't get it into your head that you can be the cute man like some of the boys that we have around here, and try to land me with the dirty jobs. You'll be up early in the morning, young fellow, if you want to get one over on me".

Frank growled and grumbled from time to time for the rest of the week and vowed that when he next met Fr. Moore he would give him a hot reception. When Fr. Moore called on Friday, however, no mention was made of his breaking Frank's laws. On the other hand Frank assured him that I would be a great asset to him and his team, and since I was young and fit I would be available for all sorts of jobs that might have to be done.

I was down at the hall about ten minutes earlier than arranged on Friday evening but even so I was met at the door by a bright faced, smiling young priest.

"You are very welcome to your new place of work

Arthur", he said, shaking my hand. "You and me have been lumbered with running this show. We are going to have to work closely together but I have a feeling since meeting you that that is not going to be a problem".

As we walked towards the stage I had feeling of confidence that I was going to enjoy working with this young man. He was friendly, very much at ease, and made people feel that he was lucky to be in their company. We sat down at the table on the stage and waited for the others to arrive.

"You know Father", I said, "you have already made a very big impact in the parish and you have only been here for three or four weeks".

He looked at me sideways with a kind of inquisitive smile. "And would that impact be good or would it be some kind of disaster?" he asked.

"I would not describe it as good at all", I answered and paused. A faint shadow of concern flashed across his face.

"Good would hardly be the word for it", I continued. "It would be truer to describe it as excellent or fantastic or something along those lines".

"And what might I have done to deserve praise like that?" he asked with a big smile. "You are very good at buttering people up, but I am sensible enough not to take it too seriously".

"Well really Father", I said, "it is the first time in my entire life that I have heard people coming out of the chapel discussing what the priest had been talking about when the sermon had nothing to do with money. I notice that you speak for a very short time and you usually have a pertinent wee story to illustrate your main point. Maybe you have been trying to imitate the parables. At any rate it is always refreshing and interesting. You have the art of grabbing peoples' attention".

Fr. Bradley sat studying his fingers as he fiddled with them on the table for a moment. "You know", he said, "a man whom I considered to be very wise, once told me that if I could not say what I wanted to say in three minutes, I should not bother to say it at all. He told me I would be wasting my time and the time of the congregation into the bargain. I have often been bored stiff myself with long, wandering sermons so I have tried to live by his advice".

"That seems to be to be a very good motto to follow", I said thoughtfully. "I have often wondered why so many men go rambling on for ages while their listeners dose off into a light sleep. Indeed in many cases there is time for a real good deep sleep and maybe a chance to dream of better things. Anyway the good advice certainly seems to be working for you".

At that point the other men began to arrive and take their places round the table. I got the impression that they were weighing us up warily and were wondering if these two young greenhorns would try to show them how to run a whist drive. The conversation opened and was friendly but guarded.

"Right men", said Fr. Bradley when introductions were completed. "I have to tell you that Arthur and myself are very aware that we know nothing at all about running this show. We have no knowledge of cards at all and are completely lost. We feel lucky, however, to have people around us like yourselves who do know and we plan to leave things in your hands. We will do whatever you want us to do and we will try not to get in your way".

I could sense the tension rapidly fading around the table and the men unconsciously leaned forward in an aura of friendship, interest and cooperation. It was agreed that Fr. Bradley and I would be 'front men' on the stage while the others would control things from the floor of the hall. Johnny Daly was recognised as a leader and expert, and he spoke for the others.

"There is one thing that we must understand", he said. "We have a few simple rules and we stick to them no matter what happens. Cards have to be checked at certain games if their holders have a potentially winning score. If a card comes up near the end and it has not been checked when it should have been, it must be rejected. I don't care who owns it, should it be the Parish Priest or my own wife, if it is not correct it must be rejected. The same goes for the tombola. We have to treat everybody the same and if we don't hold to those rules we might as well quit now".

All the men round the table nodded in agreement and the look of determination on their faces told us how important this was. They sat back to see how the priest would react.

"That makes perfect sense to me", he said. "The only thing is that for a while at least it would be good if one of you would come up on to the stage and help us check the cards. There might be things that you would see and we wouldn't".

I noticed the looks of satisfaction and slight surprise, which passed between the men. It was clear to me that Fr. Bradley was intent on building a united team and he was doing an excellent job.

"What way do you intend to handle things on the stage?" asked Patsy Donnelly who was recognised as a good man to have around.

"Fr. Bradley can do all the work with the microphone", I suggested. "I will help out with keeping things right in the background".

"It will be the other way round", said the priest with a laugh. "Arthur will be in charge of the microphone and I will be organising things at the back of the stage. I have made up my mind about that, and that's the way I want it to be".

"But", I protested, "Fr. Bradley has far more experience talking to crowds than I have. Surely he would be better at that job?"

"Have a go at it and we'll see how it turns out", said Patsy. "We can always change about but I don't think that will be necessary".

Over the following months I was aware of a spirit of great confidence in each other growing amongst the team. We had our rules, we kept to them no matter what happened and for two years Sunday nights were not only profitable but also enjoyable. In that time we raised three and a half thousand pounds, which was a vast amount of money in those days. I suppose the fact that a fine bungalow could be built and finished for under a thousand pounds will give people some idea of its value.

A Sunday night came in the late spring when a very big jackpot had built up and there was great excitement and some tension. Card sharps always came from all over the country when the money was big and the men on the floor had to be extra careful. We were confident, however, that if we kept to our rules there would be no trouble. Fr. Moore in his usual manner came over and sat at the back of the stage with his head down and looking as though everyone belonging to his had died suddenly. Everyone was aware that he only appeared when the money was big. It was easy to see how concerned he was that the jackpot should be retained if possible. Everything was going fine until the final games of the whist drive.

At that stage Fr. Moore's housekeeper sent up a card with a magnificent score, which had not been checked at any of the previous games. We had no doubt that the lady was totally honest but we had no option but to reject it.

"This card has been sent up without being checked at the twelfth and fifteenth games", I announced over the microphone. "Everyone knows our rules and we have to declare it null and void. I'm sorry but as you know those are the rules".

A murmur of agreement went round the hall mixed with some concern for a lady who had made a genuine mistake. We were about to continue with the next game when Fr. Moore jumped up and took the microphone out of my hand.

"I know Alice", he said slowly and deliberately. "I can guarantee that her card does not have to be rejected. I am directing that it be accepted and goes forward into the last games".

He stood holding the microphone towards me and there was dead silence in the hall. Only the bated breathing of the players could be heard. Very slowly I took the microphone. I knew that I had to make a key decision on my own and I could not hope to seek help.

"We here on the stage have no doubt about this player's honesty", I said. "The card does not conform to the rules, however, and it must be rejected. There can be no exceptions. Those are the conditions on which we agreed to run this whist drive and they are the conditions on which all of you agreed to take part. The rules must be the same for everyone".

Fr. Moore pulled the microphone out of my hands angrily.

"This is not a normal case", he announced curtly. "As I said I am directing that this card is genuine and can go forward".

Once again he held the microphone out towards me but this time I did not take it. I looked into his face, shook my head and walked over to take my coat from the peg where it was hanging. The priest put the microphone on its stand and followed me. The tension in the hall was so strong that I felt one could reach out and touch it.

"What do you think you are doing?" Fr. Moore asked.

"I'm sorry but I'm going home Father", I said quietly. "There's no place for me here when we have no rules".

Fr. Moore looked stunned. He was not used to people refusing to do what he said without question and he could not believe that a young teacher would dare to cross him. Finally he turned to Fr. Bradley.

"You take over for the rest of the night Father", he ordered. "We'll sort this out later".

Fr. Bradley remained sitting on his chair and slowly shook his head. He looked up at Fr. Moore sadly.

"I am in exactly the same position as Arthur Father" he said firmly. "The only thing we had to stand on was our rules and if those have been taken away I can't continue either. Since you have taken over Father, I'm afraid that you are going to have to continue on your own".

I was on the top step of the little flight that led down from the stage at this juncture. I suddenly realised that all the men in the team were standing across the front of the stage with their backs to the crowd. They were stern faced and determined. Fr. Moore went slowly back to the microphone and stood thinking while a growing volume of excited conversation arose from the hall. Peter Kernan strode purposefully across the stage and spoke loudly into the microphone.

"There's something terrible rotten in the state of Denmark", he said and walked away to get his coat. The speech was greeted with howls of surprised and uneasy laughter. Peter was one of our team and was regarded as a man well worth listening to. I had been warned a couple of years before that 'if Peter was barking at a hole there was sure to be a rabbit in it'. I found that to be very good advice.

I did not sleep easily that night. I kept going over the events of the evening in my mind and I found myself in a confused state. On the one hand I was sure that I could not have taken any other line of action but on the other I was annoyed at having to cross Fr. Moore who had been so good to me. I finally decided that I had taken the only course open to me and I would have to live with the consequences but I did not look forward to meeting the priest. It was well known that he had never admitted to being in the wrong.

To my great surprise nobody mentioned whist in school the next day. Frank had won a big prize playing golf and his only interest was in describing the great game he had played. Just after eleven o'clock on the Tuesday, my door was opened quietly and Fr. Moore slipped into my room. This was most unusual because he usually burst in with a flourish. I was teaching at the front of the room and he came over and stood beside me.

"Can you give the boys something to do, which will keep them occupied, Arthur?" he whispered. "I want to have a talk with you for a minute or two".

He sat down on the chair at the desk while I gave the class some written work. Out of the corner of my eye I noticed that the priest was in a very thoughtful mood. I took my place beside him.

"I was very surprised when you walked out on me on Sunday night Arthur", he said as I sat down. "I never thought that you would have left me in the lurch like that".

"It was something that I would never have foreseen myself doing at all, Father", I answered quietly but firmly. "As I see it you left me with no alternative. Once you dismissed our rules we did not have a leg to stand on. I have to say that if the same situation were to crop up tonight again I would do exactly the same thing".

"Humph", murmured the priest slowly. Then he turned and looked me full in the face. "I realised later", he said in a low whisper, "that I was wrong to take over and countermand your ruling. I suppose long years of being in command clouded my judgement. I have to say I'm sorry and I mean that".

"Thank you very much Father", I said. I was

astounded because I would never have imagined that this man would say he was sorry to anyone.

"I hope we can put all this behind us", he continued. "I'll go round the rest of the men this week and you can go ahead next Sunday night as usual".

"Father Moore", I said quietly, "as far as I am concerned that will not happen. I could never stand at that microphone again with any feeling of confidence and I doubt if any of the others would take part either. As I said we would not have a leg to stand on and as far as I am concerned it's all over".

"Och now Arthur", the priest replied in a surprised but very friendly tone, "it's not as bad as all that. I will explain to people before we start and that will clear the air".

"Father", I said, "I will not be in that hall next Sunday night nor any other Sunday night. I would feel an utter fool if I had to stand up there after what happened. We have lost the confidence of the crowd and we can't get it back no matter what we do. I appreciate that you did not mean any harm but the harm has been done. I hope you don't think I'm just being crooked but I won't change my mind. I can't".

The priest rose to leave and I walked over to the door with him. He turned in the doorway and smiled. "I'll call back on Friday and by that time I hope you will have seen the light and changed your mind", he said.

"You can call back on Friday surely Father",

I replied, "but I can assure you that I won't have changed my mind. By the way, Father", I added, "did you call with Frank before coming into my room?"

"Why should I?" he asked.

"Well, he gets very upset if anybody comes into the school and doesn't tell him that they are there before they pass his door", I explained.

Fr. Moore shook his head and laughed. "My heavens but all you teachers are very thin skinned", he said. "I suppose I had better say hello to him or nobody in the place will be speaking to me".

To my great surprise Frank never mentioned Fr. Moore's visit at lunch that day and I have no idea what transpired between them. He did not mention whist either and I wondered if he were playing me at my own game by keeping quiet and silent about the whole thing. The next day at lunch, however, I got the answer to my questions in no uncertain manner. I had taken my place at his desk when I noticed that he was very cross looking and had not spoken a word. I began to eat my lunch and chat as though everything were normal. Two or three minutes must have passed before he looked up and glowered at me.

"What do you mean, young fellow, by acting the cute hoor with me?" he demanded. "How dare you come into this room of mine and sit at my desk and drink my tea and still act the smart hoor for most of a week. It you want to behave like that my brave boy, I'd advise you to dine next door and look for a job somewhere else as soon as you can".

I had seen Frank in a bad mood on a number of occasions but I had never seen him as annoyed or angry as this. I had kept quiet about what was happening because I felt that Frank would not agree with the course of action I was taking and I did not want to deliberately go against his advice. I knew in my heart that some sort of confrontation was bound to come but I did not think that he would be as offended as he obviously was. There was little I could do but apologise.

"I have not been trying to be the smart fellow at all Frank", I said as calmly as I could. "It's just that I've had a lot on my mind these past few days and I have been trying to work things out for myself. I'm sorry if you feel offended because I know that you have gone miles out of your way to help me over the past few years. I know too that you have my best interests at heart. I could never hope to thank you for all that you have done".

Frank glared at me once more and it seemed as though he was even more annoyed than before. He thumped his fist down on the desk, spattering books and leaflets with tea.

"And what makes a young skitter of a teacher like you think that you can openly disagree with a man of Fr. Moore's standing?" he demanded. "After all the good work we have done to set you on the right road, you go and ruin the whole thing. And by God you have ruined it with a capital R. Do you not know that teachers can't do things like that?"

It seemed to me that even the whites of his eyes were red with bad temper.

"I did not want to stand up to Fr. Moore at all Frank", I assured him. "He pulled the whole house down on top of us last Sunday night and there was nothing that Fr. Bradley or I could do. The team of men are of one mind. We had to work together or not at all. Fr. Moore has admitted that he was wrong but I could never stand before a crowd on that stage again and if I did I would be standing on my own. My hands were tied and I had no choice".

Frank jumped up and glowered down at me once more. "Can you not understand", he pleaded, "that a teacher can't afford to treat a priest the way you are treating him? He is your employer and you do what he says. Do you not understand that he will get his own back on you and there's nothing you can do about it? Your name will be blackened all over this archdiocese. You have destroyed all the good work we did when you were here on teaching practice and since. I have to tell you that you are one damned silly, stupid fool".

I looked up at Frank who was now standing in front of the blackboard, squeezing his hands in frustration. He was also shaking his head in disbelief that anyone could be so stupid as he clearly thought I was. I sat silent for a few seconds before I said anything.

"I don't think that you are right about Fr. Moore's attitude to people", I said. "A few years ago I wrote him a very angry letter when there was a dispute about dancing in the hall in the Moy. It was none of my business and I was totally in the wrong. He did not hold that against me and I would be surprised if he takes a spite at me over this. I think he can be very overpowering in his efforts to have his own way but basically I think he is very fair. But whatever happens I don't want you to feel hurt. I'm sorry for not mentioning anything about this but I did not want to get you involved before things sorted themselves out. There comes a time when one has to stand on one's own feet and I feel deeply that I had no choice".

Frank looked up at the ceiling as though imploring assistance from on high. "Under God", he said plaintively, "has some evil spirit muddled your brain altogether? Can you not get it into your head that I have been in this job for over thirty years and I know what I am talking about. You don't walk out on a priest and leave him in the lurch the way you did and get away with it. The only thing you can do is go down to the Parochial House and make an abject apology and tell him you will do whatever he wants".

Up until this point I had been feeling very ill at ease and unsure how to mollify this man who had been so helpful to me. Suddenly I felt calm and determined.

"Frank", I said, "I know you are trying to put me on the right road but I can't do what you are suggesting. We ran that whist drive honestly and we were fair to everyone. I will not apologise to anyone for that. Fr. Moore decided to take over and run it his way and I will certainly not be going back. He took the reins out of our hands and his action made no sense at all. I told him that when he was in my room yesterday and I'm standing by it. Wild horses would not drag me to that microphone again".

Frank had been about to sit down but at my words he jumped up again and stared at me in obvious disbelief and surprise.

"Yesterday?" he roared. "Did you say yesterday? How in hell's blazes could he have been in your room yesterday? He left me and walked straight out to his car. How could he have been in your room?"

"Oh, I thought you knew he had been in my room", I muttered. "He must have come in before he called with you".

"Well, damnation to the two of you", Frank yelled. "I don't know what the hell is going on in my own school and I'm supposed to be in charge here. One of you is as bad as the other. Bloody people have no manners nowadays at all. And by the way you fairly acted the cute fellow, my smart boy, when you never told me about the piano".

I gulped, taken completely by surprise. "What piano are you talking about Frank?", I asked.

"Oh, you have a damned handy bad memory when it suits", snapped Frank. "I'm talking about the only piano that was the talk of the parish a while ago.

I'm talking about the piano that you and that Jordan fellow wrecked on Fr. Moore. But then it suited you to forget about that one, didn't it?"

"Och God Frank, sure that was months ago and it happened at the start of the holidays and it was a complete accident. Tommy and I were asked to bring it over from the Moy for a guest tea that our football team were having".

"And the two of you decided to wreck it and to make matchwood of it", hissed Frank through his teeth. "It was Fr. Moore's best piano as far as I can hear and of course you two decided that you could improve on its appearance". Frank spoke in a very sarcastic tone as though he had no intention of believing a word I said.

"Well, I don't think it was a great piano in the first place", I said. "I am told that the good piano was in another room in the hall and it's still there but the one we had did end up in bad shape. We went for it with Tommy's pick-up and a few men gave us a hand to load it. We had no rope but everyone said it would be safe enough if Tommy drove carefully. We got it to the door of that hall across the road there but we did not see a big deep pothole just in front of the door. The back wheel went into the pothole and the piano dived over the side of the pick-up. It was in a hundred pieces and there was nothing we could do about it. Fr. Moore hardly said a word about it and I have a feeling that he was secretly pleased".

"And you never said a word to me about that

escapade", Frank replied with an air of resignation. "I suppose you thought that you were one of the cute boys that we have around here".

"I didn't see you for a couple of months after it happened", I explained. "I had almost forgotten all about it and I didn't think it would be of much interest anyway".

"Well, a lot of other people seemed to think that it was of great interest and I don't know how many of them told me that anybody who trusted you and that fellow Jordan to do a job, deserved to be locked up. At any rate I can tell you one thing, Fr. Moore won't have a bad memory like you. He'll bear it in mind and when he gets the chance he'll come back at you. You didn't think to pay him for the piano did you?"

"I did not indeed", I assured him. "Tommy and I did our best and it was unfortunate that there was a big deep hole just at the door of the hall across the road there. Most people made a joke of the whole thing and it was said that the dogs for miles around were running about with the keys in their mouths. One man told me that the hounds would be playing 'Danny Boy' when the hunting season starts. But I don't honestly believe that Fr. Moore will try to punish me for what happened".

The rest of the week was pretty uncomfortable in school and especially at lunchtime. I would have liked to take Frank at his word and dine in my own room but I thought that doing so would only make things worse. I tried to make conversation each day while we ate our lunch but it was very difficult and uneasy. Frank even started to go out and walk round the field where the boys were playing as soon as he had eaten his lunch. News filtered into the school early in the next week that the whist drive on Sunday night had been a disaster. Hardly anyone had turned up and Fr. Moore did not make a good job of running it. To be fair, he did not see it as his job and did not want to be there at all. A couple of weeks later he decided that it was a lost cause and called an end to it. The tension eased a little between Frank and me but I did not really have peace of mind.

A few weeks later I was about to clear up for the evening when once more Fr. Moore came into the room. He was in obvious good form and greeted me with a big smile. To my great surprise he walked round the room and talked to each boy in turn and then he helped as they left for home. It was most unusual because the man never seemed comfortable when dealing with children. Finally he sat on the edge of my desk and explained that he wanted to have a few words with me.

"Come on out to my car and we'll let Frank lock up and go home", he said confidentially.

"Have you thought about promotion in your profession, Arthur?" he asked when we were seated in the car. The question took me completely by surprise and I found it hard to think of a sensible reply.

"Really Father", I answered slowly, "it was not something, which had been on my mind at all. The way things are here in the school, I can't see any opportunity for promotion for years to come, if ever".

"Exactly", he responded, looking into my eyes. "I know you are getting on well here but maybe you should be looking further afield. The way I see it a bit of extra money and responsibility would do you no harm at all".

I was now sure that Fr. Moore had some scheme in mind but I could not think of what it might be.

"I know you have something in mind Father", I said, looking sideways into his face. "What are you trying to tell me?"

The priest leaned his head back and looked at the ceiling of the car. "I was in Dungannon this morning and I was talking to Dr. MacLarnon" he said. "Do you know the Doctor?"

I have met him a couple of times", I said. "I have never been speaking to him though so I can't say I really know him".

"Well, he knows you and he knows all about you", Fr. Moore said with a knowing smile. "He is setting up a special class in the school and he is not satisfied with any of the people who have applied for the job. He wants you. He has assured me that if you are willing to take the post he will be able to let you have the special allowance and he will give you a post of responsibility on top of that. He tells me that it will mean about two hundred pounds a year to you. That would surely be quite a bit to a man in your position".

"Father, I am totally astounded", I gasped. "I can't see how Dr. MacLarnon has so much faith in me when he doesn't know me. I would have thought that he would have had more confidence in some of his past pupils from the Academy. This has completely taken my breath away".

"Dr.MacLarnon contacted Dr. Rogers in the training college", he answered. "It seems that Dr. Rogers left him in no doubt about who he should try to get. And then, Dr. MacLarnon knows me and I know you and remember I went to primary school with your father. If you want the job, nip into Dungannon now and see the Doctor. He told me that he would not leave the school until you arrive".

"But what about the school here, Father?" I asked. "Would I not need to tell Frank what I'm doing before I do it?"

"Young Mickey McGleenan is looking for a job and this one is made for him", replied Fr. Moore. "Don't worry about Frank. I'll handle him when it's all settled. Go straight into Dungannon this minute".

"Lord Father, I'd need to go home and change my clothes", I protested. "I'm all covered with chalk dust".

"Don't worry about that at all", Fr. Moore answered, putting a friendly hand on my shoulder. "Scoot into Dungannon. The Doctor wants a working teacher and not some sort of prima donna. I hope you enjoy your new post".

I made my way into Dungannon in a kind of daze

and found the school easily though I had never set eyes on it before that day. The Doctor met me at the door with a big smile and welcomed me in Gaelic. 'This man has really done his homework,' I thought to myself. He took fifteen minutes or so to show me round the school and by the end of that time it seemed to be taken for granted that I was taking the job although it had not been mentioned.

"You probably know that I can offer you the special class allowance", said the Doctor when we finally reached his office. "That should make a fair difference to your salary". He looked at me with a quizzical smile.

"I understood that you would also be offering a post of responsibility on top of that, Doctor", I replied, hoping that I looked sufficiently disappointed. "We were assured when we did that course in the training college that the special allowance would be no hindrance to holding a post as well".

"Oh fair enough Art", he said, gazing at me thoughtfully. "You can have the post but I don't want you to tell anyone that you have it. I have teachers here who have been with us for a year now and they have been doing a good job. They would be both angry and disappointed if they knew that someone was being given two posts. At least that is the way they would see it. Let this be a secret between you and me. And now I hope that we will be seeing you on the first of September".

I could hardly believe what had happened in such

a short time. An hour earlier I had been looking forward to the next year in primary teaching, which I was really enjoying. Now I had a completely different job and had been given a welcome rise in salary.

"Where under God have you been?" demanded my mother angrily when I walked through the door. "I have been worried sick thinking that something had happened to you. You are well over an hour late. Do you never think of people at home when you go off wandering round the country?"

I explained what had happened and she slowly cooled down and was quite pleased. My father on the other hand was delighted when he came home as he saw it as a great advancement. He had the idea that teaching in a secondary school was a much higher type of work than primary teaching. He was absolutely delighted that Fr. Moore had mentioned that they had been together in Eglish.

"Be God, it's good to see that he never forgot the way I helped him when Duffy was trying to hammer the sums and things into him", he said with a satisfied laugh. "Many's a day I saved him from a quare hiding".

Next morning Frank did not let me through the door before he confronted me.

"I saw you and Fr. Moore having a bit of a confab in his car yesterday evening", he stated bluntly. "You seemed to be having a very intimate discussion amongst yourselves and nobody else was to hear a word of it".

"I'm afraid I have to tell you that I won't be here in September Frank", I told him.

"Oh Lord Jesus, did he give you the sack?" gasped Frank. "I told you that the would not take your cheek lightly. Oh God, boy, he can't give you the road like that. We'll have to get the union on to this at once. It's a damned good job that I got you to join the union. Didn't I tell you that he would not take things lying down?"

I laughed. "No. He didn't give me the sack at all, Frank", I assured him. "In fact he came to ask me to take a job in the secondary school in Dungannon and there's reasonable promotion going with it. I was a bit worried about not having a chance to give you notice but Fr. Moore assured me it would be no problem. He says that Mickey McGleenan will be coming to take my place".

"Oh naturally, that's fine", growled Frank. "It seems like nobody bothers to tell old McAvinchey what is going on, even when it's going on in what is supposed to be his own school. Why in hell should anybody bother to tell me what is happening? I'm only the principal after all and who the hell would care about him? I've only given the best years of my life to this place".

Frank continued in this vein for a good ten minutes until it was time for class to start but by lunchtime Fr. Moore had visited him and he appeared to be quite pleased with the outcome of their conversation. As we were about to start lunch he left down his sandwiches and tea and took hold of his desk with both hands. He gazed steadily into my face.

"By God Boy", he said, "fair play to you. You stood up for what you believed to be right and you got away with it. I have to admit that you knew Fr. Moore better than I did and I thought there was not a wrinkle of him that I did not know. By God boy, I have to admire your courage all the same even though I thought at the time it was foolishness".

"I don't think it was a matter of courage at all Frank", I answered. "I saw myself as part of a team and when our trust with the crowd was broken there was nothing else I could do. It's just one of those things that seems to have turned out well. I'll be sorry to leave you and the children here all the same. I really loved primary teaching and I don't know if secondary work can ever replace it".

Frank and I parted as the best of friends and I look back on my days spent with him with satisfaction and gratitude.

"Never you dare try to act the cute boor with me".

CHAPTER 42
THE END OF THE RAINBOW

It was afternoon of a lovely day in the late spring of 1959, and at that time I had been teaching for about nine months in the school in Blackwatertown. As was usual on a dry day, I had changed my clothes after dinner and was working in the strawberry field after coming home from school. A long drill of plants had just been cleaned, and I was standing on the footrig admiring my work, and taking what I considered to be a well earned a rest, when my mother's voice hailed me from the top of the field. I looked up to see her standing near the gap, and to my surprise there was a tall young man with her. She waved to me and shouted to come on up. A thought struck me that this man might be a relative from Glasgow who had arrived on a surprise visit. I knew that I had a cousin there whom I had never met and if this were the case I was about to meet a vastly superior being according to my mother's assessment of her Scottish relations.

As I came closer to them I could see that my mother was pleased, and somewhat excited, and was talking animatedly to the young man. "This is Joey Howard", she informed me. "He has come out from Dungannon, and he wants to sell you a car. Come on into the house the two of you and I'll make a cup of tea, and you can discuss things in comfort".

To Joey she said, "I was thinking myself that Arthur has been going to school on that bicycle long enough. It's not too bad on a good day like this but in the middle of the winter it won't be so pleasant at all. And anyway when he's in a job like teaching he should have a wee car".

Joey proved to be very friendly and he explained that the car now sitting on our front street was about four years old and he could let me have it at a really good price. He had heard about me and thought that I was an ideal candidate for a sale, and he explained that he worked with his father who had a garage in Dungannon. Immediately a thought flashed into my head that the only person who might have told him about me was my mother on one of her visits to Dungannon, but I never found out if that were true. Coming away out to our house was certainly a strange thing for a car-salesman to do and it did not add up. My mother was too earnest in behaving as though his arrival was a complete surprise to her and I thought she was making a great effort to convince me that she had never seen him in her life before.

"You know, Joey", I said cautiously, "I have only been in employment for a year and a bit and I have not had the chance to save much money yet. Indeed, to tell you the truth it's not easy saving any money at all on my salary at the present time. I had no notion of buying anything big for quite a while and indeed I had no notion of buying a car at all. I have been happy enough going down to Blackwatertown on the bike and into the bargain I can't drive, and now, as you know, people have to take a driving test. I never bothered to go and buy a licence before the test started a couple of months ago".

"That is no problem at all", replied Joey in a quiet, reassuring voice. "I think it is a good thing that you didn't just get a licence. I feel certain that the test is a good thing. If you buy a car from me, I will teach you to drive and I'll not give up until you pass your test. There will be no charge for the lessons, so tell me if I can do any better than that? This is a very good wee car that I have brought out to show you".

"I would not be that keen on buying a second hand car, Joey", I replied. "If I decided to buy something I would try to get a new vehicle?"

"I must say that I'd agree with him there", chimed in my mother who had the tea ready by this time. "I never believe in buying things that other people have got rid of. I always wonder what was wrong that they were so keen to see the last of them".

"Have you had anything in mind?", Joey asked.

"Well, I was talking to Tommy Coulter, the breadman, a couple of weeks ago", I explained. "He was showing me a wee A30 van he had bought and he had put seats in the back of it. He was telling me that it was as good as any car, it was brand new, and it came a lot cheaper than a car. I had not thought of purchasing one, but the set up seemed like a good idea to me".

"If that is what you want I'll arrange it all for you", said Joey, "and I'll come out once or twice a week until you learn to drive. Now what do you say to that?"

"But what sort of money are we talking about?" I asked anxiously.

Joey considered for a while and studied a book which had taken out of his pocket. He told me that it was a car-guide and was his bible.

"Right", he said at last, "I can let you have the new van for four hundred pounds. I can guarantee you that you can search the country and you won't do better than that".

Tommy Coulter had told me that his van had cost him four hundred and twenty pounds so I knew there was nothing wrong with the offer. With a lot of encouragement from my mother, the bargain was made. Joey was as good as his word, proved to be an excellent teacher, and thanks to him I managed to get my test at the first attempt. My mother was delighted as she now had her own means of transport to the chapel or to the shops, and into the bargain, in her view, we had caught up on the neighbours to some extent. I found the van much more reliable for getting into school in a reasonable condition to appear before a class, and it meant that I was able to go to dances or other functions without looking for a lift. The ability to travel long distances, however, proved to be something that would completely change my life.

I had just passed my mid-twenties by this time, and had met lots of girls over the years, but I had never met anyone that I really felt deeply about, anyone with whom I would want to spend a lot of time and certainly not the rest of my life. I am pretty certain too that I had not left any broken hearts in my wake either. I began to think that there was something wrong with me, something lacking in my make-up and that I was incapable of really caring for anyone. It was probably only a passing thought or a fleeting fancy and it didn't worry me at all, but at the same time, somewhere in the back o my mind, there was the vision of an isolated, cold and rather lonely existence stretching into the future.

One autumn evening on the way home from school a few months after I had bought the van, I called at the village shop and met a girl who was nursing in Belfast. We began to chat about people we had known in the past and one of these was a girl whom I had met called Maureen Ó Toole from County Down. I discovered that she was back in Belfast doing midwifery, and was living with a group of girls in Eglantine Avenue, just off the Lisburn Road. I decided to write to her and ask if she would consider coming out on a date. It seemed like a completely unreasonable thing to do since the girl had not seen me for years and such a letter coming out of the blue, was likely to be treated with the disdain it deserved. Feeling rather foolish I sent my letter off, but did not expect to get any response. Chasing rainbows had never been one of my pastimes but in this case I felt somewhat like the man who spent his life looking for the crock of gold and the rainbow's end.

To my great surprise, however, Maureen agreed to my suggestion, and one evening a couple of weeks later I set out for Belfast feeling somewhat embarrassed and foolish. I told my mother that I was going to Portadown, which was of course true since I had to pass through the town, but she would have been sick with worry had she known that I was going to face the heavy traffic in the 'big city'. Maureen and I went to the pictures; it proved to be a very pleasant evening to say the least and as I drove home I realised that something unforeseen had happened. I knew that this was the girl with whom I wanted to spend the rest of my life and while we had only met, I was certain that if she parted from me, it would break my heart. As the poet, Yeats might have said, 'all was changed, changed utterly; for me a magical beauty was born'.

A few weeks after our first date Maureen was changed to Holywood to do practical midwifery and this meant that my journeys were even longer. The winter proved to be fairly difficult with quite a bit of frost and snow, but it seemed that neither of us felt the cold as the depth of our relationship was increasing all the time. We spent a lot of time together, but the hours seemed like seconds. It always felt as though I had only arrived when it was time to go home. I wondered what fool described this life and this world as 'a valley of tears' because it seemed more like earthly paradise.

One beautiful morning in the following spring Frank McAvinchey and I were chatting in the school hall before class, when I chanced to remark that the bank of trees beyond the village, and the indeed the whole countryside around, looked really beautiful. "I can see damn all beautiful about them", complained Frank with a snort. "This last while you have been seeing the whole world through rose tinted glasses. You have as bad a dose of that disease as ever I met in my life. I'll tell you one thing for nothing; any fool can find a woman and get married; it takes a very smart man to choose the right woman". With that he stomped off into his room, and slammed the door behind him. I did not consider myself particularly brilliant, but I knew that I was not making a mistake this time.

Towards the end of Maureen's term in Holywood, I was coming home one night when I was hailed by three young fellows near the start of the Sydenham by-pass. They were dressed like 'teddy boys' but I thought that they would be company for part of the journey and I stopped to give them a lift. As soon had we started off, however, I realised that it was a bad mistake. They began to talk amongst themselves about where they could go now that they had a means of transport. They made it clear that they thought they could make me do whatever they wished and I could see many reasons why they might be correct in this assumption. As we made our way towards the city I considered how I might extricate myself from this mess that I had so foolishly got myself into.

"You know", I said to the boys after a few minutes, "my petrol gauge is faulty and I'm running low on juice. I'll have to call at a station on the Stewartstown Road to fill up. It will only take a few minutes and then I'll leave you wherever you want to go".

It was an almost hopeless attempt at escape but a couple of the lads growled agreement and I began to hope that the ruse might work. While I had been living in Jimmy Andrews's house, Jimmy had introduced me to a neighbour called McCluskey who was well known as one of the 'hard men' in Belfast. We had become quite good friends, and I knew that he had later opened a petrol station at the corner of Finaghy Road North, and now I began to pray that he might be on duty.

I pulled into the petrol station and went into the shop. To my utter joy and relief Mr. McCluskey was sitting at an electric fire reading the paper. As soon as he saw me, he got up and welcomed me like a long lost brother. I explained the problem and he immediately marched out to the van without a word. He opened the passenger door, grabbed the fellow sitting there, pulled him out like a rag doll, and flung him across the yard so that he ended up crashing against a wall and fell to the ground groaning with pain. As he turned round to the van, the other two were trying to escape past the passenger seat. He grabbed them, held them at arm's length for a moment, and then pulled them together so that their heads slammed off each other with a sickening thud. He flung them from him and they too fell to the ground, obviously in a semi-conscious state. He then filled the van with petrol, would not take any money for it, and wished me a safe journey. As I made my way home I was filled with regret at the brutal treatment meted out to the boys, but that feeling was certainly mixed with relief, and gratitude. I had learned not to lift anyone I did not know, especially late at night.

A few months later we got engaged, and from that time on, some weekends I stayed for a night with Maureen's brother Dessie and his wife Jeanette, who had been married about two years at the time and had a young son, Gerard, who was a few months old when I first knew them. They lived at Raholp, which was about ten miles from Maureen's home. It was a very beautiful and historic part of the country in the Saul area where Saint Patrick is believed to have come ashore to begin his mission with the Irish. There was always plenty of craic in the house and Dessie was constantly on the look out for a chance to play tricks on everyone. The arrangement gave Maureen and I the chance of spending precious extra time together and it lessened the driving a little. In the eyes of both sets of parents we were 'at a safe distance', as one might say.

Not long after I got the van my father decided

to rebuild the chimney breast and fireplace in my bedroom, or rather he gave in to my mother's constant complaining about it. He was taking down the old structure one day when a large section of it suddenly collapsed and a fairly large piece of masonry hit him on the right leg. It was obviously painful but as usual he shook himself and assured me that it was nothing to worry about. "A man has to suffer under Pontius Pilate in this world", he said, "and sure Mick Dawley in no different from other men".

A couple of days later he was limping badly, the leg was even more swollen and he was in obvious pain. "Get yourself tidied up", I ordered, "I'm taking you up to see Dr. Garvin no matter what you say". Grudgingly after a long argument he agreed to come, still complaining that I was putting him to a lot of trouble and there was nothing wrong with him that would not rectify itself in a day or two.

The doctor got him to lie on his couch and examined his leg. "Excuse me, Mick for a minute or two", he said and left the room. A couple of minutes later he came back with a measuring tape in his hands. "Put your two legs out straight," he ordered, "and pull up that other trouser leg".

"There's damn all wrong with the other leg, Doctor", Da protested. "I only got a wee bit of a thump on that one, but to hear our boy, you'd think that it needed to come off". By the time he had finished speaking, however, he had pulled up the other trouser leg. The doctor measured the good leg and then the bad one. He stood back and looked down at Da for a few seconds. "I don't know why the hell you bothered coming to me at this time, Mick", he said. "There's only four and a half inches of difference in the two legs and if you'd waited for another fortnight there might have been a foot".

"I told you that I had no need to come here and annoy the doctor", growled Da, glaring at me and making an attempt to get up.

"Stay exactly where you are", ordered the doctor. "You are damned lucky that Arthur brought you. You have a big blood clot in that leg and it has to be treated immediately. If you'd waited much longer it would have shifted and a wooden box would be all you'd have needed then".

Da had to lie in bed for three weeks and my mother assured everyone that it was the longest three weeks of her life and he was the worst patient that any woman could be burdened with. By the end of the three weeks, however, the doctor declared that the clot had gone and while he had to rest for another fortnight or so, he could get up and sit at the fire with the leg up on a chair. Towards the end of his time in bed I came home one night to find my mother and doctor Garvin sitting by the fire chatting.

As soon as I entered the room the doctor said, "I hear, Arthur that you are going to get married in the near future. Is that right?"

"It is Doctor", I agreed. "We are getting married at the end of July".

"Would you like to take a wee bit of advice from an old man who brought you into the world?", he asked.

"I can see clearly that I'm going to get that advice anyway, Doctor", I replied.

"I was just going to warn you", he continued, "to take things very easy in the first six weeks or so, for I damn near killed myself in the first six months and I don't know if I ever got over it".

Such things had never been mentioned in our house and I was pretty embarrassed, especially by my mother's laughter.

One weekend Mrs Ó Toole had her son Willie and his family from England staying in her house, and the whole family gathered to celebrate their arrival. It so happened that Jeanette's brother, Jackie Burns was staying at Dessie's that weekend too. I had got to know Jackie fairly well and we became good friends and have remained so ever since. The house was somewhat overcrowded with the result that Jackie, Dessie and I had to share a bed for one night. As might be surmised, it was pretty late when we decided to go to bed that night. I chose the place near the wall while Jackie took the middle spot, leaving the outside place for Dessie who was last to come to bed.

Dessie pushed himself into the bed and muttered some complaints about the lack of space left for him. He was less than complimentary about the attributes of his visitors, but as far as I could make out he managed to get reasonably comfortable and settled down to sleep. It was the moment for which I had been waiting. I bent my knees up, placed my feet against the wall and pushed slowly and steadily.

It was fairly easy to move both my companions because I had the power of the lever helping me. Jackie grumbled a little and tried to move so that he would have more room. Dessie must have fallen asleep because he didn't seem to notice that he was being moved slowly towards to edge of the bed. Suddenly he landed on the floor with a dull thud, and his remarks about his visitors and their parentage could only be described as anything but friendly. It did not help when Jackie yawned, looked down at him though sleep-filled eyes and asked, "what are you doing down there, Dessie? Is it not a wee bit cold for lying on the floor?"

It was obvious from his verbal response that Dessie's opinion of his visitors had not improved!

Sammy was a friend of Dessie's and like him nursed in the mental hospital in Downpatrick, which at that time was a huge institution employing something over five hundred nurses. Sammy was very decent and very kindly but he had less concern for his own protection and well-being than any person I have ever met. Not long after I got to know him Sammy got a loan of Dessie's car one frosty winter night to got to a dance in Hilltown. As far as I know he took a little too much drink at the dance and on his way home he managed to go clean over a hedge at a bad corner and of course smashed the car but fortunately was not injured at all. Dessie was called to the police barracks and when he got there a policeman was just beginning to interrogate Sammy.

"What speed do you think you were doing?" the policeman asked, as Dessie entered the room.

"I was doing nearly sixty when I came into that corner", Sammy assured him .

"What?" gasped the policeman open-mouthed.

"Indeed you were not", interrupted Dessie. "You were doing about thirty at the very most. You were taking care on a bad road on a frosty night".

"Honest to God, Dessie," pleaded Sammy, "I was doing at least fifty so I was and sure you weren't there so you don't know what you are talking about".

"Och now", said the policeman, "I think your friend must be right. It could not have been more than thirty and it's likely to have been nearer twenty on a night like that".

Sammy pounded the table in frustration. "How could either of the two of you know what I was doing when you weren't there? I tell you I was doing about sixty".

"I'll tell you what I'll do" said the policeman, "I'll put down thirty miles an hour and that won't be too bad".

"Put down at least fifty," insisted Sammy. "I was doing far more than that so I was".

Eventually at the end of a long and heated debate the policeman put down thirty miles an hour in spite of Sammy's protests. Dessie swore that it was a miracle that he did not kill Sammy that night when he got him outside.

At the end of June and the beginning of July in 1961 a period of very hot, sunny weather set in just as the strawberry crop was beginning to ripen. One Sunday in the middle of that spell I was to meet Maureen at the Downe hospital as she came off duty at half past two in the afternoon. I decided that since there would be a big crowd at Tyrella beach, I would get up at dawn, pull a load of fruit, and see if I could sell them before two o'clock. I arrived early and took up my position beside an ice-cream van. Half an hour later the crowds began to arrive and within an hour I had sold all the fruit and the ice cream man complained that it was a pity that I did not have a bigger van.

There were still nearly two hours to spend before Maureen would be off duty and I decided to go for a walk in the sand dunes. I had not gone very far when I met Sammy and we sat down to chat. Sammy informed me that he was based at Beach House for a fortnight looking after a group of patients who were on holiday. Beach House was a holiday home which the Mental Hospital had on Tyrella at that time. We lay there on the side of a dune for well over an hour, perfectly at ease in the warm sun. Eventually I announced that it was time for me to go to Downpatrick. Sammy rose lazily and said calmly, "I had better be going too. I was sent out a couple of hours ago to find a patient who has wandered away. He's dangerous, so he is. One night last week he tried to strangle a man with his tie, and the man had not done anything on him".

On Saint Patrick's day in 1962 we arranged that Maureen, who was back in Belfast, would come on a visit to our house. She would take the train to Dungannon and I would collect her at the station. My mother was very excited and spent the previous few days making sure that the house was in tip top shape for her important visitor. While waiting to go to Dungannon I was sitting in an armchair beside the fire and my mother was flitting about the house making doubly sure that no speck of dust had escaped her attention and that her cooking was going according to plan. As we chatted I lifted a piece of wire that had been sitting on the top of the grate and I sat fiddling with it, twisting it into rings and bending it one way and then another.

It was nearly time to set out and thoughtlessly I threw the coiled wire into the blazing fire. A few seconds went by and then there was a tremendous explosion. It seemed as if the whole house shook and I thought for a moment that the grate had jumped out on to the floor. My mother who had been coming over to the fire was showered in sparks and ash. The floor near the fire got a generous coating of soot. "Jesus, Mary and Joseph", gasped my mother, "has the house been hit with a bomb? Jesus, Mary and Joseph what will that wee girl think of this house now?"

We were both in a state of shock but slowly we came to our senses and realised that no real damage had been done. Wondering what had happened we tried to bring the room back to a reasonable state, all the time debating what had caused the damage. It was some time before I remembered throwing the wire into the fire but I did not say anything about it. When I started out for Dungannon my mother was still cleaning and scrubbing and complaining that such tragedies could only happen to her when important people were coming to the house.

My father came home from the hunt in order to share a meal with us and my mother immediately showered him with information about the catastrophe that had taken place. His eyes went immediately to the grate.

"Did anybody throw anything into the fire?" he asked, but he obviously knew what had happened.

"There was a wee bit of wire on the grate", I admitted. "I was footering with it and then I threw it into the fire right enough".

"Dammit, isn't it a tarra altogether", he murmured, "that a body can't leave anything down in this house but people throw it into the fire. It seems to me that if the people in this house had more to do they might leave things that don't belong to them alone. That was a detonator that I left there and I thought that you would have had the sense and maybe even the brains to know that".

A debate ensued as to who was to blame but in

the end we probably decided to share the blame and I remember that day as truly magical. A few months later Maureen and I were married in the little church at Ballykilbeg on the thirty-first of July in 1962, my twenty-seventh birthday and without doubt the best day of my entire life. A bright dream had become reality; I had found my gold at the end of the rainbow.

Maureen has survived over forty-four years of middlin' company.

ISBN 142512552-2

9 781425 125523